Complete World Bartender Guide

Edited by Bob Sennett

BANTAM BOOKS
TORONTO • NEW YORK • LONDON • SYDNEY • AUCKLAND

COMPLETE WORLD BARTENDER GUIDE
The Standard Reference to 2000 Drinks

*A Bantam Book / published by arrangement with
Poorhouse Press*

PRINTING HISTORY

*Poorhouse edition published September 1977
6 printings through August 1979*

*Appeared in Condensed form by Profile Books-
Q Publications Miniature Book*

*Bantam edition / September 1981
Seven printings through September 1986*

ISBN 0-553-26598-9

Published simultaneously in the United States and Canada

PRINTED IN THE UNITED STATES OF AMERICA

O   16 15 14 13 12 11 10 9 8 7

Contents

INTRODUCTION

The Complete Bartender's Guide presents a compendium of popular cocktails and beverages for easy reference.

Drink recipes are listed alphabetically by their common names. The rear index orders the drinks by liquor ingredient.

The recipes are culled from professional bartenders, commercial distillers, and private collections. The Complete Guide is a valuable and comprehensive resource.

We, the editors, acknowledge the public health hazard of drinking alcohol in excess.

For this reason, we have included a section entitled "Responsible Drinking" which outlines some aspects of alcohol abuse.

We offer the Guide as a service to those who have achieved an understanding of alcohol as an intoxicant, and who have established by good judgment when drinking is appropriate for them.

TIPS
FOR BARTENDERS

GLASSES
Use freshly washed glassware. Place glasses face down on a thin towel for drying. Use a stemmed glass for cocktails served with no ice so that the hand holding the glass will not warm the drink.

FROSTING A GLASS
Keep in a refrigerator (or bury in shaved ice) until glass is frosted.
To "sugar-frost" glass, wet the rim of a pre-chilled glass with lime or lemon then dip into powdered sugar, or salt per recipe.

CHILLING A GLASS
Refrigerate or fill each glass with shaved or crushed ice before mixing. Shake out the melted ice before pouring the drink.

SHAKE AND BLENDING
Drinks containing fruit juices, sugar, eggs, cream etc. should be well shaken. To attain a frothy quality, use an electric blender. Also use a blender for punches, sours and fruit and egg drinks.

STIRRING
Stir drinks with clear liquors including ice. Stir drinks containing a carbonated mixer very gently. Don't stir liqueurs.

ADDING SUGAR
Sugar should be put in the mixing glass first, then add the liquor. Powered sugar is best used with alcohol because it dissolves easily with alcohol at low temperatures. Some bartenders prefer syrup because it blends instantly. Store syrup in bottles and keep cool. If you want to make your own, here's how: dissolve one pound of granulated sugar in one-half pint of hot water. Stir slowly adding water to make desired quantity (usually one pint).

7

USING ICE

Ice goes into the mixing glass, shaker or drinking glass before drink. Use cubes, as a rule, for old fashioneds, highballs or any on-the-rocks drinks. Cracked or cubed ice is best for stirring and shaking. Crushed or shaved ice for frappes and other tall drinks or for sipping drinks through straws.

BITTERS

Only a dash or two. Made from combinations of roots, barks, berries and herbs. They are aromatic and bitter in taste.

The four brands below are most popular:

ANGOSTURA BITTERS   made in Trinidad
ABBOTT'S AGED BITTERS   made in Baltimore
PEYCHAUD'S BITTERS   made in New Orleans
ORANGE BITTERS   made in England

TWIST OR PEEL

When using a twist of lemon peel, rub outer skin of peel around the rim of the glass to coat it with its natural oil. Add some of its oil to the drink by twisting the peel over the glass. Then add the peel itself.

FRUIT OR JUICES

Wash fruit first. Slices should be $\frac{3}{8}$" thick and slit up the center to saddle on rim of glass. Keep garnishes on a bed of ice or in a cool place. In drinks containing fruit juices you must pour in the liquor last.

SERVING BEER

Chill beer like champagne; surround with ice cubes and turn gently a few times. Don't serve it *too* cold for it goes flat. Don't shake bottle or can before opening. Open gently to prevent gushing. Once opened, serve promptly! Don't tilt glass to allow beer to slide slowly down side! Instead, pour beer into center of glass, holding bottle or can at a high angle until a head comes up. Then pour beer more slowly. Most people prefer a firm head, about 1" deep.

EGGS

To separate the white of an egg from its yolk, crack open on the edge of the glass, then shift the yolk back and forth from one half shell to the other until all the white drops into the glass. Always put the egg into the mixing glass before the liquor. When shaker is used include (cubed or cracked) ice to help blend the egg with the other ingredients.

SERVING

When serving the same cocktail for more than one, mix the drinks in one batch. Set up all the glasses in a row and partially fill each glass (half). Then go back and top off each glass

TO FLAME LIQUOR

(Brandy, Rum, Gin, Whiskey)
Prewarm the glass, vessel and liquor First preheat one spoon of liquor over a flame and set afire. Then pour flaming liquor carefully into remainder. It will set the rest aflame.

THE STRAINER

Strain cocktails into serving glasses with a wire strainer.

VERMOUTH

Vermouth is a white appetizer wine. It is often flavored with about forty different herbs, roots, berries, flowers and seeds. There are many vermouth brand labels, each with its own formula. The dry (French) has a light gold color and has a nutty flavor. Sweet (Italian) vermouth has a more syrupy quality. Keep bottle corked or it will go stale.

BAR TOOLS AND GLASSES

A glass hierarchy still exists at most public bars, but times are changing and particularly in home bars people have learned to be more flexible.

These are the glasses and tools you will need to fill most requests. Keep in mind that these are only guidelines because the styles of glasses constantly change.

TONGS

MEASURE

SHAKER

BAR STRAINER

BLENDER

CORK SCREW

MUDDLER

PARING KNIFE AND CUTTING BOARD

ICE BUCKET

LEMON/LIME SQUEEZER

POUSSE CAFE
(3-4 oz.)

CORDIAL
(PONY)
(1-2 oz.)

SHERRY
(2 oz.)

PARFAIT

COCKTAIL
(3 ½ oz.)

BRANDY
(3 oz.)

FIZZ

SOUR
(5 oz.)

OLD FASHIONED
(6 - 8 oz.)

BIG
OLD FASHIONED
(15 - 16 oz.)

SNIFTER

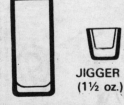
JIGGER
(1½ oz.)

TALL COLLINS
(10 - 14 oz.)

HIGHBALL
(8 oz.)

MARTINI
(4 oz.)

PILSNER
(10 oz.)

CHAMPAGNE
SAUCER
(8 oz.)

WINE
(4 - 5 oz.)

CHAMPAGNE
HOLLOW
STEM

PUNCH BOWL
AND CUP

BEER GOBLET

EGG NOG

MUG
(10 oz.)

LARGE
MIXING
PITCHER
AND
LONG
HANDLED
SPOON

MEASUREMENTS

	Standard	Metric
1 Dash	1/32 ounce	0.9 ml.
1 Teaspoon	⅛ ounce	3.7 ml.
1 Tablespoon	⅜ ounce	11.1 ml.
1 Pony	1 ounce	29.5 ml.
1 Jigger	1½ ounces	44.5 ml.
1 Wineglass	4 ounces	119ml
1 Split	6 ounces	177 ml.
1 Cup	8 ounces	257 ml.
1 Miniature (nip)	2 ounces	59.2 ml.
1 Half Pint	8 ounces	257 ml.
1 Tenth	12.8 ounces	378.88 ml.
1 Pint	16 ounces	472 ml.
1 Fifth	25.6 ounces	755.2 ml.
1 Quart	32 ounces	944 ml.
1 Imperial Quart	38.4 ounces	1.137 liter
1 Half Gallon	64 ounces	1.894 liter
1 Gallon	128 ounces	3.789 liter
Dry Wine and Champagne		
Split (¼ bottle)	6 oz.	177 ml.
"Pint" (½ bottle)	12 oz.	375.2 ml.
"Quart" (1 bottle)	25 oz.	739.0 ml.
Magnum (2 bottles)	52 oz.	1.534 liter
Jeroboam (4 bottles)	104 oz.	3.078 liter
Tappit-hen	128 oz.	3.788 liter
Rehoboam (6 bottles)		4.434 liter
Methuselah (8 bottles)		5.912 liter
Salmanazar (12 bottles)		8.868 liter
Balthazar (16 bottles)		11.829 liter
Nebuchadnezzar (20 bottles)		14.780 liter
Demijohn (4.9 gallons)		18.66 liter

STOCKING & PLANNING

Stocking for parties depends on the nature of the occasion and the kind of party, type of people, etc. Here is a general plan based on the experienced of commercial distilleries.

THE BASIC STOCK FOR THE HOME BAR

WHISKEYS Two bottles each of a good Scotch, bourbon and a serviceable blended whiskey.

GINS A bottle or two of good old American gin will do fine.

VODKA Vodka goes fast. Keep a few good-sized bottles around.

RUMS One super-dark Jamaican, one virgin white Puerto Rican and one Bacardi for special occasions.

BRANDIES Start with a bottle of fine cognac, add a bottle or two of good, inexpensive mixing brandies and one or two fruit brandies . . . apricot and blackberry are very popular.

LIQUEURS It's best to have a bottle of coffee liqueur, a bottle of Grand Marnier and a bottle of creme de cassis. In addition (and by nationality) lay in:

ITALIAN: Galliano, Tuaca
DANISH: Aquavit, Cherry Heering
DUTCH: Curacao, Creme Yvette, Kummel
FRENCH: Chartreuse, Benedictine
SCOTCH: Drambuie
BRITISH: Sloe Gin

Last, but not least, you should have a bottle of dry vermouth, a bottle of sweet vermouth and a wide assortment of bitters . . . Angostura, Orange, Abbott's Aged and Peychaud's.

15

PLANNING

The chart below is what commercial distillers generally estimate as the yield per bottle.

DRINKS PER BOTTLE (FIFTH)
(For quarts add 20% to number of drinks)

RUM	PORT	WHISKEY
16 Daiquiris	16 Drinks	16 Highballs
12 Rum Collins		14 Manhattans
12 Rum Coolers		16 Sours
		16 Old Fashioneds

GIN	LIQUEURS	SHERRY
16 Tom Collins	30 Cocktails	16 Drinks
14 Martinis	20 Frappes	
16 Fizzes		

DRY VERMOUTH	SWEET VERMOUTH
56 Martinis	28 Manhattans

CHAMPAGNE AND SPARKLING WINES
7 Drinks

PARTIES

NO. OF PEOPLE	COCKTAIL PARTY (2 HOURS)	DINNER (2 HOURS)
4	12 Drinks	8 Cocktails 8 Glasses of Wine
6	18 Drinks	12 Cocktails 12 Glasses of Wine 6 Liqueurs
8	24 Drinks	16 Cocktails 16 Glasses of Wine 8 Liqueurs

MINI-DICTIONARY

ABSINTHE– cordial with anise seed (licorice) flavor; contains wormwood (which is banned by the U.S. government). ABISANTE, ABSON, ANISETTE, HERBSAINT, MISTRA, OJEN, OXYGENE, PERNOD are substitutes.

ADES—Served tall with ice and garnished with slices of fruit. Mainly made with sweetened lemon or lime juice and a variety of liquors and filled with plain or soda water.

AGE—Often this is used as a measure of quality. It is not always dependable because rate of aging and ingredients are a factor too.

ALCOHOL (C_2H_5OH)— Common to all liquor. Ethyl alcohol, spirits distilled from grain, grape, fruit and cane are most common.

ALE—Heavier and more bitter than lager.

AMER PICON—A French cordial, bitter, orange-flavored, made from quinine and spices.

AMERICAN BLENDED LIGHT WHISKEYS—An American whiskey category. Contains 20 per cent straight whiskeys (at 100 proof) and 80 per cent of American light whiskey.

AMERICAN BRANDY— Generally distilled in California. It is usually produced by the same firms that grow the grapes. They distill, age, blend, bottle and market the brandies under their own brand names.

AMERICAN WHIS-KEY—The United States produces over thirty-three distinct types of whiskey.

ANISETTE—A cordial made from the anise seed, licorice flavor.

APPLE BRANDY, APPLE JACK OR CALVADOS—Distilled from apple cider. Calvados is produced only in Normandy, France.

ARMAGNAC—A type of brandy produced only in the Armagnac region of France.

BEER—A fermented malt beverage.

BENEDICTINE—A cordial made from a secret herb formula. Benedictine monks first made this liqueur.

BITTERS—A very concentrated flavoring agent made from roots, barks, herbs and/or berries.

BLENDED WHISKEY— Combines straight whiskeys with neutral grain spirits. Straight whiskey dominates the mix by 20%. Sold at 80 proof.

BLEND OF STRAIGHT WHISKEYS—Two or more straight whiskeys blended together and excludes neutral grain spirits.

BOCK BEER, PORTER AND STOUT—Heavier, darker, richer and sweeter than either lager beer or ale in that order. About 6% alcohol.

BOTTLED-in-BOND WHISKEY—Straight whiskey, usually bourbon or rye, produced under government control and supervision. Bonded whiskey must be at least four years old, bottled at 100 proof and produced in one distilling by the same distiller. It must be sorted and bottled at a bonded warehouse under government supervision.

BOURBON WHISKEY— Distilled from grain mash containing 51 per cent corn and aged more than four years in new (charred) oak barrels. Amber color. Bourbon gets its name from Bourbon County in Kentucky where it originated. Illinois, Indiana, Ohio, Pennsylvania, Tennessee and Missouri also produce bourbon.

BRANDY—Made (distilled) from a fermented mash of grapes or fruit. Generally they are aged in oak casks and bottled at 80 or 84 proof.

BUCKS—Made with an ounce or so of liquor and lemon juice plus ginger ale, and topped with a twist of lemon.

CANADIAN WHISKEY—A blended whiskey. Distilled from rye, corn and barley. Produced only in Canada under government control. Canadian whiskey sold in this country is at least four years old. Lighter than American whiskey, it is sold at 80 proof.

CHARTREUSE—A cordial made from herb liqueurs (either yellow or green). Carthusian monks originated this.

COGNAC—A type of brandy produced only in the Cognac region of France.

COBBLERS—Tall drinks generally served in a large goblet with shaved ice, fruit and liquor, decorated with berries, fresh fruit and a sprig of mint. Served with a straw.

COLLINS—Tall, cool punch-like drinks. Tom and John are best known. Any basic liquor with juice of lemon or lime, over ice cubes in a frosted 12-oz.

highball glass. Sugar and soda water added. Garnished with lemon slice and a cherry.

COOLERS—A tall drink made with different types of liquor, flavoring, cracked ice, carbonated beverage and fruit rinds.

CORDIAL—A liquor (or liqueur) made by mixing or redistilling neutral spirits. Fruits, flowers, herbs, seeds, roots, plants or juices are used and a sweetening is added. Most cordials are sweet, colorful and highly concentrated. Many are made from secret recipes and processes.

CREME—A cordial with a very high sugar content. It s cream-like consistency gives it its prefix. It comes in the following combinations:
CREME DE CACAO—from cacao and vanilla beans
CREME DE CASSIS—from black currants
CREME DE MENTHE—from mint
CREME YVETTE—from violets

CUPS—Made with brandy and Triple Sec, together with sweet wine, dry champagne or cider. Mixed in glass pitchers with ice cubes, served in stemmed claret glasses.

CURACAO—A cordial made of dried orange peel.

It comes from the Dutch West Indies.

DAISIES—Large cocktails made of liquor, grenadine or any other cordial with lemon or lime juice. Shaken with ice and served in a stein, metal cup or old fashioned glass over ice cubes, decorated with fruit.

DRY GIN—Gin that is very low in sweetness.

DUBONNET—An aperitif wine made from aromatics. It has a quinine taste and is mostly made in France.

EGG NOG—First achieved popularity in the American Colonies in 1775. The word "noggin" is an English word for small drinking cup. The liquors usually used in egg nog have historically been rum and brandy. Whiskey, sherry, ale and cider can also be used. It is basically a combination of eggs, milk and liquor.

FIXES—A drink mixed in the serving glass. Sometimes another name for highball. Served over lots of ice.

FIZZES—Made from liquor, citrus juices and sugar. Shaken with ice and strained into small highball glasses. Soda ("Fizz") water is then added. Any carbonated beverage, even champagne, may be used. Some add egg whites or yolks.

19

FLAVORED VODKA— American origin. Generally served straight or in mixed drinks. It is sweetened and flavored, usually with orange, lemon, lime or grape. Sold at 70 proof.

FLIPS— An egg nog and fizz combination. Made with liquor, egg and sugar with shaved ice, shaken well. Strained into short stemmed flip glasses for serving. Sprinkled with nutmeg.

FRAPPES— Small drinks. Several liqueurs combined and poured over shaved or crushed ice.

FRUIT BRANDIES— Fruit flavored liqueurs produced from blackberries, peaches, apricots, cherries and ginger. They are usually brandy-based at 70 to 80 proof.

GIN— Distilled from grain. Juniper berries and other botanicals give it its flavor. Most gin is colorless. Some gins appear golden or straw-color because of aging in barrels. Gin is bottled at proofs varying from 80 to 94.

GOLDEN GIN— A dry gin. It has a golden color that comes from its aging in wood.

GRAIN NEUTRAL SPIRITS— (Alcohol distilled from grain at 190 proof. Used in blended whiskeys for making gin and vodka and other liquors. It is almost tasteless and colorless.

GRENADINE— A flavoring for drinks. It is made from pomegranates.

HEAVY-BODIED RUMS— Dark, sweet with a pungent bouquet and a rich molasses-like body. They come from Jamaica, Demerara (British Guiana), Martinique, Trinidad, Barbados and New England.

HIGHBALLS— Any liquor served with ice, soda, plain water, ginger ale or other carbonated liquids.

HOLLAND, GENEVA OR SCHIEDAM GINS— These are highly flavored and rich in aromatic oils. They are made in Holland where gin originated.

HOT DRINKS— Made with liquor in any beverage. Served piping hot and not much liquor.

IRISH WHISKEY— A blend that contains barley malt whiskeys and grain whiskeys. The malt is dried in coal-fired kilns. The aroma of the fires does not influence the malt. Irish whiskey is heavier than Scotch and is usually 86 proof. It is produced only in Ireland.

JULEPS—Made with Kentucky bourbon and fresh mint leaves (muddled, crushed or whole). May also be made with rye, brandy, gin, rum or champagne. Served with shaved ice in an ice-frosted glass with a mint or fruit garnish and a straw.

KENTUCKY WHISKEY—A blend of straight bottled whiskies. Distilled in Kentucky.

KUMMEL—A cordial liqueur made from caraway and anise seeds with herb flavors added.

LIGHT-BODIED RUMS—Dry with slight molasses flavor. They come from Puerto Rico, Cuba and the Virgin Islands, Dominican Republic, Haiti, Venezuela, Mexico, Hawaii and the Philippines.

LAGER BEER—(3.6% alcohol) is the most popular beer.

LIGHT WHISKEY—A type of American whiskey produced at 160 to 189 proof, stored at least four years in used, charred oak containers. Light in flavor and smooth tasting. Color varies from clear to amber.

LONDON DRY GIN—Accepted as a generic term but originated in England. It sometimes appears on American-made labels.

MARASCHINO—A liqueur made from cherries. These cherries come from Dalmatia, Yugoslovia.

OLD TOM GIN—A gin that contains sugar syrup. It is made in England.

PASSION FRUIT (PASSIONOLA)—A mix made from the Passion Flower. It is nonalcoholic.

PERNOD—A liqueur, anise-flavored and used as an absinthe substitute.

PEPPERMINT SCHNAPPS—A creme de menthe that is rather light in body.

POUSSE-CAFES—Made from several cordials and liqueurs poured in series so that one floats atop another. Each has a different color and specific weight that permits "floating."

PROOF—The measure of the strength of the alcohol. One (degree) proof equals one-half of 1 per cent of alcohol. For example: 80 proof equals 40 per cent alcohol. Whiskey sold outside of America has been of more moderate, lower proofs. U.S. made whiskey and brandy is usually 80 proof.

PUNCHES—Citrus juices with two or more liquors or wines. Served cold. Hot punches use milk, eggs and cream.

RICKEYS—Made with lime, cracked ice, soda or any carbonated beverage and whiskey, gin, rum or brandy. Served with the rind of lime. Similar to a collins or sour.

ROCK AND RYE—A fruit juice that combines rock candy, rye whiskey and fruit slices.

RUM—Made by distilling the fermented juice of sugar cane, cane syrup and molasses at 190 proof (160 proof for New England rum). It is bottled and sold at 80 proof. Aged in uncharred barrels, it picks up very little color. Caramel is added to create dark rums. Most rums are a blend of several kinds.

RYE WHISKEY—Distilled from a grain mash of 80 per cent corn. It is usually aged in re-used charred oak barrels.

SANGAREES—Made with whiskey, gin, rum, or brandy, with port wine floated on top, or with wine, ale, porter or stout, with a sprinkle of nutmeg. Actually a tall, sweet, old fashioned (without bitters).

SCOTCH WHISKEY—Blended whiskies from native barley grain and Scottish pot stills. All Scotch blends contain malt whiskey and grain whiskey. The smoky flavor comes from drying malted barley over peat fires. Produced only in Scotland. Exported Scotch is at least four years old and is usualy 80 to 86 proof.

SLINGS—Made like sangarees with the addition of lemon juice and a twist of lemon peel. Served in an old fashioned glass.

SLOE GIN—A liqueur made from blackthorn bush (sloe) berries.

SWEDISH PUNCH—A liqueur made from Batavia Arak rum, tea, lemon and spices. Sometimes comes as ARRACK PUNCH AND CALORIC PUNCH. Swedish origin.

SMASHES—Small juleps. Served in old fashioned glasses. Made with muddled sugar, ice cubes, whiskey, gin, rum or brandy and soda. Garnished with sprigs of mint and fruit.

SOURS—Made of lemon juice, ice, sugar, with any basic liquor. Similar to a highly concentrated punch.

Decorated with lemon slice and cherry.

STRAIGHT WHISKEY—
A whiskey that is distilled from grain but not blended with neutral grain spirits or any other whiskey and aged in charred oak barrels for at least two years.

SWIZZLE STICK—A twig with a few forked branches on its end. It is usually inserted into the glass or pitcher and twirled rapidly between the hands. Used in cool drinks of lime, sugar, liquor, bitters, which are packed with shaved ice.

TEQUILLA—A distillate of the sap of the century plant. Sometimes called "Cactus Whiskey."

TODDIES—Served hot or cold. A lump or teaspoon of sugar dissolved in a little hot water, with liquor, ice or hot water added and stirred. Served with clove, nutmeg, cinnamon or lemon peel.

TRIPLE SEC—A cordial similar to Curacao but less sweet and colorless.

VACUUM-DISTILLED GIN—Distilled in glass-lined vacuum stills at low temperature, about 90°, to preserve the light, volatile flavors and aromas without the bitterness found in other gins.

VODKA—A refined and filtered liquor distilled at 190 proof and bottled for sale at 80 to 110 proof. Originally made in Russia from potatoes. It is usually distilled from corn and wheat in the United States. The differences between various vodkas depends on the types of grains used and the distilling and filtering processes. Most American vodkas are filtered through activated charcoal. Vodka is colorless, tasteless and odorless. It is not aged.

WHISKEY—Made from grains like corn, rye, barley, or wheat. It is distilled from a fermented mash of the grain, then aged in oak barrels. At this stage it is a water-colored liquid. During the aging period, it gradually attains its amber color, flavor and aroma. It is bottled and sold at 80 proof. Whiskey of each country is distinct from that of the others because of local grain characteristics, distillation techniques and formulas. Scotland, Ireland, U.S. and Canada are major producers.

WINE—Made from the fermented juice of grapes. If another fruit is used it appears on the label. Under 14 to 21 per cent.

ZUBROVKA—A Polish vodka in which European "buffalo" grass is steeped to give it a pale yellow color and a slight aroma.

POUSSE-CAFES

Pousse-cafes appeal to the artist in every bartender; they are layered, colorful drinks made with liqueurs of different specific gravities.

Pour over the rounded surface of a teaspoon to spread each cordial or brandy slowly and evenly over the one below without mixing. Try inserting a glass stirring rod into the glass and then slowly pour each ingredient down the rod.

Pour all ingredients in exactly the order given in the recipe.

Following is a list of beautiful suggestions. Pour them into your pony glass *in the order* listed . . . or they will not quite float.

- GREEN CREME DE MENTHE, GALLIANO, BLACKBERRY LIQUEUR AND KIRSCH-WASSER.
- CREME DE NOYAUX, ANISETTE, TUACA AND WHIPPED CREAM
- GRENADINE, WHITE CREME DE CACAO, TRIPLE SEC AND FORBIDDEN FRUIT.
- BANANA LIQUEUR, CHERRY HEERING AND COGNAC.
- PEACH LIQUEUR, KIRSCH AND PERNOD.

Each liqueur has a specific weight. The lighter ones float atop the heavier. So, the idea is to put the heaviest into the glass first, then the next lightest and so on. The following chart lists the weights of the most popular liqueurs used in Pousse-cafes.

ANISETTE LIQUEUR
  red or white (50 Proof) 17.8
CREME de NOYAUX (50 Proof) 17.7
CREME de MENTHE
  green, white or gold (60 Proof) 15.9
CREME de BANANA (50 Proof) 15.0
CREME de CACAO
  brown or white (50 Proof) 15.0
GOLD LIQUEUR (50 Proof) 15.0
MARASCHINO LIQUEUR (50 Proof) 14.9
COFFEE LIQUEUR (50 Proof) 14.2
CHERRY LIQUEUR (48 Proof) 12.7
PARFAIT AMOUR (50 Proof) 12.7
BLUE CURACAO (60 Proof) 11.7
BLACKBERRY LIQUEUR (50 Proof) 11.2
APRICOT LIQUEUR (58 Proof) 10.0
DRY ORANGE CURACAO (60 Proof) 9.8
TRIPLE SEC (60 Proof) 9.8
COFFEE FLAVORED BRANDY (70 Proof) 9.0
LIQUEUR MONASTIQUE (78 Proof) 7.9
PEACH FLAVORED BRANDY (70 Proof) 7.0
CHERRY FLAVORED BRANDY (70 Proof) 6.8
BLACKBERRY FLAVORED BRANDY (70 Proof) 6.7
APRICOT FLAVORED BRANDY (70 Proof) 6.6
ROCK & RYE LIQUEUR (60 Proof) 6.5
GINGER FLAVORED BRANDY (70 Proof) 6.4
PEPPERMINT SCHNAPPS (60 Proof) 5.2
KUMMEL (78 Proof) 4.2
PEACH LIQUEUR (60 Proof) 4.1
SLOE GIN (60 Proof) 4.0

WINES

Wine has been gaining a lot of popularity recently, and every bartender should have some knowledge of the basics of buying and serving wine.

The first thing you should know when looking for a wine is what *class* of wine you want. Most wines fit into one of five classes: appetizer, red, white, dessert, and sparkling.

Once you have determined the class of wine you want, the next step is to decide on the *generic type* of wine. Names like Burgundy and champagne were derived from the districts in which the wine was originally produced. As these wines became famous all over the world, the names came to be associated with any wine that was similar to the original, regardless of where it came from, These names are now the standard terms to describes types of wines.

A further distinction in wine selection is the *varietal type*. This refers to the name of the principal grape variety used in the wine. A Burgundy type wine can be made with many different combinations of grapes. Each combination will have the general characteristics of a Burgundy, but will have its own unique flavor. For examples, a *Gamay* wine is a Burgundy type wine made with California Gamay grapes. As you come to know wines, you will not only develop preferences for different generic types, but also different varietal types.

The following is a more extensive description of the classes of wines and listings of the characteristics of the more popular American types of wines.

APPETIZER WINES
Served before meals or as cocktails. Sherry and Vermouth are most popular.

Sherry has a nutty flavor, comes in sweet medium or dry (In dry wines all or most of the sugar has fermented into alcholol.) and ranges in color from pale to dark amber. The alcohol content of Sherry is around 20 per cent. Sherry may be served chilled or not according to taste.

Vermouth is wine flavored with herbs. There are two types; dry (French) and sweet (Italian). Alcohol content is between 15 per cent and 20 per cent. Vermouth is usually "on the rocks."

TABLE WINES (RED)

Usually dry and served with main-course red meat or dark fowl dishes. The two types, Burgundy and claret (claret is the English name for Bordeaux), usually have an alcohol content of 12 per cent. Serve at room temperature or below it. About one hour before serving, draw the cork from the bottle to allow the wine to "breathe."

A third type of red wine called Rose goes pleasantly with any food and should be served chilled.

TABLE WINES (WHITE)

These run from extremely dry to sweet and are best with white meats, fowl and seafood. Serve chilled. The three types of white table wines, sauterne, Rhine and white Burgundy, have the same alcoholic content as red table wines.

French sauternes are white wines that are somewhat sweet. American sauternes are dry, medium and sweet. Sweet sauternes are best with desserts.

German white table wines range from sweet to dry. American Rhine wines are dry and light-bodied, pale gold in color.

American white Burgundy table wines are like the white Burgundy wines of France. They are less tart than the Rhine wines but have a fruity flavor and body.

28

DESSERT WINES

Sweet, full-bodied wines served with desserts and as afternoon refreshments. Their alcoholic content is around 20 per cent. They come in port, white port, muscatel and Tokay types.

SPARKLING WINES

The most popular types are champagne and sparkling Burgundy. They are both effervescent. Champagne ranges from completely dry (usually labeled "Brut"), semi-dry (labeled "Extra Dry," "Dry" or "Sec,") and sweet (usually labeled "Doux"). Served before dinner with or without appetizers; with almost any dinner entree; and with dessert. It comes in straw color, pink or red. Always serve chilled.

Sparkling Burgundy is red and somewhat dry. Serve chilled with red meats and game.

AMERICAN WINES

Listed below are wines made in America which have over the years become popular. Professional bartenders report a growing preference for them over some European wines.

RED TABLE WINES

BARBERA: Italian type. *Varietal*. California. Robust and fruity. Excellent with Italian food.

BURGUNDY: Burgundy type. *Generic*. California, Ohio, and New York. Serve with red meats, game or cheese.

CABERNET or CABERNET SAUVIGNON: Claret type. *Varietal*. California. Rich and fruity. Serve with red and white meats and fowl.

CHARBONO: Italian type. *Varietal*. California. Similar to Barbera. Fine with Italian meals.

CHIANTI: Italian type *Generic*. California and East. American brands are not made from the same grapes as Italian Chianti. Dry, fruity and slightly tart. Goes with Italian foods.

CLARET: Claret (Bordeaux) type. *Generic*. California. and New York. Soft and fruity. Goes with red meats and fowl.

GAMAY: Burgundy type. *Varietal*. California. Soft, fragrant. Serve with red meats and cheese.

GAMAY ROSE: Rose type *Varietal*. California. Light. Serve chilled with all foods.

GRENACHE ROSE: Rose type. *Varietal*. California. Fruity fragrance. Serve chilled with all foods.

GRIGNOLINO: Italian type. *Varietal*. California. Similar to Barbera but more tart. Serve with red meats and Italian food.

MOURESTAL: Claret type *Varietal.* California. Medium body, soft with fruity aroma. Serve with red meats or fowl.

PINOT NOIR: Burgundy type. *Varietal*. California. Full-bodied, robust. Serve with red meats, game or cheese.

ROSE: Rose type. California. Light and fruity. Serve chilled with any food.

ZINFANDEL: Claret type. *Varietal*. California. Light-bodied, tart, aromatic with a fruity bouquet. A luncheon or dinner wine.

WHITE TABLE WINES

CHABLIS: White Burgundy type. *Generic*. California and New York. Light and fruity. Pale amber. Serve chilled with seafoods, white meats, and fowl.

DELWARE: Rhine wine type. *Varietal*. New York and Ohio. Fruity with a spicy bouquet. Serve chilled with seafood, fowl.

DUTCHESS: Rhine wine type. *Varietal*. New York. Very dry, light and slightly tart. Serve with seafood and fowl. Chill.

DRY SEMILLON: Sauterne type. *Varietal* California. Fruity and medium full-bodied. A dinner wine for chicken, seafood and white meats. Chill.

FOLLE BLANCHE: White Burgundy type. *Varietal*. California. A dry and delicate wine. It is thin-bodied, similar to a French Chablis. Serve with seafood and fowl. Chill.

GEWURZTRAMINER: Rhine or Alsatian type. *Varietal*. California. Aromatic with a spicy flavor. Serve chilled.

GREY RIESLING: Rhine wine type. *Varietal*. California. Soft, mild, and light in body. Serve chilled with seafood, fowl, and light entrees.

HAUTE SAUTERNE: Sauterne type. *Generic*. California, Ohio, New York. Sweet. A dessert wine.

JOHANNISBERG RIESLING: Rhine wine type. *Varietal*. California. Fragrant and fruity. Excellent with seafood and fowl. Serve chilled.

MOSELLE: Rhine wine type. *Generic*. California. Serve chilled with seafood and fowl.

PINOT BLANC: White Burgundy type. *Varietal*. California. Fragrant, lively and dry. Serve chilled with seafood and chicken.

PINOT CHARDONNAY: White Burgundy type. *Varietal*. California. Aromatic, rich body. Serve chilled with seafood and chicken.

RHINE: Rhine wine type. *Generic*. California. New York, and Ohio. Often made from table grapes. Serve with seafood and fowl.

RIESLING: Rhine wine type. *Generic*. California, New York, and Ohio. Dry, fresh and clean. Serve chilled with seafood and fowl.

SAUTERNE: Sauterne type *Generic*. California, Ohio, and New York. Varies from sweet to dry. Serve chilled.

SAUVIGNON BLANC: Sauterne type. *Varietal*. California. Fruity, extremely dry and full-bodied. Serve with almost any meal, but best with shellfish and fowl. There is also a semi-sweet Sauvignon Blanc which goes with chicken. The sweet goes with desserts. Serve chilled.

SWEET SEMILLON: Sauterne type *Varietal*. California. Rich, full-bodied, fairly sweet. Serve chilled with desserts. Excellent in punches and cups.

SYLVANER: Rhine wine type. *Varietal*. California. Light and a little tart. Goes well with seafood. Serve chilled.

TRAMINER: Rhine type. *Varietal*. California. A dry wine, fragrant and flowery in flavor. Serve chilled with chicken, seafoods, and veal.

WHITE PINOT: White Burgundy type. *Varietal*. California. Sometimes called Pinot Blanc. Made from the Chenin Blanc grape in California. Dry, light and fruity. Serve chilled with seafood, fowl, and light meats.

WHITE WINES

**CALIFORNIA AND
NEW YORK**
Chablis
Rhine Wine
Riesling

NEW YORK
Lake Delaware
Lake Dutchess
Lake Diana
Elvira
Iona

CALIFORNIA
Johannisberger Riesling
Sylvaner
Traminer
Folle Blanche
Sauvignon Blanc

OHIO
Lake Erie Island
Delaware

SAUTERNES (DRY)

**CALIFORNIA AND
NEW YORK**
Dry Sauterne

OHIO
Isle St. George

CALIFORNIA
Pinot Chardonay
Pinot Blanc
Dry Semillon
Chateau Beaulieu

SAUTERNES (MED. SWEET — SWEET)

**CALIFORNIA AND
NEW YORK**
Sauterne
Haut Sauterne

CALIFORNIA
Sweet Semillon

NEW YORK
Lake Niagara

33

RED WINES

**CALIFORNIA AND
NEW YORK**
Burgundy
Claret

NEW YORK
Lake Isabella

CALIFORNIA
Barbera
Charbono
Zinfandel
Pinot Noir
Gamay
Caberet

CHAMPAGNES

NEW YORK
Gold Seal Brut
Vindemy Brut Special
Great Western Brut Special

CALIFORNIA
Almaden Brut
Korbel Brut

THE MAJOR EUROPEAN WINE DISTRICTS

FRANCE

BURGUNDY
Chablis
Cote de Nuits
Cote de Beaune
Chalonnats
Maconnais
Beaujolais

LOIRE
Muscadet
Anjou
Saumur
Bourqueil, Chinnon
Vouvray
Pouilly-Fume
Sancerre

BORDEAUX
Medoe
Pomerol
St. Emilion
Graves
Sauternes

RHONES

Chateauneuf-du
Pape

Cole Rotic
Hermitage

Travel

ITALY

Oxvieto-Est!Est!!Est!!!
The Marches
Verdicchio
Latium
Frascati
Campania
Lacryma Christi

Piedmont
Barolo
Lombardy
Valtellina
Veneto
Soave Bardolino

Valpolicella
Emillia
Lambrusco
Tuscany
Chientl
Umbria

GERMANY

Mosel, Saar
Ruwer

Rheingau
Rheinhessen

Rheinpfalz
Franconia

SWITZERLAND

Neuchatel

Vaud
Ticino

Valais

LIQUEURS (CORDIALS)

There are over a hundred cordials on the market of which many are the special concoctions of the manufacturers known only in their own locality.

Cordials may be divided into two general categories: fruit and plant. However, some seem to fall into both. A green chartreuse can contain up to 250 ingredients. Calisay, made in Spain, contains over 125 different herbs, plants and fruits.

A cordial is an artificial liquor or spirit made by either maceration or infusion. In maceration, fruits and plants are steeped in brandy, or rectified spirit, for about six to eight months. Then other ingredients are added. In infusion; the alcohol is mixed with juice of fresh crushed fruit, spiced and sweetened. Or the oils of various plants may be mixed with alcohol, diluted with water, sweetened with sugar. Cordials prepared by the maceration method are more highly regarded by experts.

APRICOT BRANDY (ABRICOTINE): A brandy made from small French apricots.

ABSINTHE: The classic original is scarce. Traditionally it contained wormwood, claimed to be a narcotic. Modern Absinthe, minus wormwood, comes under the trade names Herbsaint or Pernod, and both are popular flavoring agents.

ANISETTE: Compounded from anise-seed oil and the oil of bitter almonds, dissolved in strong spirits.

BENEDICTINE: Made of a variety of herbs and cognac brandy. Originated by a Benedictine monk in Fecamp, France, over 400 years ago. It is still made there.

CHARTREUSE, GREEN OR YELLOW: Made in Tarragona, Spain, today, but originated in France over 300 years ago. A secret recipe of the Carthusian fathers. The yellow contains 120 ingredients (110 proof). The green is made from 250 ingredients (110 proof).

CHERRY HEERING: Made in Copenhagen, Denmark, of cherries, spice, sugar, brandy.

COUINTREAU: Sweeter than white curacao and triple sec which are similar in flavor. Made from fine brandy, with orange peel as the principal base.

CREME DE CACAO: Made from cacao beans and brandy.

CREME DE CASSIS: Made from black currants, steeped in brandy and sweetened with syrup. Called an aperitif in France, a vermouth cassis is made with equal parts of creme de cassis, dry vermouth and sparkling spring water.

CREME DE MENTHE: Made of cognac and fresh peppermint leaves. It comes in white and green.

CREME DE NOYAU: A compound of brandy, bitter almonds, nutmeg, mace and the kernals of apricot or peach pits.

CREME DE ROSE: Made of aromatic seeds and brandy and sweetened with rose petals.

CREME YVETTE: Made the same way as creme de rose, with violet petals substituted for the rose petals. Aromatic.

CURACAO: Made of bitter green orange, mace, cloves and cinnamon and sweetened with wine brandy.

DRAMBUIE: Made from Scotch whisky and wild honey.

FALERNUM: Prepared from West Indian herbs, limes and rum. Alcoholic content only 6 per cent. Sweet flavored.

FLOR ALPINA: Italian. Comes in a tall bottle containing a stalk of the tree, crystalline with a heavy encrustation of sugar. Sweet flavored.

FRAISETTE: Made of alcoholic syrup, white wine and strawberries.

FRAMBOISE: Made from raspberries, it has a high alcohol content.

GOLDWASSER: It's French name is Eau de Vie de Cantzig. It's German name is Danzig Goldwasser. The French is a distillation of fruit peels, herbs and spices with an alcohol base. The German has a caraway-seed flavor. Both have flecks of gold-leaf added. Reputed to be the oldest cordial made. It was first produced in Italy.

GRAND MARNIER: Composed of white curacao and fine champagne.

KUMMEL: Flavored with caraway and cumin seeds. Supposed to have originated in Russia but popular in Germany. Kummel means caraway seed in German.

MARASCHINO: Made with sour cherries and honey. It is white in color and is used as a flavoring agent. It bears no relationship to the popular red maraschino cherries.

PARFAIT AMOUR: Highly perfumed and very sweet made of citron, cinnamon, coriander and brandy.

PRUNELLE: Made from small Burgundian prunes and brandy.

SLIVOVITZ: Made from plums, fermented and distilled. High proof.

STREGA: Italian. Made of orange peel, spices and strong spirits. Very sweet.

SUZE LIQUEUR: Compounded from gentian, a bitter-flavored root supposed to have some medicinal qualities. In the final blending, the bitterness disappears, but the pleasant gentian flavor remains.

RESPONSIBLE DRINKING

Two-thirds of all Americans drink alcoholic beverages. Most of these people do not misuse alcohol.

But 9 million men and women are abusers.

It is unclear whether the reader of this brief article is likely to have a drinking problem; regardless, precaution taken by each and every drinker is a healthy measure.

Drinking patterns vary among people, and abuse must be judged in terms of the individual; however it can generally be stated that:

Drinking becomes a problem when it is associated repeatedly with psychological, physical, or social difficulties.

Without elaborating the long term effects that heavy drinking will have on the body, it should be known that like any other drug, addiction is a potential hazard. Also, an excess of alcohol will effect organs such as the brain, the heart, the liver.

Behavior patterns may be warning signs of misuse. If the day is frequently begun with a drink, if a drink is needed to perform at work, if friends or relatives complain about drinking, or if unusual events (such as memory losses or reckless behavior) occur while drinking, it may be time to seek professional advice.

WHAT CAN I, AS A BARTENDER, DO TO FOSTER RESPONSIBLE DRINKING?

1. Provide food with drinks, such as dairy products, fish, and meats.

2. Do not push loaded drinks onto your guests; do not insist on refilling a cocktail.

3. Offer non-alcoholic substitutes, such as fruit, vegetable, or soft drinks as attractive alternatives.

4. Do not arrange parties just for drinking; have plenty of other activities planned.

DRIVING: The risks of driving while intoxicated are demonstrated by statistics: many fatal road accidents are caused by drunk drivers.

The state limit is a blood alcohol concentration of 0.10%. This represents about two drinks taken within an hour by a man of 150 pounds.

The following chart is a useful barometer of drinking. One drink is equal to about 1.5 oz. of whisky, 5 oz. of wine or 2 bottles of beer. The shaded area indicated the range beyond the legal limit, when the pleasurable (innocuous) effects of alcohol yield to serious impairments of judgment and behavior.

Note that for each hour after drinking has stopped, .015 can be subtracted from the blood concentration, as this is the rate of elimination.

DRINKS

Body Weight	1	2	3	4	5	6
100 lbs.	.038	.075	.113	.150	.188	.225
120 "	.031	.063	.094	.125	.156	.188
140 "	.027	.054	.080	.107	.134	.161
160 "	.023	.047	.070	.094	.117	.141
180 "	.021	.042	.063	.083	.104	.124
200 "	.019	.038	.056	.075	.094	.113
220 "	.017	.034	.051	.068	.085	.102
240 "	.016	.031	.047	.063	.078	.094

RECIPES

A-Z

Use a bartender's mixing glass whenever the instructions state "combine" ingredients. Strain the drink from the mixing glass into the drinking glass suggested by the illustration alongside the ingredients.

NOTE: The number of glasses or cups shown alongside a recipe do not necessarily indicate the quantity of drinks the recipe will produce.

A-1 PICK-ME-UP

1 pint dark rum
1 lb. rock candy
1 doz. eggs
1 doz. lemons

Squeeze the juice of the lemons into a crock pot; add the eggs broken in their shells. Cover with a damp cloth and allow to stand for several days. (The shells will dissolve.) When ready strain through cheesecloth into another pot. Combine the rum and the rock candy in a saucepan; boil with a quart of water until smooth. Combine with the egg mixture and bottle for future use.

A.J.

1½ oz. apple brandy
1½ oz. unsweetened grapefruit juice
A few drops grenadine

Combine with ice; shake well. Strain and add ice.

ABBEY

1½ oz. gin
1½ oz. orange juice
1-2 dashes orange bitters

Combine with ice; shake. Strain over ice. top with a cherry.

ABBEY COCKTAIL

1½ oz. gin
¾ oz. orange juice
¼ oz. sweet vermouth
1-2 dashes of Angostura bitters

Combine with ice; shake. Strain, add ice, top with a cherry.

ABERDEEN ANGUS

2 oz. Scotch
1 oz. Drambuie
1 tbs. honey
2 tsp. lime juice

Combine the Scotch and the honey; stir until smooth. Add the lime juice. Warm the Drambuie over a low flame, turn out on a ladle; ignite and pour into the mug. Stir and serve immediately.

ABSINTHE SUISSESSE

1½ oz. absinthe substitute
1 egg white
Several drops of anisette, white creme de menthe
A few drops of orange flower water

Combine with ice; shake well. Strain straight up.

ACADIAN MEAD

2 quarts honey
12 oz. boiling water

Dissolve the honey with the water in a crock pot; allow to ferment before bottling and sealing.

ACAPULCO

1¾ oz. rum
¼ oz. Triple Sec
1 egg white
½ oz. lime juice
Sugar to taste
Mint leaves

Combine with ice; shake into pre-chilled glass. Strain. Add ice and top with one or two mint leaves, partially torn.

ADAM AND EVE

1 oz. gin
1 oz. cognac
1 oz. Forbidden Fruit
A few drops lemon juice

Combine with ice; shake. Strain over ice.

ADDINGTON

1½ oz. sweet vermouth
1½ oz. dry vermouth
Club soda

Combine everything (except the soda) with ice and shake. Strain; add ice and soda. Add a twist of lemon, plus the peel.

ADMIRAL COCKTAIL

1 oz. bourbon
1½ oz. dry vermouth
½ lemon

Combine with ice; shake. Strain. Squeeze in the lemon's juice, stir, and drop in the peel. Add ice.

ADONIS

2 oz. dry sherry
1 oz. sweet vermouth
1-2 dashes orange bitters

Combine with ice; shake. Strain over ice.

AFFINITY

¾ oz. Scotch
¾ oz. sweet vermouth
¾ oz. dry vermouth
A few dashes of Angostura bitters

Combine with ice; shake. Strain. Add ice and a twist of lemon plus peel, and top with a cherry.

For an **AFFINITY COCKTAIL** *use ¾ oz. dry sherry and ¾ oz. port instead of vermouth.*

AFTER DINNER

1½ oz. apricot brandy
1½ oz. curacao
2 oz. lime juice

Combine with ice; shake. Strain. Add a twist of lime and ice. Drop in the peel.

AFTER DINNER SPECIAL

¾ oz. cherry brandy
1½ oz. Swedish Punch
1 oz. lime juice

Combine with ice; shake. Strain over ice.

AIRMAIL SPECIAL

Follow the recipe for an **AMERICAN FLYER,** *substituting a teaspoon of honey for the sugar. Shake extra well.*

AL LONG'S SPECIAL HOT TODDY

2 oz. Drambuie
2 oz. Scotch
1 oz. raspberry syrup
1 tbs. lime juice
3 oz. water

Combine in a saucepan. Bring to a boil. Serve hot.

ALABAMA

¾ oz. brandy
¼ oz. curacao
1 oz. lime juice
½ tsp. sugar

Combine with ice; shake. Strain. Add ice, and a twist of orange. Drop in the peel.

ALABAZAM

2 oz. cognac
2 tsp. sugar syrup
1 tbs. curacao
1 tsp. lemon juice
1-2 dashes orange bitters

Combine with ice; shake well. Strain and add ice.

ALASKA

1½ oz. gin
¾ oz. yellow chartreuse
1-2 dashes orange bitters

Combine with ice; shake very well. Strain over ice.

ALBERMARLE FIZZ

2 oz. dry gin
½ lemon
1 tsp. sugar
1 tsp. raspberry syrup
Club soda
Sugar

Over three cubes of ice, add gin, squeeze in the juice of the lemon. Add sugar and the raspberry syrup and stir well. Fill glass with club soda.

ALE FLIP

2 egg whites
4 egg yolks
1 quart ale
2½ tsp. sugar syrup

Beat the egg whites until creamy; beat the egg yolks, and combine the two, adding the sugar syrup. Pour the ale into a saucepan and bring to a boil. Gradually add the egg mixture to the boiling ale, stirring it constantly. Remove from heat and transfer between two pitchers vigorously to build a frothy head. Balance out the brew between the pitchers, dust with nutmeg, and serve steaming hot.

ALE SANGAREE

½ tsp. powdered sugar
10 oz. chilled ale

Dissolve the sugar in with a few drops of water. Add the ale and dust with nutmeg.

ALEXANDER WITH PRUNELLE

1½ oz. gin
1 oz. prunelle
1 oz. cream

Combine with ice; shake well. Strain, and dust with cinnamon.

ALEXANDER YOUNG

1½ oz. bourbon
½ oz. orange juice
½ oz. pineapple juice
1 tsp. lemon juice
A few dashes of Angostura bitters
A few drops grenadine

Combine with ice; shake well. Strain over crushed ice.

ALFONSO SPECIAL

¾ oz. dry gin
1½ oz. Grand Marnier
A few drops sweet vermouth and dry vermouth
A few dashes of Angostura bitters

Combine with ice; shake. Strain and add ice.

ALGONQUIN

2 oz. rye
1 oz. dry vermouth
1 oz. pineapple juice

Combine with ice; shake. Strain and add ice.

46

ALL-WHITE FRAPPE

1 oz. anisette
1 oz. white creme de cacao
½ oz. white creme de menthe
1 oz. lemon juice

Combine with ice; shake well. Strain over crushed ice.

ALLEN

1½ oz. gin
¾ oz. maraschino
A few drops lemon juice

Combine with ice, shake well. Strain and add ice.

ALLIES

1 oz. gin
1 oz. dry vermouth
1-2 dashes kummel

Combine with ice; shake well. Strain and add ice.
For a BERLINER, increase the gin, halve the vermouth, and add ¼ oz. of lemon juice.

ALMOND COCKTAIL

2 oz. gin
1 oz. dry vermouth
A pair of almonds, peeled
A crushed peach kernel
½ tsp. powdered sugar
1 tsp. kirsch
1 tsp. peach brandy

Warm the gin; add the almonds, sugar, and kernel. Allow to cool; add the remaining ingredients and stir. Strain and add ice.

AMABILE BEONE

1 oz. Drambuie
2 oz. green creme de menthe
A few drops Pernod
Sugar

Combine with ice; shake well. Strain. "Sugar Frost" glass. Coat the rim with Pernod, and dip it in sugar.

AMARANTH

1 oz. rye
1 dash bitters
Powdered sugar
Club soda

Combine the rye, any kind of bitters, and a dash of powdered sugar in a glass. Stir well. Add ice and fill with club soda.

AMBASSADOR

2 oz. tequila
Orange juice

Pour the tequila into glass, add ice and orange juice. Add 1 oz. of sugar syrup to sweeten.

AMBER CLOUD

1½ oz. cognac
2 tbs. Galliano

Combine with ice; shake well. Pour over crushed ice.

AMBROSIA FOR TWO

3 oz. brandy
3 oz. apple brandy
Several drops of
raspberry syrup
Champagne

Combine the brandies and the syrup with ice; shake. Strain into two pre-chilled wine glasses. Fill each glass with champagne and stir.

AMER PICON COOLER

1½ oz. Amer Picon
1 oz. gin
½ oz. cherry liqueur
1 tsp. sugar syrup
1 tsp. lemon juice
Club soda

Combine with ice; shake well. Strain. Add ice and club soda.

AMERICAN BEAUTY

¾ oz. brandy
¾ oz. dry vermouth
¾ oz. orange juice
¼ oz. white creme de menthe
1 oz. port
A few drops grenadine

Combine with ice; shake well. Strain. Carefully add port, tipping the glass so that the port floats on top.

AMERICAN FLYER

1½ oz. Bacardi
1½ tsp. lime juice
A pinch sugar
Champagne

Combine the rum, juice and sugar with ice; shake. Strain; fill the glass with champagne.

AMERICAN LEGION MARGUERITA

2 oz. tequila
1 oz. Cointreau
½ oz. lemon juice
½ oz. lime juice
Salt

Combine with ice; shake well. Moisten serving glass rim with water and frost with salt. Strain.

AMERICAN ROSE

1½ oz. brandy
1 tsp. grenadine
½ ripe peach, skinned and masked
A few drops Pernod
Champagne

Combine the brandy, Pernod, grenadine, ice and peach; shake extremely well. Fill large glass with crushed ice and strain in the drink. Add the champagne.

AMERICANA

¼ oz. 100-proof bourbon
½ tsp. sugar
1-2 dashes bitters
Champagne
I peach slice

Combine the bourbon, bitters and sugar. Stir until the sugar is dissolved. Add champagne and a slice of peach.

AMERICANO

1¼ oz. Campari
1¼ oz. sweet vermouth
Club soda

Combine everything except the soda with ice. Strain, add ice and fill with club soda.

48

AMONTILLADO COCKTAIL

1 oz. Amontillado
1 oz. Dubonnet

Combine in a wide champagne glass; stir gently. Touch it up with a twist of lemon and add ice.

ANCHORS AWEIGH

1 oz. bourbon
2 tbs. heavy cream
2 tsp. apiece Triple Sec, peach brandy and maraschino
A few drops cherry juice

Combine with ice; shake well. Strain and serve straight up.

ANDALUSIA

1½ oz. dry sherry
½ oz. cognac
½ oz. white rum
A few dashes of Angostura bitters

Combine with ice; shake well. Strain and add ice.

ANDALUSIAN WINE

1 pint red wine
1 pint water
Sugar to taste
Lemon slices

Combine in a pitcher; fill with ice.

ANGEL FACE

1 oz. dry gin
1 oz. apricot brandy
1 oz. apple brandy

Combine with ice; shake well. Strain and add ice.

ANGEL'S DELIGHT

¼ oz. grenadine
¼ oz. Triple Sec
¼ oz. Creme Yvette
¼ oz. cream

Carefully add in above order, tipping glass so ingredients float on top of each other.

ANGEL'S RUM PUNCH

1 bottle Jamaican rum
1 quart milk
1 tsp. honey

Combine; stir gently to dissolve the honey. Serve with ice; stir a few times to frost the glass before drinking.

ANGEL'S TIP

1 oz. dark creme de cacao
½ oz. heavy cream

Pour the creme de cacao into a pony glass, tip it and carefully add the cream, floating it on top.

For a KING ALPHONSE spear a maraschino cherry and bridge it over serving glass.

ANGEL'S WINGS

½ oz. creme de violette
½ oz. raspberry syrup
½ oz. maraschino

Pour each ingredient as shown, tipping glass so that the ingredients do not mix but float on top of each other.

49

ANGELICA RATAFIA

4 small bunches angelica stalks, with leaves
1 tbs. whole angelica seeds
Nutmeg, ground cinnamon, crushed cloves
4 lbs. sugar

Pound the angelica stalks and leaves on the bottom of a crock pot; add the seeds and spices and store in a cool place for two months. Strain. Boil the sugar in enough water to make a syrup; combine with the spiced angelica; stir well and re-strain; bottle for future use.

ANGLER'S COCKTAIL

1½ oz. dry gin
A few drops of grenadine
1-2 dashes Angostura bitters
1-2 dashes orange bitters

Combine with ice; shake. Strain. Add ice if desired.

ANISE VODKA

1 pint vodka
2 oz. whole anise seeds
2 oz. rock candy

Combine in a large bottle; seal tightly and allow to stand at room temperature for at least one week. Strain clean and re-bottle for future use.

ANISETTE DE BORDEAUX

7 oz. whole, green anise seeds
3 oz. star anise seeds
1½ oz. fine tea
1 tbs. apiece ground coriander and fennel
10 pints sugar
3½ gallons cooking alcohol

Pound the anise seeds into a powder; combine with the remaining spices and steep in the alcohol for two weeks. Strain. Boil the sugar in enough water to make a thick syrup; mix with anisette. Bottle and store in a cool place until fermented. Strain and re-bottle for future use.

ANKLE BREAKER

1½ oz. cherry brandy
1 oz. lime juice
1 oz. 151-proof rum
2 tsp. sugar syrup

Combine with ice, shake well. Strain over ice.

ANNE

1½ oz. apple brandy
¾ oz. Cointreau
¾ oz. Dubonnet
1-2 dashes Angostura bitters

Combine without ice; stir until well-blended. Pour over ice, decorate with one red and one green cherry, a slice of orange and a slice of lime.

ANNIVERSARY PUNCH

1 bottle whiskey
1 pint orange juice
8 oz. pineapple juice
8 oz. brown sugar
4 oz. lemon juice
1 quart pineapple sherbet
1 bottle club soda
2 bottles ginger ale
Orange and pineapple slices

Combine everything except the sherbet, sodas and garnishes; stir well. Before serving, add the ginger ale and soda. Use the sherbet instead of ice; garnish with cherries.

APPENDECTOMY

6 oz. gin
1½ oz. lime juice
¾ oz. Grand Marnier
1 egg white

Combine with ice; shake extremely well. Serves two. Strain into a goblet or split in two old-fashioned glasses over ice.

APPENDICITIS

12 oz. gin
3 oz. lemon juice
1½ oz. curacao
1 whole egg

Combine with ice; shake extremely well. Serves four.

APPLE BLOW

2 oz. apple brandy
1 tsp. sugar
1 egg white
Lemon juice
Club soda
Cider

In a mixing glass filled with ice, combine the apple brandy, sugar, egg white and several drops of lemon juice. Shake well. Strain over ice into a glass and fill with half soda and half cider.

For an **APPLE BLOW FIZZ**, omit the cider and fill the glass entirely with soda.

APPLE BRANDY COCKTAIL

1½ oz. apple brandy
½ tsp. grenadine
½ tsp. lemon juice

Combine with ice; shake well. Strain and add ice.

For an **APPLE BRANDY SOUR**, increase the brandy, eliminate the grenadine and strain straight up.

APPLE BRANDY COOLER

2 oz. brandy
1 oz. white rum
1 tsp. lime juice
Apple juice
1 tsp. Jamaican rum

Combine the brandy, rum and lime juice with ice, then almost fill the glass with apple juice and stir well. Float the Jamaican rum on top. Top with a slice of lime.

APPLE BRANDY HIGHBALL

2 oz. apple brandy
Ginger ale

Pour the apple brandy over ice. Add ginger ale and a twist of lemon. Stir well.

APPLE BUCK

1½ oz. apple brandy
1 tsp. ginger brandy
1 tsp. lemon juice
1 chunk preserved ginger
Ginger ale

With ice, combine the apple brandy, ginger brandy and lemon juice; shake well. Strain over ice, fill with ginger ale. Top with the preserved ginger.

APPLE BYRRH

1½ oz. calvados
¼ oz. Byrrh
½ oz. dry vermouth
½ tsp. lemon juice

Combine with ice; shake well. Strain. Add ice and a twist of lemon, plus the peel.

APPLE COCKTAIL

2 oz. brandy
1 oz. apple brandy

Combine with ice; shake well. Strain and add ice.

APPLE DUBONNET

1½ oz. calvados
1½ oz. Dubonnet

Combine with ice; shake well. Strain, add ice and top with a slice of lemon.

APPLE GINGER FIX

1 oz. apple brandy
1 oz. ginger brandy
Sugar syrup
Lemon juice

Combine the brandies with ice. Add several drops of sugar syrup and a teaspoon of lemon juice; shake well. Strain over crushed ice. Top with a slice of lemon.

APPLE GINGER SANGAREE

1½ oz. apple brandy
½ oz. green ginger wine

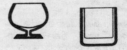

Combine with ice; shake well. Strain, add ice and decorate with an orange slice.

APPLE KNOCKER

2½ oz. apple brandy
3 oz. orange juice
½ oz. sweet vermouth
1 tsp. lemon juice
1½ tsp. sugar syrup

Combine with ice; shake well. Strain with crushed ice.

APPLE LILLET

1½ oz. calvados
1½ oz. Lillet

Combine with ice; shake well. Strain, add ice, and top with an orange slice.

APPLE RUM RICKEY

¾ oz. apple brandy
¾ oz. white rum
Club soda

Combine the rum and the brandy with ice; shake well. Strain over ice into a glass and fill with club soda. Add a twist of orange and lime; stir and drop the peels into the drink.

APPLE SMILE

1½ oz. gin
1 tbs. apple brandy
2 tsp. lime juice
A few drops grenadine

Combine with ice; shake well. Strain and add ice.

APPLE SWIZZLE

1½ oz. apple brandy
1 oz. white rum
1 tsp. lime juice
1 tsp. powdered sugar
A few dashes of Angostura bitters

Combine with ice; shake well. Strain over crushed ice.

APPLE WINE

4 lbs. apples
1½ lbs. sugar

Slice the apples in their skins; place them in a large pot and add 1 gal. of water which has been boiled clean and cooled. Store at room temperature for at least a week, stirring every day. Strain the juice a bit and allow to stand until the sugar dissolves naturally. Pour off into bottles; seal and allow to ferment for a week to ten days.

APPLE STRAWBERRY CORDIAL

1 dozen apples
½ peck strawberries
1 lb. brown sugar

Whiskey
Allspice, nutmeg, mace

Peel and core the apples. Simmer them in a pint of water for several minutes; add the spices and simmer twice as long. Add the strawberries and the sugar, plus approximately five more cups of water and simmer several more minutes. Allow to cool; strain and double the amount of liquid with whiskey. Bottle for future use.

APPLECAR

¾ oz. apple brandy
¾ oz. curacao
1 tbs. lemon juice

Combine with ice; shake well. Strain and add ice. Cointreau can be used instead of curacao.

APPLEHAWK

1¼ oz. apple brandy
1¼ oz. unsweetened grapefruit juice
½ tsp. sugar syrup

Combine with ice; shake well. Strain and add ice.

APPLEJACK NO. 1

1½ oz. apple brandy
1 tsp. sugar syrup
1-2 dashes Angostura bitters
1-2 dashes orange bitters

Combine the brandy and the sugar syrup with ice. Add bitters; shake well. Strain and add ice.

APPLEJACK NO. 2

Substitute ½ oz. sweet vermouth for the sugar syrup.

APPLEJACK ALGONQUIN

1½ oz. apple brandy
1 tsp. baked apple
1 cube sugar
Nutmeg

In a glass, combine apple brandy and the baked apple. Drop in the sugar; fill with hot water and stir well. Garnish with nutmeg.

APPLEJACK COCKTAIL

2 oz. apple brandy
¼ oz. curacao
1 tsp. powdered sugar
1½ tbs. lime juice

Combine with ice; shake well. Strain over crushed ice.

APPLEJACK PUNCH

2 bottles apple juice
1 bottle ginger ale
1 bottle vodka
1 pint orange juice
Mint sprigs

Combine everything except the mint and ginger ale in a large punch bowl; stir well. Add the ginger ale plus chunks of ice. Decorate with mint.

APPLEJACK RABBIT

1½ oz. apple brandy
½ oz. lemon juice
½ oz. lime juice
½ tsp. maple syrup

Combine with ice; shake very well. Dip glass rim in water or maple syrup and line with sugar. Strain in the drink and add ice.

APPLEJACK SOUR

2 oz. apple brandy
½ oz. lemon juice
1½ tsp. sugar syrup

Combine with ice; shake well. Strain into a sour glass and serve straight up or in an old-fashioned glass over ice.

For a **SOUR RED APPLEJACK,** *add a few drops of grenadine and a few drops of lime juice, halving the sugar.*

APRICOT ANISE FIZZ

1 ¾ oz. gin
½ oz. apricot brandy
¼ oz. anisette
1 tsp. lemon juice
Club soda
½ apricot

Combine with ice; shake well. Strain and add ice. Almost fill with club soda. Add a twist of lemon, drop in the peel and stir. Add the apricot.

APRICOT BRANDY

1 lb. apricots
1 lb. sugar
4 oz. brandy

Boil the apricots whole in enough water to cover them; lower heat and simmer until tender. Remove the skins. Boil the sugar in enough water to make a syrup and pour it over the apricots. Allow to stand for at least a day. Pour out into a jug or large bottle; add the brandy, seal and store a year. Strain and bottle when ready for future use.

APRICOT BRANDY

2 oz. apricot brandy
Several drops grenadine
Club soda

Pour the apricot brandy into glass. Add the grenadine and ice; stir well. Fill with club soda. Twist in a lemon and an orange peel. Top with fruit slices.

APRICOT COOLER

1 ¼ oz. apricot brandy
¾ oz. lemon juice
1 tbs. sugar syrup
1 peeled, pitted apricot

Cook and cool the apricot. Mash well and put in a mixing glass filled with ice, along with the apricot brandy, the lemon juice and the sugar syrup. Shake extremely well. Pour unstrained into glass and serve with a straw.

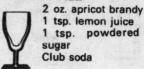

APRICOT FIZZ

2 oz. apricot brandy
1 tsp. lemon juice
1 tsp. powdered sugar
Club soda

Combine brandy, juice and sugar with ice; shake well. Strain, add ice and fill with club soda. Top with fruit slices.

APRICOT LADY

1 oz. apricot brandy
1½ oz. white rum
½ tsp. curacao
1 tsp. lime juice
1 egg white

Combine in an ice-filled mixing glass; shake very well. Strain over crushed ice. Top with an orange slice.

APRICOT NO. 1

2 oz. apricot brandy
1 oz. orange juice
1 oz. lemon juice
A few drops gin

Combine with ice, shake well. Strain and add ice.

APRICOT NOG

4 oz. white rum
4 oz. heavy cream
4 oz. apricot nectar
2 oz. apricot brandy
1 egg, well beaten
4 oz. crushed ice

Combine in blender at a high speed until smooth. Serve garnished with nutmeg.

APRICOT PIE

1 oz. white rum
1 oz. sweet vermouth
¼ oz. apricot brandy
½ tsp. lemon juice
Several drops grenadine

Combine in a mixing glass filled with ice; shake well. Strain, add ice and twist in an orange peel.

APRICOT VODKA

1 lb. apricots, peeled and pitted
3 cups cooking alcohol
2 cups sugar
Grated lemon rinds

Boil the sugar in enough water to make a syrup; add the apricots and simmer for several minutes. Strain and allow to cool. Add the alcohol, 2 cups of water and the rinds; pour off into a bottle and store for at least a month. Strain and re-bottle for future use when ready.

AQUAVIT FIZZ

5 oz. aquavit
1 oz. Cherry Heering
2 tbs. sugar syrup
1 oz. lemon juice
1 egg white
Club soda

Combine (except soda) with ice; shake well. Strain and fill with club soda. Serves two.

AQUAVIT RICKEY

1½ oz. aquavit
1 tsp. kummel
Club soda

Combine aquavit and kummel in a highball glass, add ice and fill with club soda. Squeeze a slice of lime into the drink, drop in the peel and stir well.

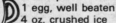

AQUEDUCT

1½ oz. vodka
¼ oz. curacao
¼ oz. apricot liqueur
1 tsp. lime juice

Combine with ice; shake well. Strain, add ice and a twist of orange.

ARCHBISHOP PUNCH

1 bottle claret
1 large orange
6 cloves
Sugar

Stick the cloves into the orange and bake in a medium-hot oven (300°). When the orange browns, remove it, quarter it, take out the seeds and place it in a saucepan. Pour in the bottle of claret, and a tablespoon of sugar; simmer until steaming. Serve hot.
For a **BRANDY BISHOP** *pour ⅛ oz. of Brandy into each mug when serving.*

ARGENTINE JULEP

1 oz. brandy
1 oz. light claret
1 oz. orange juice
1 oz. pineapple juice
¼ oz. Cointreau
A mint sprig

Combine (except mint) with ice. Add sugar; shake well. Strain over crushed ice. Top with an orange slice and a mint sprig.

ARRACK PUNCH

1½ oz. Arrack
1 oz. orange juice
1 oz. lemon juice
1 tsp. sugar
Several tea leaves

Combine the Arrack, juices and sugar in a large mug. Add boiling water; infuse with dark tea several minutes. Stir well. Decorate with pineapple slice.

ARTILLERY

2 oz. gin
¾ oz. sweet ver-
mouth
A few dashes of
Angostura bitters

Combine with ice; shake well. Strain, add ice and twist in a lemon peel.

ARTILLERY PUNCH

1 gallon hard cider
1 bottle bourbon
1 bottle dark rum
1 quart orange juice
1 quart strawberries
6 large pineapples
1 dozen bottles champagne

Slice the pineapple; cut out all the meat. Squeeze and save all the juice. Slice and squeeze the strawberries; combine the juice with the pineapple and orange juice in a large punch bowl. Add the rum, whiskey and cider; stir well and allow to stand overnight. Add the champagne plus ice when ready to serve.

ASTRONAUT

1½ oz. Jamaican rum
1½ oz. vodka
1½ tsp. lemon juice
A few drops of passion fruit juice

Combine with ice; shake well. Strain and add ice. Touch it up with lemon and drop in the peel.

AUNT AGATHA

2 oz. white rum
4 oz. orange juice
1 dash Angostura bitters

Pour the rum and the orange juice into a wide glass. Stir gently and then drop in a few cubes of ice. Float the Angostura bitters on top.

AUNT BETSY'S FAVORITE

1 bottle dry red wine
2 cups dark port
1 cup brandy
4 tsp. sugar
Peels of two oranges
6 cloves
12 cinnamon sticks

Combine the wines and brandy in a saucepan. Add the sugar, peels, cloves and cinnamon sticks. Heat slowly and do not bring to a boil. Serves 10-12.

AUNT JEMIMA

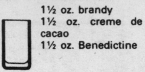

1½ oz. brandy
1½ oz. creme de cacao
1½ oz. Benedictine

Combine, carefully tilting the glass so that each ingredient floats upon the other.

AVIATION

2 oz. gin
½ oz. lemon juice
¼ oz. maraschino

Combine with ice; shake very well. Strain and add ice.

AZTEC PUNCH

5 gallons grapefruit juice
1 gallon tequila
3 cups lemon juice
1 cup sugar syrup
2 quarts dark tea

Combine in a large punch bowl and add a block of ice before serving.

YOUR OWN RECIPE

YOUR OWN RECIPE

Use a bartender's mixing glass whenever the instructions state "combine" ingredients. Strain the drink from the mixing glass into the drinking glass suggested by the illustration alongside the ingredients.

The glass pictured for each drink is our suggestion; other drinking cups may be used as well.

B & B

1 oz. Benedictine
1 oz. brandy

Stir together, serve straight up.

B & B COLLINS

2 oz. cognac
1 tbs. sugar syrup
1 tsp. lemon juice
1 tsp. Benedictine
Club soda

Combine cognac, juice and sugar syrup with ice; shake well. Strain, add ice, almost fill with club soda. Stir gently. Float Benedictine on top. Decorate with lemon slice.

B.V.D.

¾ oz. dry gin, white rum and dry vermouth

Combine with ice; shake well. Strain and add ice.

BACARDI SPECIAL

1½ oz. Bacardi
1 oz. lime juice
¾ oz. gin
1 tsp. grenadine

Combine with ice; shake well. Strain and add ice.

BACHELOR'S BAIT

2 oz. gin
½ tsp. grenadine
1-2 dashes orange bitters
1 egg white

Combine with ice; shake extremely well. Strain and add ice.

BADMINTON

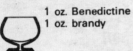

1 bottle red wine
2 oz. sugar
A pinch of nutmeg
Cucumber slices
½ pint club soda

Combine the wine and sugar in a pitcher; stir until the sugar is dissolved. Add plenty of ice. Garnish with nutmeg; decorate with cucumber slices. Add the soda before serving.

BAIRN

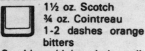

1½ oz. Scotch
¾ oz. Cointreau
1-2 dashes orange bitters

Combine with ice; shake well.

BALI HAI

1 oz. gin
1 oz. white rum
1 oz. okolehao
1 oz. lemon juice
3 oz. lime juice
Champagne

Combine everything except the champagne with ice; shake well. Strain over crushed ice. Add several drops champagne.

BALTIMORE BRACER

1 oz. brandy
1 oz. anisette
1 egg white

Combine with ice; shake extremely well. Strain and add ice.

BANANA BIRD

1 oz. bourbon
1 oz. heavy cream
2 tsp. creme de banana
2 tsp. Triple Sec

Combine with ice; shake very well. Drain into a sour glass straight up.

BANANA CHARTREUSE

4 bananas, barely ripe
4 oz. yellow chartreuse
Butter
Ground ginger

Peel the bananas. Slice them into quarters; first the long way, then in half. Saute the banana slices in a generous amount of butter; sprinkle with ginger and pour the chartreuse over them. Ignite; burn for no more than sixty seconds and serve at once.

BALTIMORE EGG NOG

½ pint cognac, Jamaican rum, apple brandy and peach brandy
1 doz. eggs
½ lb. sugar
1½ quarts milk
1 pint ice cream (any flavor)
½ pint heavy cream

Separate eggs. Lightly beat yolks in a large saucepan; add liquors and heat until eggs are cooked. Gently beat in sugar, milk, ice cream and heavy cream. Cool and refrigerate. A half-hour before serving, beat egg whites until stiff and fold into the dessert. Top with nutmeg or cinnamon. Serves 4-6.

BANANA COCKTAIL

1¼ oz. vodka
1 tsp. banana liqueur
½ lime
Club soda
Mint sprigs

Combine the vodka and banana liquer with ice; shake well. Strain, squeeze in the lime and drop in the peel. Add ice and fill with club soda. Stir gently and top with sprigs of mint.

BANANA DAIQUIRI

2 oz. white rum
1½ tsp. lime juice
1 tsp. banana liqueur
½ banana, sliced
4 oz. crushed ice

Combine in an electric blender; blend at a low speed for no more than 15 seconds. Strain.

BANANA MANGO

1½ oz. white rum
½ oz. mango nectar
¾ tsp. banana liqueur
2 tsp. lime juice
1 mango slice

Combine with ice; shake well. Strain, add ice. Top with mango slice.

BANANA RUM FRAPPE

½ oz. white rum
½ oz. banana liqueur
½ oz. orange juice

Combine with ice; shake well. Strain over crushed ice.

BANANA SQUASH

4 oz. white rum
3 tsp. lime juice
2 brown bananas, sliced
6 oz. crushed ice

Soak the banana slices with the rum in a deep bowl for several hours. Combine this with the lime juice and ice in a blender at a high speed for 15 seconds. Turn out straight up. (Bananas can be browned by storing in a refrigerator.)

BANANA VODKA

1 pint vodka
1 ripe banana, peeled and sliced
1 lemon, sliced in the skin
12 oz. rock candy

Combine in a large bottle; seal tightly and allow to stand at room temperature for at least a week, or until all the rock candy has dissolved. Shake gently at least once each day. Strain when ready, squeeze in the lemon juice and re-bottle for future use.

BANSHEE

1 oz. white creme de cacao
1 oz. creme de banana
1 oz. light cream

Combine with ice; shake very well. Strain. Serve straight up.

BARBARY COAST

½ oz. dry gin, Scotch, white rum, white creme de cacao and heavy cream

Combine with ice; shake very well. Strain and add ice.

BARLEY CIDER

12 gallons sweet cider
5 lb. brown sugar
2 lb. raisins
2 quarts barley
2 oz. olive oil

Combine in a large wooden cask; stir well. Seal and allow to ferment. When ready, strain off into another cask to age.

BARNUM

1½ oz. gin
½ oz. apricot brandy
A few dashes of Angostura bitters
A few drops lemon juice

Combine with ice; shake well. Strain and add ice.

BARTON SPECIAL

1½ oz. calvados
¾ oz. Scotch
¾ oz. dry gin

Combine with ice; shake well. Strain, add ice and a twist of lemon; drop in the peel.

BATIDO DE PINA

2½ oz. white rum
2/3 cup crushed pineapple
1 tsp. powdered sugar

Combine the rum with the crushed pineapple in an electric blender; blend until smooth.

BAYARD FIZZ

2 oz. gin
2 tsp. maraschino
1 tsp. lemon juice
1 tsp. raspberry syrup
2 raspberries
Club soda

Combine (except the soda and the raspberries) with ice; shake well. Strain and add ice. Fill with soda. Stir gently. Float raspberries on top.

BARROSA CUP

1 bottle blackberry brandy
1 bottle peach brandy
1 pint cherry whiskey, dark curacao and maraschino
4 oz. sherry and kummel
3 oz. sugar
1 tsp. almond extract
Lemon rinds, cucumber peels
1 pint champagne

Combine everything except the champagne; stir until blended. Strain clean. Add champagne plus chunks of ice before serving.

BAYBERRY PUNCH

2 quarts brandy
½ pint curacao
2 cups cold tea
10 oz. powdered sugar
6 oz. grenadine
1 doz. sliced lemons
½ doz. sliced oranges
1½ quarts cold water

Combine in a large punch bowl; mix well. Add ice a half-hour before serving. Fruit slices can be squeezed in before mixing, if desired.

BAYOU

1¾ oz. brandy
2 tsp. lime juice
1 tsp. mango nectar
Several drops peach liqueur
1 peach slice

Combine (except peach slice) with ice; shake well. Strain and add ice. Top with peach slice.

BAYOU BEER

There are any number of ways to make beer. This is one.

1 oz. hops
A cake of yeast
1 lb. molasses

Combine in a large saucepan; bring to a boil and stir constantly. Allow to cool and ferment before bottling in a crock pot or stone jug, (it should only take a few days).

BEACHCOMBER

1½ oz. rum
1 tsp. lime juice
1 tsp. Triple Sec
Several drops maraschino
Sugar

Combine with ice; shake well. Line the rim of glass with water, press it in sugar. Strain in drink, add ice.

BEACHCOMBER'S BRACER

1 oz. white rum
1 tbs. orange curacao
1 tbs. bourbon
1 tsp. powdered sugar
A few dashes of Angostura bitters
Lemon juice

Dissolve the sugar with a few drops of lemon juice in a mug; add the remaining ingredients. Fill the mug with boiling water and stir well.

BEACHCOMBER'S GOLD

1½ oz. white rum
½ oz. dry vermouth
½ oz. sweet vermouth

Combine with ice; shake well. Strain; add crushed ice.

BEAUTY SPOT

1 oz. dry gin
½ oz. sweet vermouth
½ oz. dry vermouth
1 tsp. orange juice
1 drop grenadine

Combine everything except grenadine with ice; shake well. Pour grenadine into small glass; add ice, strain in the drink. Do not stir.

BEE'S KISS

1½ oz. white rum
1 tsp. honey
1 tsp. heavy cream

Combine with ice; shake very well. Strain and add ice.

BEE-BEE

Bourbon
Honey
The skins of 2 oranges, 3 lemons and 4 limes

Dice fruit skins and place in the coffee receptacle of a percolator. Pour several teaspoons of honey over the skins and percolate in bourbon. Serve hot.

BEEF AND BULL

2 oz. beef bouillon
1 oz. bourbon
Cucumber slices
A pinch salt

Combine everything except the cucumber slices with ice; shake well. Strain with ice; garnish with cucumber.

BEER BUSTER

2 oz. cold, 100-proof vodka
1-2 dashes Tabasco sauce
Cold beer

Pour vodka into a beer mug. Add Tabasco sauce; fill the mug with cold beer and stir.

BEER PANACHEE

10 oz. beer
12 oz. lime soda
2 tbs. sugar
1 tsp. lime juice

Combine with chunks of ice before serving; stir to blend.

BEER PUNCH

10 oz. beer
12 oz. grapefruit or orange juice
1 bottle ginger ale
4 oz. sugar
2 tbs. lime juice

Combine with chunks of ice before serving; stir gently.

BELLINI PUNCH

Peaches
Iced champagne
1 tbs. lemon juice
Sugar

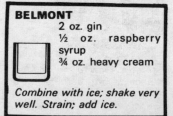

Puree enough peaches to generously fill bottom of a small punch bowl. Add three times as much champagne, plus the lemon juice and sugar to taste. Stir very well.

BELMONT

2 oz. gin
½ oz. raspberry syrup
¾ oz. heavy cream

Combine with ice; shake very well. Strain; add ice.

BELVUE EGG NOG

1 doz. eggs
1 cup sugar
1 pint cognac
½ pint Jamaican rum
½ pint heavy cream
1 pint milk

Separate the eggs. Beat yolks well; add sugar, cognac and rum. Stir until smooth and well-blended. Whip the heavy cream; add milk. Beat egg whites until stiff; fold cream mixture and stiff egg whites into the liquor. Season with nutmeg and refrigerate until ready to serve. For a less sweet eggnog, don't whip the cream, halve the sugar and add a little more cognac.

BENEDICT

1 oz. Scotch
1 oz. Benedictine
Ginger ale

Over a few cubes of ice pour the Scotch and the Benedictine. Fill glass with ginger ale and stir.

BENEDICTINE COCKTAIL

3 oz. Benedictine
A few dashes of Angostura bitters
Powdered sugar
½ lemon

Combine Benedictine with bitters. Shake only a few seconds. Rub the lemon around the rim of a glass and press the rim in powdered sugar. Drop a cherry into the glass; add the Benedictine plus ice.

BENNETT

2 oz. gin
1½ oz. lime juice
A few dashes of Angostura bitters
1 tsp. powdered sugar

Combine with ice; shake well. Strain and add ice.

BERMUDA BOUQUET

1½ oz. dry gin
1 oz. apricot brandy
1 tsp. powdered sugar
½ tsp. grenadine
½ tsp. curacao

Combine with ice; shake well. Strain. Add ice, a twist of orange; drop in the peels.

BERMUDA HIGHBALL

1 oz. gin
1 oz. brandy
1 oz. dry vermouth
Club soda

Combine the gin, brandy and vermouth; add ice and fill with club soda; stir gently.

BERMUDA ROSE

1½ oz. gin
1 tbs. lime juice
A few drops of grenadine
A few drops apricot brandy

Combine with ice; shake well. Strain and add ice.

BETSY ROSS

1½ oz. brandy
1½ oz. port
A few drops curacao
A few dashes of
Angostura bitters
Combine with ice;
shake well. Strain.
Add ice.

BETTY COCKTAIL

1½ oz. dry gin
½ oz. Swedish
Punch
½ lemon

*Fill a small glass with ice;
pour in the gin and Swedish
Punch. Squeeze in the lemon;
drop in the peel and stir well.*

BETWEEN THE SHEETS

1 oz. brandy
1 oz. Cointreau
1 oz. white rum
1 tsp. lemon juice

*Combine with ice; shake well.
Strain and add ice.*

BIG APPLE

1 oz. apple brandy
3 oz. apple juice
3 tbs. baked apple
A pinch ground
ginger

*Heat the juice and the ginger;
simmer for a few minutes.
Warm a glass tumbler; add
the baked apple. Pour the apple brandy into a ladle; ignite
and pour over the baked apple. Put out the fire with the
warm, spiced juice. Stir gently. Serve warm with a spoon
to eat the apple.*

BIG JOHN'S SPECIAL

2 oz. grapefruit juice
2 tbs. gin
1 tbs. vodka
1 tbs. orange juice
A few drops orange
flower water
A few maraschino
cherries
A few drops cherry
juice
An orange slice, cut
into small pieces
2 oz. crushed ice

*Combine in a blender at a
high speed until smooth.
Serve unstrained.*

BILLY TAYLOR

2 oz. gin
1½ oz. lime juice
1 tsp. powdered
sugar
Club soda

*Combine everything except
the club soda with ice; shake
well. Strain; add ice and fill
the glass with club soda.*

BIMBO PUNCH

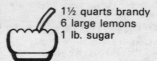

1½ quarts brandy
6 large lemons
1 lb. sugar

*Slice the lemons and steep in
the brandy overnight. Strain
the brandy out. Dissolve the
sugar in enough boiling
water to make a watery
syrup; cool; add to the brandy,
and refrigerate. One-half
hour before serving, pour the
punch into a large bowl filled
with chunks of ice and
decorate with slices of fruit.*

BIRD OF PARADISE

2 oz. gin
2 tbs. lemon juice
1 tsp. powdered sugar
1 tsp. grenadine
1 egg white
Club soda

Combine (except the soda) with ice; shake extremely well. Strain. Add ice and fill with soda.

BISCAYNE

1 oz. gin
½ oz. white rum
½ oz. Forbidden Fruit
1 tsp. lime juice

Combine with ice; shake well. Strain and add ice. Decorate with lime slice.

BISHOP

2 oz. orange juice
1½ oz. lemon juice
1 tsp. powdered sugar
1 tsp. rum
Burgundy

Half fill glass with crushed ice; combine the orange juice, lemon juice and powdered sugar. Almost fill glass with Burgundy and stir well. Float rum on top and decorate with orange slice.

BISHOP'S COCKTAIL

2 oz. gin
2 oz. ginger wine

Combine with ice; shake well. Strain and add ice.

BITTER BANANA COOLER

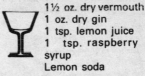

1½ oz. white rum
2 oz. pineapple juice
½ oz. lime juice
1-2 dashes Peychaud's bitters
½ banana, sliced
Lemon
4 oz. crushed ice

Combine (except soda) in an electric blender; blend at a low speed for no more than 15 seconds. Strain, add more ice and fill with soda.

BITTER LEMON COOLER

1½ oz. dry vermouth
1 oz. dry gin
1 tsp. lemon juice
1 tsp. raspberry syrup
Lemon soda

Combine (except the soda) with ice; shake well. Strain; add ice and fill with soda. Add a twist of lemon; stir and drop in the peel.

BITTERSWEET

1¼ oz. sweet vermouth
1¼ oz. dry vermouth
1-2 dashes Angostura bitters
1-2 dashes orange bitters

Combine with ice; shake well. Strain into a martini glass straight up or in an old-fashioned glass filled with ice. Add a twist of orange and drop in the peel.

BLACK BEAUTY

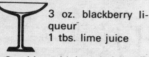

3 oz. blackberry liqueur
1 tbs. lime juice

Combine with ice; shake well. Strain into a chilled champagne glass straight up.

BLACK DAIQUIRI

1½ oz. Jamaican rum
2 tsp. lime juice
1 tsp. honey

Combine with ice; shake very well. Strain into a sour glass.

BLACK EYE

1½ oz. vodka
2 tsp. blackberry brandy
2 tbs. lime juice

Combine with ice; shake well. Strain straight up. Decorate with a slice of lime.

BLACK HAWK

1¼ oz. whiskey
1½ oz. sloe gin

Combine with ice; shake well. Strain into a martini glass straight up or over ice in an old-fashioned glass. Top with a cherry.

BLACK PEARL

1½ oz. gold rum
1 tsp. apricot brandy
2 tsp. pineapple juice
1 tsp. Jamaican rum

Combine with ice; shake well. Strain. Serve straight up.

BLACK RUSSIAN

1½ oz. vodka
¾ oz. Kahlua

Combine with ice; shake well. Strain and add ice. For a **BLACK MAGIC** *add a few drops of lemon juice before shaking.*

BLACK STRIPE

3 oz. Jamaican rum
1 tsp. dark molasses

Mix the rum with the molasses in a mug. Fill the mug with boiling water; add a twist of lemon and stir very well. Serve hot.

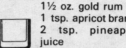

BLACK VELVET

Fill a tall glass with equal parts champagne and stout. Stir gently.

BLACKBERRY CORDIAL

1/2 gallon blackberry juice
1 pint cognac
4 cups sugar
Ground cloves
Allspice

Combine everything except the cognac in a large saucepan; bring to a boil several times, stirring occasionally. Add the brandy and bottle, cork and seal the cordial while still hot. Store in a cool, dark place for several months. Eight quarts of blackberries can be used to extract 1/2 gallon of juice, if you wish to start from scratch.

BLACKBERRY COOLER

1 1/2 oz. blackberry brandy
1/2 oz. lemon juice
Club soda

Combine the brandy and lemon juice; add ice and fill with club soda. Stir well.

BLACKBERRY WINE

1/2 peck crushed blackberries
1 gallon hot water
Sugar

Combine the crushed berries with the water in a large crock pot and allow to stand for two days. Strain and add three parts sugar for each part juice; stir, seal and allow to stand for several months.

BLACKJACK

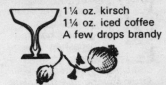

1 1/4 oz. kirsch
1 1/4 oz. iced coffee
A few drops brandy

Combine the kirsch and the coffee in a wide champagne glass filled with crushed ice. Add the brandy and gently stir.

BLACKTHORN

1 1/2 oz. Irish whiskey
1 1/2 oz. dry vermouth
Several drops Pernod
Several dashes Angostura bitters

Combine with ice; shake well. Strain and add ice. Sloe gin can be used instead of the whiskey.

BLANCHE

1 oz. Cointreau
1 oz. white curacao
1 oz. anisette

Combine with ice; shake well. Strain and add ice.

BLENDED COMFORT

2 oz. whiskey
1 oz. Southern Comfort
1 oz. orange juice
½ oz. dry vermouth
2 tbs. lemon juice
¼ peach, skinned
4 oz. crushed ice

Combine in an electric blender; blend at a low speed no more than 15 seconds. Strain and fill glass with crushed ice. Top with a lemon slice and an orange slice.

BLENHEIM

1 oz. apple brandy
½ oz. apricot brandy
1 tbs. lemon juice
1 tsp. grenadine
1-2 dashes Angostura bitters

Combine with ice; shake well. Strain and add ice.

BLENTON

2 oz. gin
Several drops dry vermouth
1-2 dashes Angostura bitters

Pour the gin into a mixing glass filled with ice; add the vermouth and bitters. Shake well. Strain. Add a twist of lemon and drop in the peel.

BLINKER

1½ oz. rye
2 oz. grapefruit juice
1 tbs. grenadine

Combine with ice; shake well. Strain and add ice.

BLIZZARD

3 oz. bourbon
1 oz. cranberry juice
1 tbs. lemon juice
2 tbs. sugar syrup
4 oz. crushed ice

Combine in a blender until the drink is thick. Serve straight up.

BLOOD AND SAND

¾ oz. Scotch, cherry brandy, sweet vermouth and orange juice

Combine with ice; shake well. Strain and add ice.

BLOODHOUND

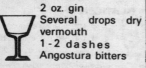

1 oz. gin
½ oz. sweet vermouth
½ oz. dry vermouth
1 tsp. strawberry liqueur
1 strawberry

Combine everything except the strawberry with ice; shake well. Strain and add ice. Top with the strawberry.

BLOODY MARIANA

2 oz. vodka
6 oz. V-8 vegetable juice
1 tsp. lime juice
A few drops Tabasco sauce
A few drops Worchestershire sauce
A pinch of white pepper
A pinch of celery salt
A pinch of oregano

Combine with ice; shake. Strain and add ice.

BLOODY MARY

1½ oz. vodka
3 oz. tomato juice
1 tbs. lemon juice
Several drops
Worchestershire
sauce
Several drops
Tabasco sauce

Combine with ice; shake well. Strain and serve straight up. Add salt and pepper to taste. For a **BLOODY MARIE** *halve the lemon juice and add several drops of Pernod. For a* **BLOODY MARIA** *use tequila instead of vodka.*

BLUE ANGEL

½ oz. blue curacao, vanilla parfait, brandy and heavy cream

Combine with ice; shake very well. Strain and serve straight up.

BLUE BELL

1½ oz. whiskey
1 tbs. dry vermouth
1-2 dashes
Angostura bitters

Combine with ice; shake well. Strain and add ice.

BLUE MOON

1½ oz. gin
¾ oz. dry vermouth
1-2 dashes orange bitters
1-2 dashes Creme Yvette

Combine with ice; shake well. Strain and add ice.

BLUE MOUNTAIN

1½ oz. Jamaican rum
1½ oz. orange juice
¾ Tia Maria
¾ oz. vodka

Combine with ice; shake well. Strain and add ice.

BLUE PACIFIC

3 oz dry gin
A few drops of dry vermouth
1-2 dashes vodka
1-2 dashes blue food coloring

Combine without ice; stir until blended. Pour out over ice. Decorate with a black olive.

BLUE SHARK

1½ oz. tequila
1½ oz. vodka
1-2 dashes blue food coloring

Combine with ice; shake well. Strain and add ice.

BLUE TAIL FLY

1½ oz. blue curacao
1 tbs. white creme de cacao
1 tbs. light cream

Combine with ice; shake very well. Strain. Serve over ice.

BLUEBERRY CORDIAL

1 quart blueberries
12 oz. sugar
whiskey

Boil the berries for at least half an hour in enough water to cover them. Add the sugar; stir and allow to simmer until thick. Strain the syrup clean and add the same amount of whiskey as syrup. Stir well. Bottle and seal to use as a cordial.

BLUEBERRY RUM FIZZ

2½ oz. white rum
½ oz. Triple Sec
1 tbs. lemon juice
1 tsp. blueberry syrup
A few blueberries
Club soda

Combine (except the soda and blueberries) with ice; shake well. Strain; add ice and fill glass with soda. Top with blueberries and a lemon slice.

BLUEBIRD

2½ oz gin
½ oz. curacao
Several dashes Angostura bitters

Combine with ice; shake well. Strain and add ice. Add a twist of lemon and drop in the peel. Top with a cherry.

BLUEBLAZER

3 oz. Scotch
3 oz. boiling water
Powdered sugar

Pour the Scotch into one mug, the boiling water in another. Ignite the Scotch; toss the burning liquor and the water from mug to mug. When throughly mixed, the mixture will look like a stream of fire. Pour it all into one of the mugs; add a teaspoon of powdered sugar and a twist of lemon. Stir and wait until it cools enough to drink.

BOB DANBY

2 oz. Dubonnet
1 oz. strong brandy

Combine with ice; shake well. Strain and add ice.

BOBBY BURNS

1½ oz. Scotch
¾ oz. sweet vermouth
¾ oz. dry vermouth
1-2 dashes Benedictine

Combine with ice; shake well. Strain and add ice. For a sweeter drink, increase the Benedictine to a teaspoon and omit the dry vermouth.

BOILERMAKER

Drink 2 oz.of whiskey straight up and wash it down with a large mug of beer. The whiskey and the beer can be combined in a highball glass, if desired. Scotch can be used instead of blended whiskey.

For a **DOG'S NOSE** *substitute gin for the whiskey and mix with the beer.*

BOLERO

1½ oz. white rum
¾ oz. apple brandy
Several drops sweet
vermouth

Combine with ice; shake well. Strain and add ice. Add a twist of lemon and drop in the peel.

BOLO

3 oz. white rum
1½ oz. orange juice
1 oz. lime juice
1 tsp. powdered
sugar

Combine with ice; shake well. Strain and add ice.

BOMB

2 pints sherry
2½ oz. Cointreau
2½ oz. orange juice
Several dashes
orange bitters
Several dashes
Pimento Dram
Olives

Combine with ice and stir very well. Serve with crushed ice. Top each glass with an olive.

BOMBAY

1 oz. brandy
1 oz. sweet
vermouth
½ oz. dry vermouth
1-2 dashes curacao
A few drops Pernod

Combine with ice; shake well. Strain and add ice.

BOMBAY PUNCH

1 bottle cognac
1 bottle dry sherry
4 oz. curacao
4 oz. maraschino
9 oz. lemon juice
Sugar to taste
2 bottles club soda
4 bottles champagne

Combine all but the champagne and soda. Add the champagne and soda, plus ice.

BOMBE GLACEE TULLAMORE

1 quart vanilla ice
cream
1 pint coffee ice
cream
4 oz. Irish Mist
1 tsp. almond extract

Line the sides of a bombe or similar deep dish with the coffee ice cream. In a separate bowl, combine the Irish Mist and vanilla ice cream; stir until well-blended. Add the almond extract. Pack the ice cream and liqueur into the coffee ice cream mold; freeze. Keep frozen until ready to use.

BONNIE PRINCE

1¼ oz. gin
½ oz. Lillet
Several drops Drambuie

Combine with ice; shake well. Strain and add ice. Add more Drambuie, if you want a stronger drink.

BONSONI

3 oz. sweet vermouth
1½ tbs. Fernet Branca
1-2 dashes sugar syrup
1-2 dashes Pernod

Combine with ice; shake well. Strain and add ice. For a less sweet drink, eliminate the sugar syrup and the Pernod.

BOOMERANG

2 oz. gin
1 oz. dry vermouth
A few dashes of Angostura bitters
1-2 dashes maraschino

Combine with ice; shake well. Strain. Add a twist of lemon and drop in the peel. Serve straight up.

BOOSTER

2½ oz. brandy
¼ oz. curacao
1 egg white

Combine with ice; shake extremely well. Strain and add ice. Dust with nutmeg.

BORDEN CHASE

1½ oz. Scotch
½ oz. sweet vermouth
1-2 dashes orange bitters
Several drops Pernod

Combine with ice; shake well. Strain and add ice.

BORINQUEN

1½ oz. white rum
½ oz. orange juice
½ oz. passion fruit juice
1 tbs. lime juice
1 tsp. high-proof rum
Gardenia or jasmine flowers

Combine with ice; shake well. Strain over crushed ice; decorate with gardenia or jasmine. For a thicker drink, mix all the ingredients in an electric blender with ½ cup crushed ice.

BOSOM CARESSER

½ oz. Madeira
¼ oz. brandy
¼ oz. curacao
1 tsp. grenadine
1 egg yolk

Combine with ice; shake extremely well. Strain; serve straight up.

BOSTON COCKTAIL

1 oz. dry gin
1 oz. apricot brandy
1 tsp. lemon juice
1 tsp. grenadine

Combine with ice; shake well. Strain and add ice.

BOSTON FISH HOUSE PUNCH

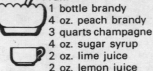

1½ quarts Jamaican rum
1 bottle brandy
4 oz. peach brandy
3 quarts champagne
4 oz. sugar syrup
2 oz. lime juice
2 oz. lemon juice

Combine the sugar syrup, lemon juice and lime juice in a large punch bowl. Add the rum, brandies and champagne; stir gently. Serve over ice.

BOSTON SIDECAR

1 oz. brandy
1 oz. rum
1 oz. Triple Sec
1 tbs. lime juice

Combine with ice; shake well. Strain and add ice.

BOSTON SOUR

2 oz. whiskey
1½ oz. lemon juice
1 tsp. powdered sugar
1 egg white
Club soda

Combine (except the soda) with ice; shake well. Strain, add ice and fill the glass with club soda. Top with a lemon slice and a cherry.

BOURBON A LA CREME

2 oz. bourbon
1 oz. dark creme de cacao
1-2 vanilla beans

Combine with ice and allow to stand in the refrigerator for at least one hour. When ready, shake well and strain straight up.

BOURBON AND EGG SOUR

2 oz. bourbon
1½ tsp. lemon juice
1 tsp. powdered sugar
1 egg
Several drops of bitters (Angostura touched up with rum and maraschino is best)

Combine with ice; shake well. Strain.

BOURBON BRANCA

2 oz. bourbon
1 tsp. Fernet Branca

Combine in an old-fashioned glass; stir well. Add ice. Touch it up with a twist of lemon.

BOURBON CARDINAL

1½ oz. 100-proof bourbon
1 tbs. grapefruit juice
1 tbs. cranberry juice
1 tbs. sugar syrup
2 tsp. lemon juice
A few drops cherry juice

Combine with ice; shake well. Strain. Serve straight up; decorate with a pair of maraschino cherries.

BOURBON COLLINS

2 oz. 100-proof bourbon
½ oz. lemon juice
1 - 2 dashes Peychaud's bitters
1 tbs. sugar syrup
Club soda

Combine (except the soda) with ice; shake well. Strain, add ice and fill with soda. Top with a lemon slice.

BOURBON DAISY

2 oz. bourbon
1 tbs. lemon juice
1 tsp. grenadine
1 tsp. Southern Comfort
Club soda
1 pineapple stick

Combine the bourbon, lemon juice and grenadine with ice; shake well. Strain, add ice and fill with soda. Float the Southern Comfort on top and top with a slice of orange and the pineapple stick.

BOURBON EGG NOG

1 doz. eggs
1½ cups sugar
1 quart heavy cream
1 quart milk
1 quart bourbon

Separate the eggs. Combine the yolks with sugar and beat until well-blended. In another bowl, beat the heavy cream until stiff but not whipped; add the milk and slowly stir in the bourbon. Combine this with the yolks. Beat the egg whites until stiff and fold them into the egg nog. Refrigerate until ready to serve. Dust with nutmeg.

BOURBON PUNCH

1 quart bourbon
4 oz. grenadine
4 oz. sugar
3 oz. lemon juice
6 oz. orange juice
1 quart club soda

Dissolve the sugar with the fruit juices. Add the grenadine and the whiskey and stir until blended.

BOURBON SLOE GIN

1½ oz. bourbon
½ oz. sloe gin
½ oz. lemon juice
1 tsp. sugar syrup

Combine with ice; shake well. Strain over crushed ice. Top with a lemon slice and a peach slice.

BOURBON SOUR

2 oz. bourbon
2 tbs. lemon juice
2 tsp. sugar syrup

Combine with ice; shake well. Strain straight up; decorate with a slice of orange.

BOURBONVILLE

1½ oz. bourbon
1½ tsp. lime juice
Club soda

Combine the bourbon and the lime juice with ice; shake well. Strain; add ice and fill the glass with soda. Touch it up with a twist of lime.

BOURGOGNE A L'ORANGE

2 bottles Burgundy
2 oranges
1 cup sugar
Cloves

In a wide bowl, combine the soft, inner skins of the oranges with the sugar. Pour in 4 oz. of boiling water and allow to stand for at least 15 minutes.
Squeeze in the juice of half of one orange and strain the mixture into a large saucepan. Add the Burgundy. Heat and stir; do not bring to a boil. Serve hot. Decorate each mug with slices of orange stuck with cloves.

BOXCAR

1¼ oz. Cointreau
1¼ oz. gin
1 tsp. lime juice
1 egg white
1-2 dashes grenadine
Sugar

Combine with ice; shake extremely well. Line the rim of a glass with water and press it in sugar. Strain in the drink straight up.

BRANDIED APRICOT

1½ oz. brandy
½ oz. apricot brandy
2 tsp. lemon juice

Combine with ice; shake well. Strain, add ice and a twist of orange; drop in the peel.

BRANDIED APRICOT FLIP

1½ oz. brandy
1 oz. apricot brandy
1 tbs. sugar syrup
1 egg

Combine with ice; shake extremely well. Strain into a small glass straight up. Dust with nutmeg.

BRANDIED BANANA COLLINS

1½ oz. brandy
1 oz. banana liqueur
2 tsp. lemon juice
Club soda
1 banana slice

Combine (except the soda and banana slice) with ice; shake well. Strain, add ice and fill with club soda. Decorate with the banana slice and a lemon slice.

BRANDIED BOAT

1 oz. dark port
1 oz. brandy
2 tsp. lemon juice
1 tsp. maraschino

Combine with ice; shake well. Strain and add ice. Decorate with and orange slice.

BRANDIED CORDIAL MEDOC

1½ oz. brandy
½ oz. Cordial Medoc
2 tsp. lemon juice

Combine with ice; shake well. Strain and add ice. Add a twist of lemon and drop in the peel.

BRANDIED GINGER

1 oz. brandy
½ oz. ginger brandy
1 tsp. lime juice
1 tsp. orange juice
1 chunk ginger

Combine (except the ginger chunk) with ice; shake well. Strain and add ice. Decorate with the ginger.

BRANDIED MADEIRA

1 oz. brandy
1 oz. Madeira
2 tsp. dry vermouth

Combine with ice; shake well. Strain. Add ice and a twist of lemon; drop in the peel.

BRANDIED PEACH FIZZ

2 oz. brandy
2 tsp. peach brandy
2 tsp. lemon juice
1½ tsp. sugar syrup
1 tsp. banana liqueur
Club soda
1 peach slice

Combine everything except the soda and the peach slice with ice; shake well. Strain, add ice and fill with soda. Decorate with peach slice.
For a **BRANDIED PEACH SLING,** *eliminate the banana liqueur, put peach slice into the drink.*

BRANDIED MOCHA PUNCH

1 quart hot dark coffee
1 quart hot chocolate
10 oz. brandy
Whipped cream
Chocolate chips
Cinnamon

Combine the coffee and hot chocolate in a large punch bowl and allow to cool. Stir in the brandy and add ice. Decorate with whipped cream, chocolate chips and cinnamon. Serve over ice, making sure each gets a bit of the garnish.

BRANDIED NIGHT

1¼ oz. brandy
1 oz. gin
Several drops dry vermouth
1 olive

Combine (except the olive) with ice; shake well. Strain and decorate with the olive. Serve straight up.

BRANDY ALEXANDER

1½ oz. brandy
1 oz. dark creme de cacao
1 oz. heavy cream

Combine with ice; shake well. Strain and serve straight up. For an **ALEXANDER'S SISTER,** *substitute Kahlua for the dark creme de cacao.*

BRANDY AND AMER PICON

2 oz. cognac
2 tsp. Amer Picon

Combine with ice; shake well. Strain and add ice. Add a twist of lemon and a twist of orange; drop in the peels.

BRANDY APRICOT FRAPPE

¾ oz. brandy
½ oz. apricot brandy
¼ oz. creme de noyaux

Combine with ice; shake well. Strain over crushed ice.

BRANDY BERRY FIX

2 oz. brandy
2 tsp. lemon juice
1½ tsp. sugar syrup
1 tsp. strawberry liqueur

Combine with ice; shake well. Strain over crushed ice.

BRANDY BLAZER

2 oz. brandy
1 cube of sugar

Place the sugar cube on the bottom of a small, wide bowl. Pour in the brandy and stir until the sugar is dissolved. Add a twist of lemon and a twist of orange; ignite for a few seconds. Extinguish the blaze and serve hot, strain and serve straight up.

BRANDY BOAT

2 oz. brandy
2 tsp. sugar syrup
1 tsp. pineapple juice
1 tsp. lemon juice
Several drops lime juice
A few drops rum
Club soda
Fruit slices

Combine (except the rum, soda and fruit slices) with ice; shake well. Strain. Add a few drops of club soda and fill with crushed ice. Float the rum on top; decorate with fruit slices.

BRANDY BUCK

1½ oz. brandy
½ oz. lemon juice
¼ oz. white creme de menthe
Ginger ale
Seedless grapes

Combine (except the ginger ale and grapes) with ice; shake well. Strain, add ice and fill with ginger ale. Decorate with a couple of seedless grapes.

BRANDY CHAMPARELLE

¼ oz. curacao, yellow chartreuse, anisette and brandy

Combine and stir gently.

BRANDY COBBLER

1½ oz. brandy
2 tsp. curacao
2 tsp. lemon juice
1½ tsp. sugar syrup
1 tsp. kirschwasser
1 pineapple stick

Combine (except the pineapple stick) with ice; shake well. Strain over crushed ice. Top with the pineapple stick.

BRANDY CRUSTA

2 oz. brandy
2 tsp. curacao
2 tsp. lemon juice
1 tsp. maraschino
1-2 dashes bitters
1 spiral lemon peel

Combine (except the lemon peel) with ice; shake well. Strain over ice and lemon peel.

BRANDY DAISY

2 oz. brandy
1 tbs. lemon juice
2 tsp. grenadine
Skinned, pressed peaches
Cooked apples and apricots

Combine the brandy, lemon juice and grenadine with ice; shake well. Strain. Add the peaches, apples and apricots.

BRANDY EGG NOG

2½ oz. brandy
1 cup milk
1 egg
2 tbs. powdered sugar

Combine with ice; shake extremely well. Strain and garnish with nutmeg. Serve straight up.

BRANDY FINO

1½ oz. brandy
2 tsp. dry sherry
2 tsp. Drambuie

Combine with ice; shake well. Strain. Add ice and a twist of lemon; drop in the peel. Decorate with an orange slice.

BRANDY FIX

1¼ oz. brandy
¾ oz. cherry brandy
1 tsp. lime juice
1 tsp. sugar syrup

Combine with ice; shake well. Strain over crushed ice and serve with a straw.

BRANDY FIZZ

1¼ oz. brandy
1 tbs. lemon juice
2 tsp. sugar syrup
Several dashes yellow chartreuse
Club soda

Combine all but the soda with ice; shake well. Strain, add ice and fill with soda.

BRANDY FLIP

2 oz. brandy
1 tsp. sugar syrup
½ tsp. curacao
1-2 dashes bitters
1 mint sprig

Combine (except the mint) with ice; shake well. Strain and add ice. Add a twist of lemon and drop in the peel; top with mint.

BRANDY GRUEL

8 oz. brandy
6 oz. barley water
8 oz. sugar
2 egg whites

Combine the barley water with the sugar plus a few teaspoons of boiling water in a saucepan. Slowly add the brandy, stirring constantly. Allow to cool. In a separate bowl, beat the egg whites until foamy; then fold them into the gruel. Serve in large mugs.

BRANDY HOT TODDY

2 oz. brandy
1 cube sugar

Drop the sugar cube in a mug and fill 2/3 with boiling water. Add the brandy and stir until the sugar is completely dissolved. Add a twist of lemon; drop in the peel. Garnish with nutmeg; serve steaming hot.

BRANDY MILK PUNCH

2 oz. brandy
8 oz. milk
1 tsp. powdered sugar

Combine with ice; shake well. Strain over ice and garnish with nutmeg.

BRANDY MINT FIZZ

2 oz. brandy
½ oz. white creme de menthe
¼ oz. white creme de cacao
2 tsp. lemon juice
1 tsp. sugar syrup
Club soda
Mint leaves

Combine everything except the soda and the mint with ice; shake well. Strain, add ice and fill with soda. Decorate with mint leaves, partially torn.

BRANDY MINT FLOAT

1½ oz. white creme de menthe
1 tbs. brandy

Pour the creme de menthe over ice in a small liqueur glass; carefully float the brandy.

BRANDY MINT JULEP

3 oz. brandy
1 oz. sugar syrup
Mint sprigs
Fruit slices

Place a few sprigs of mint on the bottom of a wide glass. Pour in the sugar syrup and crush the leaves in it. Add the brandy. Fill with crushed ice, packing the ice as solidly as possible and stirring until very cold. Decorate with fruit and serve with a straw.

BRANDY OLD FASHIONED

2½ oz. brandy
1 cube sugar
1-2 dashes Angostura bitters

Combine the bitters, a twist of lemon and sugar cube. Pour in the brandy and stir until the sugar is completely dissolved. Add ice.

BRANDY PUNCH

3 quarts brandy
8 oz. Jamaican rum
3 oz. lemon juice
1 oz. curacao
1 gallon water
Sliced raspberries, chopped pineapple, and orange slices

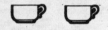

Combine everything except the fruit in a large punch bowl; sugar to taste and stir well. Decorate with the fruit. A half-hour before serving, add ice. Serve very cold.

BRANDY SANGAREE

2 oz. brandy
¼ oz. Madeira
1 cube sugar
Club soda

Dissolve sugar cube in a tablespoon of club soda. Pour in the brandy and the Madeira; add a few more drops of soda. Stir well and add ice. Garnish with nutmeg. Add a twist of orange and drop in the peel.

BRANDY SHRUB

10 oz. lemon juice
1 quart brandy
1 quart sherry
1½ lb. sugar
Lemon peels

Place the peels in a large bowl. Add the lemon juice and the brandy; stir and allow to stand at room temperature at least 3 days. When ready, pour in the sherry. Add the sugar and stir until the sugar is completely dissolved. Strain into a large pitcher and refrigerate until ready to serve.

BRANDY SOUR

2 oz. brandy
2 tsp. lemon juice
1 tsp. orange juice
1 tsp. sugar syrup

Combine with ice; shake well. Strain, decorate with a lemon slice and serve straight up.

BRANDY STEW

4 oz. cognac
2 oz. sugar
1 tbs. butter
Grated nutmeg, ground cloves, cinnamon and allspice

Dissolve the sugar with the butter over low heat in a large saucepan; add the spices and simmer several minutes before adding the cognac. Stir constantly and do not allow the cognac to burn. Serve immediately.

BRANDY STINGER

1½ oz. brandy
1 tbs. white creme de menthe

Combine with ice; shake well. Strain into an old-fashioned glass and add ice. Touch it up with a twist of lemon.

BRANDY TIPPLE

16 oz. dark coffee, warm
8 oz. cognac
1 oz. sugar syrup
2 eggs

Beat the eggs; add the syrup, cognac and coffee. Shake well with ice until cool. Turn out over ice.

BRAWNY BROTH

1 oz. vodka
A pinch of pepper
A pinch of salt
A lemon slice
1 packet powdered beef bouillon

Combine; fill mug with boiling water and stir well.

BRAZIL

1½ oz. sherry
1½ oz. dry vermouth
A few drops Pernod
1-2 dashes Angostura bitters

Combine with ice; shake well. Strain and add ice. Add a twist of lemon and drop in the peel.

BRIDE'S BOWL

3 bottles gold rum
1 quart pineapple juice
2 cups lemon juice
2 cups sugar
1 pint whole strawberries
Pineapple chunks
2 bottles club soda

Boil the sugar with enough water to make a syrup; combine with fruit chunks and juices and stir to blend. Pour in the rum and store in the refrigerator for a few hours. Add the soda plus chunks of ice before serving; float the strawberries.

BRIGHTON PUNCH

1 oz. bourbon
1 oz. cognac
¾ oz. Benedictine
2 tsp. lemon juice
Club soda

Combine (except the club soda) with ice; shake well. Strain, add ice and fill with soda. Decorate with an orange slice and a lemon slice

BRITISH ATOLL

1 oz. dry gin
1 oz. creme de banana
1 oz. orange juice

Combine with ice; shake well.

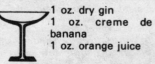

BRITTANY

1½ oz. gin
2 tsp. Amer Picon
1 tsp. orange juice
1 tsp. lemon juice

Combine with ice and a twist of orange; drop in the peel.

BROKEN SPUR

1½ oz. white port
1 tsp. dry gin
1 tsp. anisette
1 tsp. sweet vermouth
1 egg yolk

Combine with ice; shake extremely well. Strain and add ice.

BRONX COCKTAIL

1½ oz. gin
1 oz. lemon juice
2 tsp. orange juice
2 tsp. dry vermouth
2 tsp. sweet vermouth

Combine with ice; shake well. Strain and add ice.
*For a **BLOODY BRONX COCKTAIL** substitute the juice of ¼ blood orange for the orange juice.*

BRONX SILVER

1 oz. dry gin
1 tbs. orange juice
2 tsp. dry vermouth
1 egg white

Combine with ice; shake extremely well. Strain and add ice.

BROUSSARD'S ORANGE BRULOT

1 orange
2 cubes sugar
Brandy

Make cups out of the orange by slicing the skin around its circumference (without cutting the fruit) and sliding the skin away gently with a spoon. Drop a cube of sugar into each cup; pour in as much brandy as you wish and ignite. Stir gently while burning; drink when cooled. Brandy burns best when previously warmed.
*For a **LIZARD SKIN** do not ignite brandy.*

BROWN

1¼ oz. bourbon
1¼ oz. dry vermouth
1-2 dashes orange bitters

Combine with ice; shake well. Strain and add ice.

BRUNELLE

1 oz. Pernod
3 oz. lemon juice
1½ tsp. powdered sugar

Combine with ice; shake well. Strain and add ice.

BUBY

2 oz. gin
3 tbs. lemon juice
1 tsp. grenadine

Combine with ice; shake well. Strain and add ice.

BUDDHA PUNCH

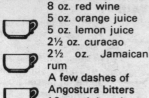

8 oz. red wine
5 oz. orange juice
5 oz. lemon juice
2½ oz. curacao
2½ oz. Jamaican rum
A few dashes of Angostura bitters
16 oz. club soda
1 bottle champagne
Fruit slices
Mint leaves

Combine (except soda, champagne and garnishes) in a large punch bowl; stir well. Just before serving, add the soda, champagne and ice. Decorate with the fruit and mint leaves.

BUL

10 oz. beer
2 bottles club soda
3 oz. sugar
2 tbs. lime juice

Combine with chunks of ice before serving; stir gently to blend.

BULL'S MILK

1½ oz. brandy
1 oz. rum
8 oz. milk
1 tsp. powdered sugar

Combine with ice; shake well. Strain and add ice. Dust with nutmeg and cinnamon.

BULLSHOT

1 dash Worcestershire sauce
4 oz. beef bouillion
1½ oz. vodka

Combine; add ice and a twist of lemon.

BUNNY BONANZA

1½ oz. tequila
1 oz. apple brandy
2 tsp. lemon juice
1½ tsp. sugar syrup
½ tsp. curacao

Combine with ice; shake well. Strain, add ice and decorate with lemon slice

BUNNY HUG

¾ oz. gin
¾ oz. whiskey
1 tbs. Pernod

Combine with ice; shake well. Strain and add ice.

BUNNY MOTHER

1½ oz. vodka
1½ tbs. lemon juice
1½ tbs. orange juice
1½ tsp. sugar syrup
1 tsp. Cointreau
1 tsp. grenadine

Combine (except the Cointreau) with ice; shake well. Strain and add ice. Float the Cointreau on top and decorate with a slice of orange and a cherry.

BURGUNDY COCKTAIL

3 oz. Burgundy
1 oz. brandy
Several drops of maraschino

Combine with ice; shake well. Strain straight up. Decorate with a slice of lemon.

BURGUNDY CUP

2½ oz. whiskey
1¼ oz. curacao
1¼ oz. Benedictine
3 oz. sugar
8 oz. club soda
1½ bottles Burgundy

Combine the whiskey, curacao and Benedictine in a large pitcher; add the sugar and stir until the sugar is completely dissolved. Add the Burgundy, club soda and ice. Decorate with fruit slices.

BURNING BLUE MOUNTAIN

5 oz. Jamaican rum
2 tsp. powdered sugar
The rind of one orange and one lime, in pieces
A lemon peel

Warm the rum in a wide chafing dish. Add the sugar and fruit rinds; stir until the sugar has dissolved. Ignite and serve. Ladle out with a long-handled spoon.

BURGUNDY PUNCH

2 bottles Burgundy
8 oz. port
5 oz. orange juice
4 tsp. lemon juice
2 quarts cold bottled water
Sugar
Cucumber slices

Combine the Burgundy, port and juices in a large punch bowl; sugar to taste and stir well. Add the water and ice just before serving; top with cucumber slices.

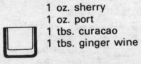

BURLESQUE

1 oz. bourbon
1 tsp. parfait amour
2 tsp. lemon juice
2 tsp. Triple Sec

Combine with ice; shake well. Strain. Serve straight up.

BUSHRANGER

1 oz. Dubonnet
1 oz. white rum
A few dashes of Angostura bitters

Combine with ice; shake well. Strain. Add ice and a twist of lemon; drop in the peel.

BYCULLA

1 oz. sherry
1 oz. port
1 tbs. curacao
1 tbs. ginger wine

Combine with ice; shake well. Strain and add ice.

YOUR OWN RECIPE

YOUR OWN RECIPE

Use a bartender's mixing glass whenever the instructions state "combine" ingredients. Strain the drink from the mixing glass into the drinking glass suggested by the illustration alongside the ingredients.

NOTE: The number of glasses or cups shown alongside a recipe do not necessarily indicate the quantity of drinks the recipe will produce.

CABARET

1 oz. dry gin
1 oz. Dubonnet
A few dashes of Angostura bitters
A few drops Pernod

Combine with ice; shake well. Strain and add ice. Top with a cherry.

CABARET NO. 2

1½ oz. gin
½ tsp. dry vermouth
A few dashes of Angostura bitters
A few drops Benedictine

Combine with ice; shake well. Strain and add ice. Top with a cherry.

CABLEGRAM

2 oz. whiskey
1 tsp. powdered sugar
1 tsp. lemon juice
Ginger ale

Combine (except the ginger ale) with ice; shake well. Strain, add ice, and fill the glass with ginger ale.

CADIZ

¾ oz. amontillado
¾ oz. blackberry liqueur
2 tsp. Triple Sec
2 tsp. heavy cream

Combine with ice; shake very well. Strain and add ice.

CAFE BRULOT

8 oz. brandy
1 pint boiling coffee
2 sugar cubes
6 cloves
1 chopped vanilla bean
1 cinnamon stick

Pour the brandy into a small, wide bowl. Add one cube of sugar, cloves, and vanilla. Toss in a cinnamon stick and slices of orange and lemon; stir well. Pour in the coffee. Dunk the remaining cube of sugar in brandy; place the cube on a spoon, ignite it, and dip the spoon into the bowl, igniting the punch. Serve hot.

CAFE CACAO

1½ oz. dark creme de cacao
4 oz. iced coffee

Combine. Stir gently.

CAFE COCKTAIL

1½ oz. dark, iced coffee
1½ tsp. sugar syrup
¾ oz. dark creme de cacao
¾ oz. cognac

Combine with ice; shake well. Strain, add ice and a twist of lemon.

CAFE DE PARIS

2 oz. gin
¼ oz. heavy cream
1 egg white
Several drops Pernod

Combine with ice; shake extremely well. Strain and add ice.

CAFE DIABLE

4 cups hot, strong coffee
6 oz. cognac
1 oz. sugar
Whole cloves, cinnamon sticks
Grated orange and lemon rinds

Combine the sugar, rinds, and spices in a chafing dish. Add all but 1 tablespoon of the cognac; ignite the remaining spoon of cognac and slowly enter it into the sugar. Allow to burn until the sugar has dissolved. Pour in the coffee; stir, and serve.

CAFE GROG

2 oz. Jamaican rum
¾ oz. brandy
1-2 cubes sugar
4 oz. hot black coffee

Combine. Stir well. Add a twist of lemon.

CAJUN NOG

2 bottles whiskey
8 oz. Jamaican rum
Vanilla ice cream
Nutmeg
6 eggs
4 oz. brown sugar

Separate the eggs. Combine the yolks with the brown sugar; stir until smooth. Carefully add the whiskey and the rum to this egg mixture, stirring constantly. Refrigerate. Beat the egg whites in another bowl until stiff. Serve cold. Top each glass with a spoon of ice cream and dust with nutmeg.

CALIFORNIA PUNCH

2 bottles California Sauterne
2 bottles California champagne
1 quart orange sherbet
2 6-oz. cans frozen orange juice concentrate
1 6-oz. can frozen lemonade concentrate
Orange slices, whole strawberries

Combine the frozen fruit juice concentrates with the Sauterne in a large punch bowl; stir well to blend. Add the champagne immediately before serving. Use the sherbet instead of or in conjunction with chunks of ice; garnish with the orange slices and strawberries.

CAMBRIDGE MILK PUNCH

2 quarts milk
1 pint rum
8 oz. brandy
8 oz. sugar, in cubes
2 eggs, well-beaten
Grated lemon rind

Combine the milk, sugar cubes, and rinds in a saucepan; bring to a boil, stirring constantly until the sugar dissolves. Strain out the peels. Remove from heat; add the eggs, rum, and brandy. Beat until foamy and serve in pre-warmed mugs.

CAMPFIRE BRULOT

1 bottle brandy
A pot of hot coffee
Cinnamon sticks, whole cloves, soft shelled nuts, lemon and orange peels, nutmeg

Ideal for the camper. Pour the brandy into an iron pot or small kettle; add the spices and ignite. Slowly pour in the coffee while the liquor burns; cool and enjoy.

CANADIAN

1½ oz. curacao
1½ oz. lemon juice
1 tsp. powdered sugar
Several dashes Jamaican rum

Combine with ice; shake well. Strain and add ice.

CANADIAN AND CAMPARI

1 oz. Canadian whiskey
1 oz. dry vermouth
2 tsp. Campari

Combine with ice; shake well. Strain and add ice. Add a twist of lemon.

CANADIAN APPLE

1½ oz. Canadian whiskey
½ oz. calvados
1½ tsp. sugar syrup
1 tsp. lemon juice
1-2 dashes cinnamon

Combine with ice; shake well. Strain and add ice. Decorate with lemon slice.

CANADIAN BLACKBERRY FIX

1½ oz. Canadian whiskey
½ oz. blackberry liqueur
2 tsp. lemon juice
1 tsp. sugar syrup
1 blackberry

Combine with ice; shake well. Strain over tightly packed crushed ice. Decorate with a lemon slice and a blackberry.

CANADIAN CHERRY

1½ oz. Canadian whiskey
½ oz. Cherry Heering
1 tsp. lemon juice
1 tsp. orange juice
Sugar

Combine with ice; shake well. Sugar frost glass with Cherry Heering. Strain in the drink and add ice.

CANADIAN DAISY

14 oz. Canadian whiskey
2 tsp. lemon juice
1 tsp. raspberry syrup
Club soda
Whole raspberries
1 tsp. brandy

Combine the whiskey, juice, and syrup with ice; shake well. Strain. Add ice. Fill with club soda. Decorate with raspberries and float the brandy.

CANADIAN OLD· FASHIONED

1½ oz. Canadian whiskey
½ tsp. curacao
Several drops lemon juice
1-2 dashes Angostura bitters

Combine with ice; shake well. Strain and add ice. Add a twist of lemon and of orange.

CANADIAN PINEAPPLE

1½ oz. Canadian whiskey
2 tsp. pineapple juice
2 tsp. lemon juice
Several drops maraschino
1 pineapple stick

Combine with ice; shake well. Strain and add ice. Top it with the pineapple stick.

CAPE CODDER

2 oz. vodka
1 tbs. lime juice
Cranberry juice

Combine the vodka and lime juice. Stir. Add ice and fill the glass with cranberry juice; stir again until the glass begins to frost.

CAPRI

1½ oz. white creme de cacao
2 tbs. blue curacao
1 tbs. green creme de menthe

Combine with ice; shake well. Strain and add ice.

CAPRICE

2 oz. gin
1 oz. sweet vermouth
1 oz. Campari

Combine with ice; shake well. Strain into a martini glass straight up.

CARA SPOSA

1 oz. Tia Maria
1 oz. curacao
½ heavy cream
3 oz. crushed ice

Combine in a blender at a low speed for 15 seconds. Strain and serve straight up.

CARDINAL COCKTAIL

2 oz. white rum
1½ tbs. lime juice
1 tsp. almond extract
1 tsp. grenadine
1 tsp. Triple Sec

Combine with ice; shake well. Strain and add ice. Top with a lime slice.

CARDINAL PUNCH

1 bottle champagne
2 quarts claret
1 quart club soda
1 pint brandy
1 pint Jamaican rum
8 oz. sweet vermouth
6 oz. powdered sugar
3 cups lemon juice

Combine all but soda and champagne, stir with ice. When ready to serve, add soda and champagne; top with fruit slices.

CARIB COCKTAIL

1½ oz. white rum
1 oz. lime juice
1 oz. pineapple juice

Combine with ice; shake well. Strain and add ice.

CARIBBEAN CHAMPAGNE

4 oz. champagne
½ tsp. white rum
½ tsp. banana liqueur
1-2 dashes orange bitters
1 banana slice

Combine (except the banana slice) in a wide champagne glass straight up; stir gently. Decorate with the slice of banana. Crushed ice optional.

CARIBBEAN COCKTAIL

2 oz. white rum
8 oz. pineapple juice
2 tbs. lime juice
1 oz. sugar syrup
1-2 dashes orange bitters
Club soda

Combine (except the soda) with ice; shake. Strain; add ice and soda.

CARIBBEAN JOY

1½ oz. Scotch
2 tsp. lime juice
1 tsp. powdered sugar
Several drops Cointreau

Combine with ice; shake well. Strain and add ice.

CARIOCA COOLER

1½ oz. white rum
1 oz. honey
1 oz. lime juice
2 tsp. mandarin liqueur
2 oz. crushed ice

Combine in a blender at a high speed for 10 seconds. Strain into a pre-chilled glass filled with crushed ice. Top with a slice of lime.

CARLTON

3 oz. orange juice
2 tbs. Grand Marnier
1 egg white
A few drops of peach bitters
Champagne

Combine everything except the champagne with ice; shake very well. Strain; add champagne and stir gently. Decorate with a cherry.

CAROLINA

3 oz. Centenario or aged tequila
1 oz. heavy cream
1½ tsp. grenadine
Several drops vanilla extract
1 egg white

Combine with ice; shake well. Strain; serve straight up. Dust with cinnamon. Top with cherry.

CARROL

1½ oz. brandy
1 tbs. sweet vermouth

Combine with ice; shake well. Strain and add ice. Top with a cherry.

CARROT WINE

4 lbs. carrots, pared clean
2 oz. hops
3 lbs. sugar, moistened in water
1 tbs. yeast

Boil the carrots in 1 gal. of water for 15 minutes; add the hops and boil another 10 minutes. Strain into a large pot; add the moist sugar. When lukewarm, spread the yeast on a slice of toast and drop the toast and yeast into the pot. Seal and allow to ferment for a day and a half. When fermented, strain clean and seal up in bottles. Store for at least a month before using.

CASA BLANCA

2 oz. Jamaican rum
1 tsp. lime juice
A few dashes of Angostura bitters
A few drops of curacao
A few drops of maraschino

Combine with ice; shake well. Strain and add ice.

CASA BLANCA SPECIAL

2 oz. dark rum
3 tsp. sugar syrup
3 tsp. lime juice
1 tsp. apiece of Cointreau, cherry brandy, and grenadine
1-2 dashes Angostura bitters

Combine with ice; shake well. Strain. Decorate with a cherry and a slice of orange.

CASINO

2 oz. gin
½ tsp. maraschino
1-2 dashes orange bitters
A few drops lemon juice

Combine with ice; shake well. Strain and add ice.

CASSIS PUNCH

13 bottles white wine
4 oz. creme de cassis
2 cups strawberries

Steep the strawberries in the creme de cassis for 1-2 hours before serving. Strain the creme de cassis. Add the wine plus chunks of ice. Float the strawberries.

CASTLE DIP

1½ oz. apple brandy
1½ oz. white creme de menthe
A few drops Pernod

Combine with ice; shake well. Strain and add ice.

CASTLE SPECIAL

2 oz. dark rum
1½ tsp. lime juice
A few drops of curacao
A few drops of rock candy syrup
Mint leaves

Combine (except the mint leaves) with ice; shake. Strain and add ice. Top with mint.

CELERY WINE

1 large bunch of celery
3 lb. sugar
2 cakes of yeast, moistened
Lemon slices

Boil the celery in a gallon of water for at least 15 minutes. Strain and allow to cool; combine with the sugar, lemon slices, and the yeast and store in a warm place for several days. Re-strain; seal in a crock pot and allow to ferment for several weeks. Store in bottles for future use.

CHABLIS COOLER

1 oz. vodka
2 tsp. grenadine
2 tsp. lemon juice
A few drops vanilla extract
Chablis
Sugar

Sugar frost the glass. Pour in all the ingredients except the Chablis and stir well. Add ice and fill with Chablis.

CHABLIS CUP

1 bottle Chablis
4 oz. Grand Marnier
4 oz. kirsch
2½ cups sliced peaches, strawberries, lemons, and oranges
Mint sprigs

Combine all but the Chablis and mint. Refrigerate for one hour. When ready, pour the fruit in. Top with mint.

CHAMPAGNE AND APPLE PUNCH

2 quarts apple juice
2 bottles white rum
2 bottles champagne
1 tbs. Angostura bitters

Combine the juice, rum, and bitters. Stir. Add the champagne plus chunks of ice before serving; stir very gently to mix.

CHAMPAGNE BAYOU

2 oz. gin
2 tsp. sugar syrup
1 tsp. lemon juice
Champagne

Combine the gin, syrup, and juice with ice; shake well. Strain, add ice and fill the glass with champagne. Flavored brandies can be used instead of the gin.

CHAMPAGNE BRUNCH PUNCH

2 bottles cognac
8 oz. curacao
12 oz. orange juice
9 oz. lemon juice
8 oz. grenadine
Sugar to taste
Orange peels, in spirals
1 bottle champagne

Combine everything except the champagne; stir well. Add the champagne plus chunks of ice before serving.

CHAMPAGNE CASSIS

Serve your champagne as always, adding a few drops of creme de cassis.

CHAMPAGNE CIDER

9 gallons hard cider
2½ pints maple syrup
1½ pints cooking alcohol
1 cup skimmed milk
A few drops apiece orange flower water and neroli

Combine the cider, maple syrup, and alcohol in a wooden cask; seal and store for several weeks. When ready, skim the surface clean; add the milk, flower water, and neroli. Stir well and bottle. Store the bottles on their sides for aeration.

CHAMPAGNE COOLER

1 oz. brandy
1 oz. Cointreau
Champagne
Mint sprigs

Pour the brandy and the Cointreau over packed crushed ice. Fill with champagne and stir. Top with mint sprigs.

CHAMPAGNE CUP

2 oz. brandy
2 oz. curacao
1 pint club soda
1 bottle champagne
Slices of pineapple
and strawberries
Cucumber peels

*Combine the brandy and the
curacao with ice; add the fruit
slices and peels. Stir well.
Pour in the soda and the
champagne before serving.*

CHAMPAGNE JULEP

1½ oz. brandy
1 tbs. sugar syrup
Champagne
A few mint sprigs

*Crush the mint in the sugar
syrup on the bottom of a
glass. Fill with crushed ice;
add the brandy. Pour in the
champagne. Stir gently.
Decorate with more sprigs of
mint.*

CHAMPAGNE POLONAISE

Blackberry liqueur
1 tsp. blackberry
brandy
Cognac
Several drops cham-
pagne
Sugar

*Sugar frost a glass with a lit-
tle blackberry liqueur. Pour in
the brandy; add the cognac.
Fill with champagne and
gently stir.*

CHAMPAGNE PUNCH

4 bottles champagne
1 quart club soda
1 pint curacao
1 pint brandy
8 oz. maraschino
8 oz. powdered
sugar
3 cups lemon juice

*Combine all except the
champagne. Stir well. Add the
soda plus chunks of ice
before serving.*

*There are many variations to
a* **CHAMPAGNE PUNCH:**

*You can substitute rum for
the brandy, halve the lemon
juice and add orange juice to
make it up, and add pineapple
juice for the maraschino
(omitting the curacao and
club soda).*

*If you like the taste of other li-
quors with champagne, make
the punch with rum, brandy,
and bourbon (a bottle each),
halving the champagne and
the sugar, and using orange
juice instead of the lemon
juice altogether. Seal it with
1 quart of strong cold tea instead of the club soda.
Orange bitters can be added
for a zingier punch. Fruit
slices are for topping.*

*Ancient
Royal
Drinking Horn*

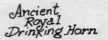

CHAMPAGNE SHERBET PUNCH

2 bottles chilled champagne
1 quart lemon sherbet
1 bottle chilled sauterne

Place the sherbet in the center of a punch bowl. Pour the champagne and sauterne around it. Serve with a scoop, putting half sherbet and half wine into each glass.

CHAMPAGNE ST. MORITZ

1 tbs. dry gin
1 tbs. apricot brandy
1 tbs. orange juice
Champagne

Combine everything except the champagne with ice; shake well. Strain into a wide champagne glass straight up. Fill with champagne and stir.

CHANCELLOR

1½ oz. Scotch
1½ tsp. dry vermouth
1½ tsp. port
1-2 dashes bitters

Combine with ice; shake well. Strain and add ice.

CHANTICLEER

2½ oz. gin
1½ oz. lemon juice
1 tbs. raspberry syrup
1 egg white

Combine with ice; shake well. Strain and add ice.

CHAPALA

1½ oz. tequila
2 tsp. orange juice
lemon juice, and grenadine
A few drops orange flower water

Combine with ice; shake well. Strain and add ice. Top with an orange slice.

CHAPEL HILL

1½ oz. whiskey
½ oz. curacao
2 tsp. lemon juice

Combine with ice; shake well. Strain and add ice. Top with an orange slice.

CHARLES

1½ oz. brandy
1½ oz. sweet vermouth
A few dashes of Angostura bitters

Combine with ice; shake well. Strain and add ice.

CHARLIE CHAPLIN

2½ oz. sloe gin
2½ oz. apricot brandy
1½ tbs. lime juice

Combine with ice; shake well. Strain over crushed ice.

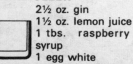

CHARTREUSE CHAMPAGNE

4 oz. champagne
Several drops green chartreuse
Several drops cognac

Combine and gently stir. Add a twist of lemon.

CHARTREUSE COGNAC FRAPPE

1 tbs. yellow chartreuse
1 tbs. cognac
Lemon soda

Combine with ice; shake well. Strain, add ice, and fill with lemon soda. Decorate with an orange slice.

CHATEAU D'ISSOGNE

1½ oz. bourbon
1½ oz. sweet vermouth
1 tbs. aquavit
A few drops of Campari

Combine with ice; shake well. Strain straight up.

CHATHAM

1¼ oz. gin
2 tsp. ginger brandy
1 tsp. lemon juice
1 piece preserved ginger

Combine the gin, brandy, and lemon juice with ice. Shake well. Strain, add ice, and drop in the piece of ginger.

CHATHAM ARTILLERY PUNCH

1½ gallons rose wine
1½ quarts rye
1 quart brandy
1½ gallons dark iced tea
½ gallon rum
1 quart dry gin
8 oz. Benedictine
1½ gallons orange juice
2 lb. brown sugar
12 oz. lemon juice
1 case champagne

Combine everything but the champagne in a large punch bowl; refrigerate for at least 48 hours. Before serving, pour in the champagne, add chunks of ice, and stir.

CHAUNCEY

½ oz. rye
½ oz. gin
½ oz. sweet vermouth
½ oz. brandy
1-2 dashes orange bitters

Combine with ice; shake well. Strain and add ice.

CHELSEA SIDECAR

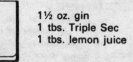

1½ oz. gin
1 tbs. Triple Sec
1 tbs. lemon juice

Combine with ice, shake well. Strain and add ice.

CHERRY BLOSSOM

1½ oz. brandy
1 tbs. cherry liqueur
A few drops of curacao
A few drops of grenadine
½ oz. lemon juice
Sugar

Combine. Shake with ice. Sugar frost the glass with cherry brandy. Strain in the drink.

CHERRY BOUNCE

1 quart Jamaican rum
5 pints whole cherries
Brown sugar

Muddle the cherries (unstoned). Pour the rum over them and allow to stand at room temperature for at least one week. After this time, strain the drink clean; add brown sugar to taste, and allow to stand another week before serving. Serve over ice.

CHERRY COBBLER

1½ oz. gin
2 tsp. Cherry Heering
2 tsp. creme de cassis
2 tsp. lemon juice
1½ tsp. sugar syrup

Combine the liquors, lemon juice, and sugar syrup with ice; shake well. Strain over ice. Decorate with a lemon slice and a cherry.

CHERRY DAIQUIRI

1½ oz. white rum
2 tsp. lime juice
2 tsp. cherry liqueur
A few drops kirsch

Combine with ice; shake well. Strain, add ice and a twist of lime.

CHERRY GINGER FRAPPE

1 oz. cherry liqueur
1 tsp. kirschwasser
1 tsp. ginger brandy
1 piece preserved ginger

Combine the liquors without ice and mix well. Pour over crushed ice. Spear a cherry and the ginger on a toothpick and bridge the pick across the drink.

CHERRY RUM FIX

1½ oz. vodka
2 tsp. Cherry Heering
2 tsp. lemon juice
1 tsp. sugar

Into 2 oz. of water, add the sugar and stir until completely dissolved. Fill with crushed ice and pour in the vodka, Cherry Heering, and lemon juice. Decorate with a lemon slice.

CHERRY SLING

1½ oz. gin
2 tsp. Cherry Karise
2 tsp. lime juice

Combine with ice; shake well. Strain and add ice.

CHICAGO

1½ oz. brandy
A few drops curacao
Powdered sugar
1-2 dashes
Angostura bitters
Champagne
Sugar

Combine the brandy, curacao, and bitters with ice. Shake well. Sugar frost the glass with lemon juice. Strain in the drink and fill with champagne.

CHICAGO BOMB

2 oz. vanilla ice cream
1 tsp. white creme de cacao
1 tsp. green creme de menthe

Combine in a blender at a high speed for a few seconds. Serve straight up.

CHICAGO FIZZ

1 oz. white rum
1 oz. port
1½ tsp. lemon juice
1 tsp. powdered sugar
1 egg white
Club soda

Combine (except the club soda) with ice; shake well. Strain, add ice, and fill the glass with club soda.

BIBLICAL WINE JUG

CHINA

2 oz. gold rum
1 tsp. curacao
A few drops grenadine
A few drops passion fruit juice
A few dashes of Angostura bitters

Combine with ice; shake well. Strain and add ice.

CHINESE COCKTAIL

1½ oz. Jamaican rum
1 tbs. grenadine
A few dashes curacao
A few dashes maraschino
1-2 dashes Angostura bitters

Combine with ice; shake well. Strain and add ice.

CHIQUITA

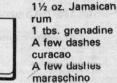

1½ oz. vodka
2 tsp. banana liqueur
2 tsp. lime juice
2 oz. sliced bananas
1 tsp. sugar
2 oz. crushed ice

Combine in a blender at a low speed for 15 seconds. Strain and serve straight up.

CHIQUITA PUNCH

¾ oz. banana liqueur
¾ oz. orange juice
¾ oz. heavy cream
1 tsp. grenadine
6 oz. crushed ice

Combine in a blender at a high speed for 15 seconds. Strain and serve straight up.

CHOCOLATE EGG NOG

1 doz. eggs
1 bottle bourbon
4 tbs. rum
12 oz. sugar
1½ quarts heavy cream
Bittersweet chocolate, in pieces

Separate the eggs. Beat the yolks with 1 cup of the sugar; add the bourbon and the rum in small amounts, stirring constantly. Beat the egg whites with the remaining sugar until stiff; whip the cream. Fold them both carefull into the nog. Garnish with the chocolate.

CHOCOLATE ORANGE FRAPPE

1 oz. white creme de cacao
1 oz. orange juice
1 tsp. Roiano

Combine without ice; pour over crushed ice.

CHOCOLATE RUM

1 oz. white rum
2 tsp. white creme de cacao
2 tsp. white creme de menthe
2 tsp. heavy cream
1 tsp. high-proof rum

Combine the white rum and creams with ice; shake well. Strain and add ice. Float the high-proof rum on top.

CHOCOLATE SOLDIER

1½ oz. gin
1 tbs. Dubonnet
1 tbs. lime juice

Combine with ice; shake well. Strain and add ice.

CHRISTMAS DELIGHT

10 oz. white rum
3 egg yolks
8 oz. sugar
1 tsp. vanilla extract
14 oz. undiluted evaporated milk

Combine the yolks and the sugar in a saucepan; slowly add the milk and stir until smooth. Heat for no more than two minutes, stirring rapidly. Remove from heat; add the vanilla and the rum. Stir well.

CHRISTMAS RUM PUNCH

½ gallon cider
1 bottle Jamaican rum
½ doz. oranges
Cloves
Sugar
Cinnamon
Nutmeg

Stick the oranges with cloves and bake until the oranges begin to brown. Slice the oranges and place them in a large punch bowl; pour in the rum and add sugar to taste. Ignite; extinguish with the cider after a few minutes. Garnish with cinnamon and nutmeg; serve hot.

CHRISTMAS TEA PUNCH

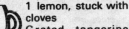

2 bottles red wine
1 bottle dark rum
3 cups hot tea
2 lbs. sugar
3 oz. orange juice
1 oz. lemon juice

Combine the wine, juices, tea, and all but one oz. of the rum; heat thoroughly but do not allow to boil. Turn out into a large chafing dish; add all but 2 oz. sugar and stir until the sugar has dissolved. Combine the leftover sugar and rum in a ladle; ignite and infuse into the warm punch. Serve immediately.

CHRISTMAS WINE

2 gallon bottles red wine
1 bottle port
1 pint brandy
1 lemon, stuck with cloves
Grated tangerine peels
Some ginger, mace, nutmeg, and cinnamon

Combine in a large saucepan; heat thoroughly but do not allow to boil. Serve warm in mugs.

CHRISTOPHER'S MOTHER

2 oz. gin
1 oz. white rum
2 tsp. orange juice
1 tsp. lemon juice
A few drops of whiskey

Combine with ice; shake well. Strain and add ice.

CHRYSANTHEMUM

2 tbs. dry vermouth
2 tbs. Benedictine
Several dashes Pernod

Combine with ice; shake well. Strain, add ice and a twist of orange.

CHURCHILL

1½ oz. Scotch
½ oz. Cointreau
½ oz. sweet vermouth
2 tsp. lime juice

Combine with ice; shake well. Strain and add ice.

CIDER CUP

1 quart cider
2 tbs. maraschino
2 tbs. brandy
12 oz. club soda

Combine all the ingredients in a large pitcher with ice cubes. Garnish with a twist of lemon or orange; stir.

CIDER HEADACHE MEDICINE

1 quart hard cider
2 oz. whole white mustard seeds
2 oz. whole burdock seeds
1 horse-radish root, cut into small pieces

Combine in a large jar or bottle; cover tightly. Allow to stand for several hours before using. Drink in moderation.

CIDER NIGHT CAP

½ gallon hard cider
3 oz. powdered sugar
9 eggs, separated
Grated nutmeg, allspice

Combine the egg yolks with the sugar; beat until creamy. In a separate bowl, beat the whites until foamy; combine with the sweetened yolks in a large bowl. Heat the cider in a large saucepan; when it begins to boil pour it over the eggs, stirring constantly. Top with the garnishes and serve in mugs.

CIDER SYLLABUB

1 pint hard cider
1 pint heavy cream
4 oz. brandy
2 egg whites
2 oz. sugar
Grated lemon rind; tsp. lemon juice

Combine the brandy with the cider in a large crock; add the lemon juice, rind, and sugar. Stir very well to blend and store in a cool place overnight. When ready, beat together the cream and egg whites until thick and fold into the cider.

CIDER POSSET

1 quart heavy cream
1 pint cider
8 oz. Madeira
10 egg yolks
4 egg whites
Grated nutmeg

Combine the cream and the cider in a saucepan; beat the yolks and the whites in separate bowls until thick and creamy and add to the cider and cream. Pour in the Madeira and nutmeg to taste and simmer over low heat until saucy; do not allow to boil. Serve warmed in mugs.

CIDER SMASH

2 oz. brandy
1 tbs. powdered sugar
Pineapple chunks
Lemon slices
Cider

Dissolve the sugar with the brandy; add fruit slices plus plenty of crushed ice. Fill the glass with cider and stir gently.

CITY SLICKER

1½ oz. brandy
¾ oz. curacao

Combine with ice; shake well. Strain and add ice.

CITRONELLE

The rinds of 3 doz. lemons
The rinds of 5 oranges
6 cups of sugar
1 gallon cooking alcohol
Ground cloves, nutmeg

Grate the rinds and combine in a pot with ground cloves and the alcohol. Seal the pot and allow to steep for at least two weeks. Strain clean and add the sugar, diluted in a quart of water. Bottle and store in a cool, dark place.

CLARET COBBLER

1 tsp. powdered sugar
1 tsp. lemon juice
A few drops of maraschino
Claret
1 oz. crushed ice
1 pineapple stick

Over crushed ice, add sugar, lemon juice, and maraschino. Stir well. Fill with claret. Top with pineapple.

CLARET COCKTAIL

1 oz. claret
1 oz. brandy
1 tsp. curacao
1 tsp. lemon
½ tsp. anisette

Combine with ice; shake well. Strain and add ice and a twist of orange.

CLARET COOLER

4 oz. claret
1 oz. orange juice
2 tsp. brandy
2 tsp. lemon juice
3 oz. club soda
1 long sliver orange rind

Pour the wine, brandy, soda, and juices over ice and stir well. Drop in the orange rind and add a twist of lemon.

CLARET CUP

1 bottle claret
1 bottle club soda
8 oz. sherry
2½ oz. Triple Sec
2½ oz. brandy
1 lemon rind, pared
Powdered sugar
Fruit slices
Fresh mint

Combine in a small punch bowl and stir well. Add powdered sugar to taste. Decorate with fruit and mint. Let stand a few hours before serving.

CLARET FRUIT CUP

1 bottle claret
3 oz. orange juice
3 tsp. lemon juice
Grated lemon rind
1½ oz. sugar
2 oz. brandy
1 cucumber slice
2 bottles club soda

Soak the claret with the sugar in a punch bowl for at least one hour. Stir and add the juices and brandy. Garnish with the rinds. When ready to serve, add the soda plus enough crushed ice to fill the bowl and stir gently.

CLARET PUNCH

3 cups lemon juice
1 cup powdered sugar
3 quarts claret
8 oz. curacao
8 oz. brandy
1 quart club soda
Fruit slices

In a large punch bowl, combine the lemon juice with the sugar. Stir vigorously to dissolve sugar. Pour in the wine, curacao, brandy, and soda. Stir. Top with fruit. Add chunks of ice a half-hour before serving.

CLARET RUM COOLER

3 oz. claret
1 oz. white
2 tsp. kirschwasser
2 tsp. Falernum
1 strawberry

Combine with ice; stir well. Drop in the strawberry or add a twist of orange.

CLARIDGE COCKTAIL

¾ oz. dry gin
¾ oz. dry vermouth
2 tsp. apricot brandy
2 tsp. Triple Sec

Combine with ice; shake well. Strain and add ice.

CLASSIC

1½ oz. brandy
2 tsp. lemon juice
1 tsp. maraschino
1 tsp. curacao

Combine with ice; shake well. Strain and add ice.

CLOISTER

1½ oz. gin
2 tsp. grapefruit juice
1 tsp. lemon juice
1 tsp. yellow chartreuse

Combine with ice; shake well. Strain and add ice.

CLOVER CLUB

1½ oz. gin
2 tbs. lime juice
2 tbs. grenadine
1 egg white

Combine with ice; shake well. Strain and add ice.

CLOVER CLUB ROYAL

1½ oz. gin
1 tbs. lemon juice
1 tsp. grenadine
½ egg yolk

Combine with ice; shake well. Strain and add ice.

CLUB MARTINI

1½ oz. gin
2 tsp. sweet vermouth

Combine with ice; shake well. Strain. Decorate with an olive and serve straight up.

COCICE

1½ oz. white rum
1 oz. coconut milk
1 tsp. sugar syrup
6 oz. crushed ice

Combine in a blender at a high speed for 25 seconds. Pour out straight up.

COCONUT BRANDY BOWL

3 oz. brandy
1½ banana liqueur
2 large coconuts
Crushed ice

Slice off the eyes of the coconuts; drain and save the milk. Gouge out the meat of the coconuts; saving as much milk from that as possible. Combine the brandy, banana liqueur, and all the coconut milk in a blender with 3-4 oz. of crushed ice. Blend at a high speed for 15 seconds. Serve the drink in the two coconut shells.

COCONUT COOLER

1½ oz. white rum
1 oz. cream of coconut
1 oz. heavy cream
4 oz. crushed ice
1 coconut

With a very sharp knife or cleaver, cleanly chop off the top of a coconut, nearest the eyes; save the juice. Combine the remaining ingredients with 2 oz. of the coconut juice in a blender at a high speed for 15 seconds. Strain this into the coconut shell and serve in a large dish filled with crushed ice.

COCONUT CORDIAL

White rum
Sugar
A large coconut

Slice off the eye of the coconut and drain. Fill the coconut with water and measure the amount of water you put in. Combine the rum and sugar (at a ratio of 2:1) to equal the amount of water. Stir until the sugar has dissolved and pour it into the coconut. Seal it with wax and store at room temperature for at least a month. Uncork and bottle. Serve as a cordial.

COCONUT GIN

1½ oz. gin
2 tsp. lemon juice
1 tsp. maraschino
1 tsp. cream of coconut

Combine with ice; shake. Strain and add ice.

COCONUT GROVE COOLER

1½ oz. bourbon
2 tsp. apiece of orange juice, lemon juice, orange curacao, grenadine, and pineapple juice
1 tsp. Passionola

Combine with ice; shake well. Strain over crushed ice. Decorate with orange and pineapple slices, a cherry, and a mint sprig.

COCONUT RUM

1 large coconut
Brown sugar

Slice off the eyes of the coconut and drain out the milk. Fill with brown sugar and seal very tightly. Allow the sugar in the coconut ferment in a cool, dark place for several months. When ready, you will be able to smell and taste a most delicate, coconut-scented rum. Serve pieces of coconut meat on the side.

COCONUT TEQUILA

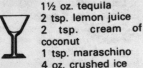

1½ oz. tequila
2 tsp. lemon juice
2 tsp. cream of coconut
1 tsp. maraschino
4 oz. crushed ice

Combine in a blender at a low speed for 15 seconds. Strain and serve straight up.

COEXISTENCE COLLINS

2 oz. vodka
2 tsp. lemon juice
1½ tsp. sugar syrup
1 tsp. kummel
1 cucumber peel
Club soda

Combine the vodka, juice, sugar, and kummel with ice; shake well. Strain, add ice, and fill with club soda. Top with the cucumber peel and a twist of lemon.

COFFEE ALEXANDER

1½ oz. brandy or gin
1 oz. Galacafe
1 oz. heavy cream
Sugar

Wet the rim of a glass with Galacafe and press in sugar. Combine all the liquids and shake in a mixing glass. Strain into the frosted glass.

COFFEE BLAZER

1 tbs. coffee liqueur
1 tbs. cognac
Sugar
Lemon slice
Hot coffee
Whipped cream

Warm the coffee liqueur and cognac over a low flame. Line the rim of an old-fashioned glass with the juice of the lemon slice; press it in sugar and drop in the slice. Warm the glass to melt the sugar; pour in the warmed liquor and ignite. Pour in the coffee; stir well. Garnish with whipped cream.

COFFEE COCKTAIL

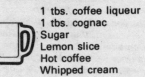

1½ oz. apple brandy
1½ oz. port
1 egg yolk
1 oz. coffee

Combine with ice; shake. Strain and add ice. Top with nutmeg.

COFFEE COOLER

1½ oz. vodka
1 oz. heavy cream
1 oz. Kahlua
1½ tsp. sugar syrup
4 oz. iced coffee
1 scoop coffee ice cream

Combine all (except ice cream) with ice; shake. Strain, add ice and the ice cream.

COFFEE EGG NOG

1½ oz. whiskey
1 oz. Kahlua
2 tsp. heavy cream
1½ tsp. sugar syrup
1 egg
½ tsp. instant coffee
4 oz. milk
Ground coriander

Combine all (except the coriander) with ice; shake. Strain and add ice. Dust with coriander.

COFFEE FLIP

1½ oz. cognac
1 oz. port
1½ tsp. sugar syrup
1 egg
1 oz. coffee

Combine with ice; shake. Strain. Dust with nutmeg and serve straight up.

COFFEE GRAND MARNIER

¾ oz. Kahlua
¾ oz. Grand Marnier
1 tbs. orange juice

Combine without ice.; stir well. Pour over crushed ice. Top with an orange slice.

COFFEE GRASSHOPPER

¾ oz. coffee liqueur
¾ oz. white creme de menthe
¾ oz. heavy cream

Combine with ice; shake very well. Strain and add ice.

COFFEE KIRSCH

1 oz. kirsch
1 egg white
4 oz. coffee
A pinch of sugar

Combine with ice; shake well. Strain and add ice.

COFFEE LIQUEUR

5 cups cooking alcohol
4 lb. sugar
8 oz. brewed ground coffee beans

Combine the coffee with 1 cup of alcohol in a pot; allow to stand for at least one week. Boil the sugar in water to make a syrup; remove from heat. Add the unused alcohol and the prepared coffee; stir, strain, and bottle. Store for several months before using.

COFFEE NO. 2

1½ oz. brandy
1 tbs. port
1-2 dashes curacao
1 tsp. sugar syrup
1 egg yolk
1 oz. coffee

Combine with ice; shake well. Strain and add ice; garnish with nutmeg.

COFFEE ROIANO

1½ oz. Roiano
2 tsp. coffee liqueur
2 tsp. cream
3 oz. crushed ice

Combine in a blender at a low speed for 15 seconds. Strain and serve straight up.

COFFEE VIENNESE

5 cups fresh, hot coffee
1 quart vanilla ice cream
8 oz. brandy
Whipped cream
Grated nutmeg

Combine the coffee and the brandy in a large chafing dish to keep hot. Fill several tall glasses with alternate layers of brandy and coffee and scoops of ice cream, stirring to blend until every glass is almost full. Garnish with whipped cream dusted with nutmeg.

COGNAC MINT FRAPPE

1 oz. green creme de menthe
1 tsp. cognac
Mint leaves, partially torn

Combine the creme de menthe and the cognac without ice; stir well. Pour over crushed ice; top with the mint leaves.

COKE AND DAGGER

2 oz. Jamuican rum
Cola
1-2 drops orange bitters

Combine the rum and the bitters. Stir well. Add ice and fill with cola; stir gently. Touch it up with a twist of orange.

COLD APPLE TODDY

1 quart apple brandy
1 pint peach brandy
1 pint sherry
1 doz. apples
10 oz. sugar
2 quarts boiling water

Bake the apples; mash while hot. Add the sugar and boiling water and stir well. Pour in the brandies; stir. Cover and allow to cool. Strain when cool, add the sherry, and serve over ice.

COLD DECK

1½ oz. brandy
¾ oz. sweet vermouth
¾ oz. white creme de menthe
1-2 dashes Pernod

Combine with ice; shake well. Strain and add ice.

COLD DUCK

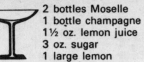

2 bottles Moselle
1 bottle champagne
1½ oz. lemon juice
3 oz. sugar
1 large lemon

Dissolve the sugar with the lemon juice on the bottom of a large punch bowl; add the Moselle and stir gently. Carefully peel the lemon in one long, spiral strip. Hook the end of the peel over the side of the bowl and place the whole, peeled lemon in the wine. Add the champagne before serving.

COLD IRISH

1½ oz. Irish whiskey
½ oz. Irish Mist
A few drops creme de cacao
Whipped cream
Coffee soda

Pour the whiskey and the Irish Mist over ice. Fill with coffee soda and stir. Touch up the whipped cream with the creme de cacao and use it to top the drink.

COLD WINE FLIP

3 oz. claret, burgundy, or sherry
1 egg
1 tsp. powdered sugar

Combine the wine and the egg with ice; shake well. Dissolve the sugar with a few drops of water. Strain over ice and stir gently. Garnish with nutmeg.

COLONIAL CAUDLE

1 pint white wine
8 oz. sugar
8 oz. oatmeal water
3 tsp. orange juice
Grated lemon rind

Simmer the oatmeal water with lemon rinds (to taste) for several minutes. Strain clean into a separate bowl. Add the sugar, orange juice, and wine; stir until well-blended. Serve in mugs.

COLONIAL TEA PUNCH

12 lemons, thinly pooled
1 quart dark iced tea
1 quart Jamaican rum
1½ oz. brandy
12 oz. sugar

Combine the juice of the lemons, their peels, the tea, and the sugar. Steep for 1-2 hours. Then, a half-hour before serving add the rum, brandy, and chunks of ice.

COLUMBIA SKIN

1 lemon, thinly peeled
9 oz. Scotch
2 cups boiling water

Slice the fruit and place its peels and the slices on the bottom of a small, heat-proof pitcher. Pour in the Scotch and the boiling water; stir. Serve hot, topped with lemon slices.

COLUMBIA SKIN NO. 2

3 oz. rum
1½ oz. lemon juice
1 tsp. curacao
2 cubes sugar
1 tbs. water

Combine in a saucepan; heat and stir but do not boil. Pour out into a warm glass; serve hot. Brandy or gin can be used for the rum.

COMBO

2½ oz. dry vermouth
¼ oz. cognac
½ tsp. curacao
1 tsp. sugar syrup
A few dashes of Angostura bitters

Combine with ice; shake. Strain and add ice.

COMMODORE

1 oz. bourbon
1 oz. dark creme de cacao
1 oz. lemon juice
1-2 dashes grenadine

Combine with ice; shake well. Strain and serve straight up.

COMMONWEALTH

1¾ oz. Canadian whiskey
½ oz. Van der Hum liqueur
1 tsp. lemon juice

Combine with ice; shake well. Strain; add ice and a twist of orange.

CONCHITA

1 oz. tequila
1 oz. grapefruit juice
A few drops lemon juice

Combine with ice; shake well. Strain and add ice.

CONCH SHELL

4 oz. white rum
2 tsp. lime juice

Combine with ice; shake well. Strain and add ice.

CONNECTICUT SYLLABUB

This one is from the first cookbook ever published in New England, written by Miss Amelia Simonds of Hartford: "Sweeten a quart of cyder with refined sugar, grate nutmeg into it, then milk your cow into your liquor."

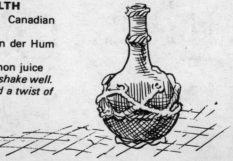

CONSTANT COMMENT PUNCH

1 quart tea, iced
1 pint orange juice
8 oz. lemon juice
8 oz. sugar
1 bottle ginger ale
Bourbon
Fruit slices, cherries, mint sprigs

Combine everything except the soda, bourbon, and garnishes. Stir well to blend. Add the ginger ale plus ice before serving; top with the fruit slices, cherries, and mint. Spike the punch with bourbon to taste.

CONSTANTIA PUNCH

1 bottle claret
4 oz. Van der Hum
4 oz. brandy liqueur
7 oz. sugar
Whole cloves
1 orange, peeled and sliced

Combine the wine with the orange slices, sugar, and cloves in a saucepan; heat thoroughly but do not allow to boil. Add 1 pint of already boiling water plus the brandy liqueur and the Van der Hum and stir well. Allow to cool and serve garnished with nutmeg.

CONSTITUTION FLIP

1 pint hard cider
2 oz. rock candy
1 egg
Whole cloves
A cinnamon stick

CONTINENTAL SOUR

1¼ oz. rye
1½ tbs. lemon juice
1 tsp. sugar syrup
1 egg white
1 tbs. claret

Combine (except the claret) with ice; shake extremely well. Strain, add ice, and float the claret on top.

COOCH BEHAR

1½ oz. pepper vodka
3 oz. tomato juice

Combine with ice; shake well. Strain and add ice.
To make your own pepper vodka, drop a hot chili pepper into a bottle of vodka and let it stand for a week or so.

COOL COLONEL

1½ oz. bourbon
1 oz. Southern Comfort
3 oz. dark iced tea
½ oz. lemon juice
3 tsp. sugar syrup
Club soda

Combine all (except the soda); add ice and stir well. Splash in some soda and add a twist of lemon.

Crush the rock candy and the cinnamon stick together into a powder; add to the cider and stir well. Beat in an egg; stir briskly until the drink foams. Serve in two large mugs; heat with a hot mulling poker.

COOL CUP

1 quart cider
1½ cups sherry
1 large lemon
6 oz. sugar, in cubes
Grated nutmeg
Mint sprigs

Peel the lemon; rub the cubes against the rinds until the cubes turn yellow. Drop them on the bottom of a large pitcher; squeeze the juice of the fruit over them and stir until dissolved. Add the cider, sherry, and nutmeg; stir well. Top with mint.

COPA DE ORO

1 oz. gold rum
3 tsp. lime juice
2 tsp. sugar syrup
A few drops of maraschino
3 oz. crushed ice
A few drops Pernod

Combine everything except the Pernod in a blender at a high speed for 10 seconds. Strain into a deep-dish champagne glass straight up. Float the Pernod.

COPENHAGEN

1 oz. gin
1 oz. aquavit
1 tsp. dry vermouth

Combine with ice; shake well. Strain and add ice. Top with an olive.

COPENHAGEN SPECIAL

1 oz. aquavit
1 oz. Arrack
1½ tbs. lemon juice

Combine with ice; shake well. Strain and add ice.

CORDIAL MEDOC CUP

1 oz. Cordial Medoc
½ oz. cognac
1½ tbs. lemon juice
1 tsp. sugar syrup
Champagne

Combine all (except the champagne) with ice; shake. Strain, add ice, and fill with champagne. Top with a slice of orange.

CORDIAL MEDOC SOUR

1½ oz. gin
½ oz. Cordial Medoc
2 tsp. lemon juice

Combine with ice; shake well. Strain. Top with a slice of orange and serve straight up.

CORKSCREW

1½ oz. white rum
½ oz. peach liqueur
2 tsp. dry vermouth

Combine with ice; shake well. Strain and add ice. Top with a lime slice.

CORSON

1½ oz. sherry
1½ oz. gin
1 oz. lemon juice
A few drops of sweet vermouth, dry vermouth, curacao, cherry brandy, and white creme de cacao

Combine with ice; shake well. Strain and add ice.

COSTA DEL SOL

2 oz. gin
1 oz. apricot brandy
1 oz. Cointreau

*Combine with ice; shake well.
Strain straight up.*

COTE D'AZUR COOLER

1 oz. brandy
2 tsp. lemon juice
2 tsp. pineapple juice
A few drops of maraschino
Club soda

Combine all except the club soda with ice; shake well. Strain straight; add soda and stir.

COUCOU CUMBER

1½ oz. vodka
2 tsp. sugar syrup
1 tsp. Pernod
1 large cucumber

Combine everything except the cucumber with ice; shake well. Slice one end off the cucumber, use an apple corer on the other end to hollow out all the meat. Strain in the drink; add crushed ice to fill the cucumber, and serve on a flat dish for support.

COUNSELLOR'S CUP

8 oz. cognac
2 large, sweet oranges
4 oz. sugar, in cubes
3 tsp. lemon juice

Peel the oranges; rub the sugar cubes against the rinds until they turn orange. Combine the cubes in a pint of water in a large saucepan; bring to a boil. Lower heat and simmer. Squeeze in the juice of the oranges; add the lemon juice, and bring back to a boil; stir well. As soon as it boils, remove from heat and pour into a heatproof bowl; add the cognac and stir. Serve immediately in warmed mugs.

CRANBERRY CHRISTMAS PUNCH

1 quart cranberry juice
1 bottle Sauterne
8 oz. brandy
Sugar
Lemon slices
1 bottle club soda

Combine the wine, juice, brandy, and lemon slices in a large pot; stir well and allow to stand, covered, at room temperature for several hours. Add sugar to taste if needed. Turn out into a large punch bowl; add the soda plus chunks of ice before serving.

CREAM AND COFFEE PUNCH

1 quart vanilla ice cream
½ bottle Jamaican rum
3 quarts hot dark coffee

Place the ice cream in a punch bowl; add the coffee and stir until the ice cream has melted. Pour in the rum and add ice.

CREAMY ORANGE

1 oz. cream sherry
1 oz. orange juice
2 tsp. heavy cream
2 tsp. brandy

Combine with ice; shake very well. Strain and add ice.

CREAMY SCREWDRIVER

2 oz. vodka
6 oz. orange
1 egg yolk
1½ tsp. sugar syrup
¾ cup crushed ice

Combine in a blender at low speed for 15 seconds. Strain over ice.

CREME DE CACAO

1 lb. cacao beans
2 cups sugar
2 bottles brandy
1 tbs. vanilla extract

Roast the beans until nearly charred; soak in the brandy for a week. Boil the sugar in water to make a thick syrup; allow it to cool and then combine with the brandy. Add the vanilla extract; strain and bottle for future use.

CREME DE LAURIER

3 oz. laurel leaves, crushed
2 oz. myrtle flowers
6 pints sugar
Whole cloves, chopped nutmeg
3 bottles brandy

Pound and blend the laurel leaves, myrtle flowers, cloves, and nutmeg; pour the brandy over them. Boil the sugar in enough water to make a syrup; allow to cool and combine with the spiced brandy. Strain and bottle for future use.

CREME DE MENTHE

1 lb. mint sprigs, as fresh as possible
7 pints cognac
4 pints sugar
2 tbs. peppermint extract
Grated lemon rinds

Wash the mint sprigs; chop into fine pieces. Combine with the lemon rinds in a flat bowl; pound as finely as possible. Soak in the brandy for a week. Strain; distill, and add the peppermint extract. Boil the sugar in enough water to make a syrup; allow to cool. Add to the brandy and stand for a half-hour. Strain and bottle for future use.

Old English Leather "Bottel" (Wine)

CREOLE

1 oz. whiskey
1 oz. sweet
vermouth
1-2 dashes
Amer Picon
1-2 dashes
Benedictine

Combine with ice; shake well. Strain. Add ice and a twist of lemon.

CREOLE CHAMPAGNE PUNCH

1 bottle champagne
1 bottle white wine
8 oz. curacao
1 pint lemon juice
2 cups sugar
1 pineapple, half grated, half sliced
Whole strawberries
2 bottles club soda

Dissolve the sugar with the lemon juice. Add the wine, champagne, and curacao. Stir well. Garnish with the grated and sliced pineapple and the strawberries. Add the soda plus chunks of ice before serving; stir to blend.

CREOLE DOWNFALL

1 pint corn whiskey
1 pint ginger ale
Mint sprigs

Muddle the mint in a large jar; add the whiskey and the ginger ale. Seal the jar tightly and refrigerate for at least a week. Serve straight up or as a mixer like straight whiskey.

CREOLE LADY

1½ oz. whiskey
1½ oz. Madeira
1 tsp. grenadine
1 green cherry
1 red cherry

Combine with ice; shake well. Strain and add ice. Top with the cherries.

CREOLE WHITE WINE PUNCH

2½ bottle Sauterne
1 pint lemon juice
8 oz. brandy
2 cup sugar
Grated and sliced pineapple
Cherries, mint sprigs
1 bottle club soda

Combine everything except the soda, wine, and mint leaves and allow to stand at room temperature for one hour. Add the wine and soda plus chunks of ice

CREOLE CLARET PUNCH

2½ bottles claret
1 pint lemon juice
1 pint sugar
2 lemons, thinly sliced
1½ bottles club soda

Combine everything except the soda; stir well. Add the soda plus chunks of ice before serving.

CRIMEAN CUP

16 oz. cognac
8 oz. dark rum
8 oz. maraschino
3 oz. sugar
10 oz. lemon juice
3 cup sugar syrup
2 tsp. almond extract
Grated lemon rinds
2 bottles club soda
2 bottles champagne

Muddle the rinds with the sugar. Add the lemon juice and the soda; stir until the sugar is dissolved. Add the sugar syrup and beat until foamy. Pour in the cognac, maraschino, and rum and allow to stand until marinated. Add the champagne plus chunks of ice.

CRIMSON

2 oz. gin
1 oz. port
½ oz. lemon juice
1 tsp. grenadine

Combine the gin, juice, and grenadine with ice; shake well. Strain; add ice and float the port.

CUBAN SPECIAL

1 oz. white rum
½ tsp. curacao
¾ oz. pineapple juice
¾ oz. lime juice
1 pineapple stick

Combine (except the pineapple stick) with ice; shake well. Strain, add ice and decorate with the pinapple.

CUCUMBER CHAMPAGNE

1 oz. Benedictine
2 tsp. lemon juice
8 oz. champagne
1 long, narrow cucumber peel

Pour the Benedictine and lemon juice over the peel. Add the champagne and stir gently. Let it stand a bit.

CULROSS

1½ oz. gold rum
½ oz. Lillet
1 tsp. apricot brandy
1 tsp. lime juice

Combine with ice; shake well. Strain and add ice.

CUPID

3 oz. sherry
1 egg
1 tsp. powdered sugar
1 pinch cayenne pepper

Combine with ice; shake extremely well. Strain and add ice.

CURACAO COOLER

1 oz. blue curacao
1 oz. vodka
2 tsp. lime juice
2 tsp. lemon juice
Orange juice

Combine the curacao, vodka, and lemon and lime juice with ice; shake well. Strain, add ice, and fill the glass with orange juice. Add a twist of lemon, orange, and/or lime.

YOUR OWN RECIPE

YOUR OWN RECIPE

Use a bartender's mixing glass whenever the instructions state "combine" ingredients. Strain the drink from the mixing glass into the drinking glass suggested by the illustration alongside the ingredients.

D

DAFFODIL

1 oz. apple brandy
1 oz. white port
2 tsp. apricot brandy
2 tsp. lemon juice
Yellow gumdrops

Combine everything except the gumdrops with ice; shake well. Strain straight up. Cut the gumdrops and use toothpicks to spear them; then bridge the glass with the speared gumdrops.

DAIQUIRI

2 oz. white rum
1 oz. lime juice
1 tsp. sugar syrup

Combine with ice; shake well. Strain and add ice.

DAISY

2 oz. tequila
2 tsp. lemon juice
2 tsp. grenadine
2 tsp. club soda

Combine with ice; shake well. Strain and add ice.

DAMN THE WEATHER

1 oz. gin
2 tsp. sweet vermouth
2 tsp. orange juice
1 tsp. curacao

Combine with ice; shake well. Strain and add ice.

DAMSON WINE

7 lb. damsons
2 lb. sugar
4 oz. brandy
1 oz. yeast, spread on a piece of toast

Slice the fruit; place them in a large pot and pour in a gallon of boiling water. Close tightly and allow to stand for several days; stir occasionally. Strain out the juice into a separate pot; add the sugar and brandy plus the yeast on toast. Seal and allow to ferment. Strain when ready and store a year before used.

DANCING LEPRECHAUN

1½ oz. Irish Whiskey
1½ oz. lemon juice
Club soda
Ginger ale

Combine the whiskey and the juice; shake with ice. Strain and add ice. Fill the glass with equal parts soda and ginger ale; stir gently. Touch it up with a twist of lemon.

DANIEL DE ORO

1 oz. tequila
Orange juice
½ tsp. Creme
Damiana

Pour the tequila into a glass; add ice and fill with orange juice. Top it off with the Creme Damiana.

DANISH GIN FIZZ

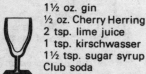

1½ oz. gin
½ oz. Cherry Herring
2 tsp. lime juice
1 tsp. kirschwasser
1½ tsp. sugar syrup
Club soda

Combine all (except the soda) with ice; shake well. Strain, add ice and fill the glass with club soda. Add a lime slice.

DANNY'S SPECIAL

2 oz. bourbon
1 oz. Cointreau
3 tbs. lemon juice
1 tsp. Grand Marnier

Combine with ice; shake well. Strain and add plenty of ice.

DARE COCKTAIL

¾ oz. dry vermouth
¾ oz. dry gin
1 tbs. apricot brandy
1 tsp. lemon juice

Combine with ice; shake well. Strain and add ice.

DE RIGUEUR

1 oz. whiskey
2 tsp. grapefruit juice
2 tsp. honey

Combine with ice; shake and strain. Serve over ice.

DEAUVILLE

¾ oz. brandy
¾ oz. apple brandy
¾ oz. Cointreau or Triple Sec
1½ tbs. lemon juice

Combine with ice; shake well. Strain and add ice.

DEEP SEA

1 oz. Old Tom gin
1 oz. dry vermouth
1-2 dashes Pernod
1-2 dashes orange bitters
1 olive

Combine with ice; shake well. Strain, add ice and a twist of lemon.

DELTA

1½ oz. whiskey
½ oz. Southern Comfort
2 tsp. lime juice
1 tsp. sugar syrup
1 peach slice

Combine all but the peach with ice; shake well. Strain and add ice. Top with the peach.

DEMPSEY

1 oz. gin
1 oz. apple brandy
1-2 dashes Pernod
1-2 dashes grenadine

Combine with ice; shake well. Strain over ice.

DEPTH BOMB

1¼ oz. apple brandy
1¼ oz. brandy
A few drops of grenadine
A few drops lemon juice

Combine with ice; shake well. Strain and add ice.

DERBY NO. 1

1½ oz. gin
1-2 dashes peach bitters
Mint sprigs

Combine the gin and the bitters with ice; shake well. Strain and add ice. Decorate with mint.

DERBY NO.2

1 oz. whiskey
2 tsp. sweet vermouth
2 tsp. white curacao
1½ tbs. lime juice
1 mint leaf

Combine all but the mint leaf with ice; shake well. Strain and add ice. Decorate with the mint.

DERBY DAIQUIRI

1½ oz. white rum
1 oz. orange juice
2 tsp. lime juice
2 tsp. sugar syrup
3 oz. crushed ice

Combine in a blender at a low speed for 15 seconds. Strain and serve straight up.

DERBY FIZZ

1½ oz. whiskey
1½ tsp. sugar syrup
1 tsp. lemon juice
1 egg
A few drops of curacao
Club soda

Combine (except the soda) with ice; shake well. Strain, add ice, and club soda.

DERBY RUM FIX

2 oz. white rum
2 tsp. lime juice
1½ tsp. sugar syrup
1 oz. orange juice

Combine without ice; stir. Strain over crushed ice. Decorate with a slice of orange and a cherry.

DEVIL'S TAIL

1½ oz. gold rum
1 oz. vodka
2 tsp. lime juice
2 tsp. grenadine
1 tsp. apricot liqueur
3 oz. crushed ice

Combine in a blender at a low speed for 15 seconds. Strain, add a twist of lime and serve straight up.

DEWBERRY CORDIAL

1 quart dewberries
1 gallon water
1.5 lb. sugar
A cake of yeast

Mash the berries and combine them with the water in a large crock pot. Add the sugar and yeast and stir until blended. Allow to ferment for at least one month before straining and re-bottling it as a liqueur.

DIABLO

1½ oz. dry white port
1 oz. vermouth
A few drops lemon juice

Combine with ice; shake well. Strain, add ice and a twist of lemon.

DIAMOND PUNCH

1 bottle champagne
6 oz. raspberry syrup
4 oz. gin
2 oz. orange juice
3 tsp. lemon juice
3 tsp. lime juice

Combine with chunks of ice before serving.

DIANA

2 oz. white creme de menthe
2 tsp. brandy

Pack a small wine glass with crushed ice and pour in the creme de menth. Float the brandy.

DIKI-DIKI

2 oz. apple brandy
2 tsp. grapefruit juice
2 tsp. dry gin

Combine with ice; shake well. Strain and add ice.

DINAH

1½ oz. whiskey
¾ oz. lemon juice
½ tsp. powdered sugar

Combine. Shake with ice. Pour on ice. Decorate with mint.

DIPLOMAT

3 oz. dry vermouth
1 oz. sweet vermouth
A few drops of maraschino

Combine with ice; shake very well. Strain and add ice.

DIPLOMAT SPECIAL

2 oz. Scotch
1 tbs. dry vermouth
Several drops Pernod

Combine with ice; shake well. Strain into a pre-chilled martini glass, straight up; add a twist of lemon.

Ancient Wooden cup...British. Called a QUAIGH

126

DIXIE

¾ oz. gin
1½ oz. orange juice
2 tsp. Pernod
2 tsp. dry vermouth
1-2 dashes grenadine

Combine with ice; shake. Strain and add ice.

DIXIE WHISKEY

2 oz. whiskey
¼ oz. lemon juice
½ tsp. powdered sugar
½ tsp. white creme de menthe
A few drops curacao

Combine with ice; shake. Strain and add ice.

DOBBS

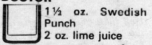

White creme de menthe
Fernet Branca

Pour the creme de menthe into a glass filled with crushed ice. Top with few dashes of Fernet Branca.

DOCTOR

1½ oz. Swedish Punch
2 oz. lime juice

Combine with ice; shake. Strain and add ice.

DOCTOR FUNK

3 oz. Jamaican rum
¾ oz. lemon juice
1 tbs. Pernod
1 tsp. grenadine
1 tsp. powdered sugar
Club soda
1 small lime

Squeeze the lime into a mixing glass; drop in the fruit. Add ice and everything else except the soda; shake well. Strain; add ice and club soda.

DOLORES

¾ oz. cherry brandy
¾ oz. creme de cacao
¾ oz. Spanish brandy
1 egg white

Combine with ice; shake extremely well. Strain and add ice.

DOOLITTLE SPECIAL

1¼ oz. whiskey
A few dashes sugar syrup
½ lemon

Muddle the lemon on the bottom of a glass; add the whiskey, sugar, and ice. Stir.

DORADO COCKTAIL

2 oz. tequila
1½ oz. lemon juice
1 tbs. honey

Combine with ice; shake well. Strain and add ice.

DOUBLE DERBY

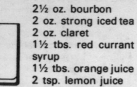

2½ oz. bourbon
2 oz. strong iced tea
2 oz. claret
1½ tbs. red currant syrup
1½ tbs. orange juice
2 tsp. lemon juice

Combine; add ice and stir very well. Decorate with a slice of orange. Heat the red currant jelly in a teaspoon with warm water to make the syrup. Stir again.

DOUBLE STANDARD SOUR

¾ oz. whiskey
¾ oz. dry gin
1½ tsp. lemon juice
½ tsp. powdered sugar
½ tsp. grenadine

Combine with ice; shake. Strain straight up and decorate with a slice of lemon and a cherry.

DRAGOON PUNCH

3 pints porter stout
3 pints ale
½ pint brandy
½ pint sherry
4 oz. sugar syrup
3 lemons, sliced
2 bottles champagne

Combine all but the champagne. Stir well. A half-hour before serving, add the champagne and chunks of ice.

DREAM COCKTAIL

1½ oz. brandy
1 tsp. curacao
A few drops anisette

Combine with ice; shake well. Strain and add ice.

DRY COLD DECK

1¾ oz. brandy
2 tsp. dry vermouth
1 tsp. white creme de menthe

Combine with ice; shake well. Strain and add ice.

DRY MANHATTAN COOLER

2 oz. whiskey
1 oz. dry vermouth
2 oz. orange juice
2 tsp. lemon juice
2 tsp. almond extract
Club soda

Combine all but the soda. Shake with ice. Strain. Pour on ice.

DRY VERMOUTH COBBLER

3 oz. dry vermouth
3 oz. club soda

Half-fill a glass with crushed ice. Add the vermouth and soda; stir well. Top with a lemon slice.

DUBARRY COCKTAIL

¾ oz. dry vermouth
1½ oz. gin
Several drops Pernod
1-2 dashes bitters

Strain and add ice.

DUBONNET COCKTAIL

1¼ oz. Dubonnet
1¼ oz. gin

Combine with ice; shake. Strain. Add ice and a twist of lemon.

DUBONNET FIZZ

3 oz. Dubonnet
2 oz. orange juice
1 tsp. cherry brandy
1 tbs. lemon juice
Club soda

Combine (except the soda) with ice; shake. Strain, add ice, and club soda. Top with a lemon slice and a cherry. For an extra kick, add 1 teaspoon of kirschwasser.

DUBONNET MANHATTEN

1½ oz. Dubonnet
1½ oz. whiskey

Combine with ice; shake well. Strain. Add ice and top with a cherry.

DUBONNET ON THE ROCKS

Twist a lemon peel into a glass; drop in the peel. Add ice and Dubonnet. Stir well.

DUBONNET PUNCH

1 bottle Dubonnet
1 pint gin
1 quart club soda
½ doz. limes
Mint leaves

Combine the juice of the limes, the Dubonnet, and the gin in a pitcher. Add the lime rinds, club soda, and ice. Serve with crushed ice and mint leaves.

DUCHESS

¾ oz. Pernod
¾ oz. dry vermouth
¾ oz. sweet vermouth

Combine with ice; shake well. Strain and add ice.

DUKE OF MARLBOROUGH

1½ oz. sherry
1½ oz. sweet vermouth
2 oz. lime juice
Several dashes raspberry syrup

Combine with ice; shake. Strain and add ice.

DULCET

1 oz. vodka
2 tsp. curacao
2 tsp. anisette
2 tsp. apricot liqueur
1 tsp. lemon juice
½ brandied apricot

Combine all but the apricot with ice; shake well. Strain and add ice and the apricot.

DUNDEE

1 oz. gin
2 tbs. Scotch
2 tsp. Drambuie
1 tsp. lemon juice

Combine with ice; shake well. Strain and add ice. Decorate with a cherry and a twist of lemon.

DURANGO

1½ oz. tequila
2 tbs. grapefruit juice
1 tsp. almond extract
Mint sprigs
Calistoga spring water

Combine the tequila, juice, and almond extract with ice; shake well. Strain into a large tumbler; add ice and fill with spring water. Garnish with mint.

DUTCH TRADEWINDS

1½ oz. gin
1 tbs. curacao
3 tbs. lemon juice
1 egg white
1 tsp. sugar syrup

Combine with ice; shake very well. Strain and add ice.

English
Tankard
1600

YOUR OWN RECIPE

YOUR OWN RECIPE

Use a bartender's mixing glass whenever the instructions state "combine" ingredients. Strain the drink from the mixing glass into the drinking glass suggested by the illustration alongside the ingredients.

NOTE: The number of glasses or cups shown alongside a recipe do not necessarily indicate the quantity of drinks the recipe will produce.

EARTHQUAKE

1½ oz. tequila
1 tsp. grenadine
2 strawberries
1-2 dashes orange bitters
3 oz. crushed ice

Combine in a blender at a high speed for 15 seconds. Strain straight up with a lime slice and a strawberry.

EAST INDIA

1½ oz. brandy
1 tsp. pineapple juice
1 tsp. red curacao
A few dashes of Angostura bitters

Combine with ice; shake well. Strain and add ice.

EAST INDIAN SPECIAL

1½ oz. sherry
1½ oz. dry vermouth
1-2 dashes orange bitters

Combine with ice; shake well. Strain and add ice.
(A few variations: reduce the sherry; use peach bitters instead of orange bitters and garnish with mint; touch up with maraschino.)

ECLIPSE

1½ oz. sloe gin
1 oz. gin
2 tsp. grenadine
1 cherry

Combine the gins with ice; shake well. Drop the cherry into a glass and cover it with grenadine. Carefully strain in the gins so that they float on the grenadine; add a twist of orange.

EGG AND WINE

1 oz. sherry
1 egg
1 tbs. sugar
Grated nutmeg

Separate the egg. Beat the yolk with the sugar until creamy; add the sherry and stir well. Beat the white until stiff. Fold the whites with the wine mixture into a wine glass; top with nutmeg.

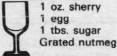

EGG LEMONADE

1¼ oz. brandy
3 tsp. lemon juice
1½ tsp. sugar syrup
1 egg
Club soda

Combine all but the soda with ice. Shake extremely well. Strain; add ice and fill with club soda.

EGG NOG FOR ONE

1 egg
2 tsp. powdered sugar
A few dashes of Angostura bitters
2 oz. milk
4 oz. rum

Heat the rum, but do not boil. Break the egg into a serving glass; add the sugar, bitters, and milk. Pour in the hot rum and stir well. Serve hot.

EGG NOG NASHVILLE

1 quart bourbon
1 pint Jamaican rum
1 pint brandy
3 quarts heavy cream
2 cups sugar
18 eggs, separated

Combine the liquors and egg yolks; stir well. Combine the cream and sugar; blend into the liquor mixture. Beat the egg whites until stiff and gently fold them in. Garnish with cloves and nutmeg.

EGG SOUR

1½ oz. brandy
1½ oz. curacao
2 tbs. lemon juice
1 tsp. powdered sugar
1 egg

Combine with ice; shake extremely well. Strain and add ice.

EL DIABLO

1½ oz. tequila
½ oz. creme de cassis
1½ tsp. lime juice
Ginger ale

Pour the lime juice into a glass. Add the tequila and creme de cassis; drop in a few ice cubes and ginger ale. Stir gently; add a lime twist.

EL PRESIDENTE

1½ oz. white rum
½ oz. curacao
2 tsp. dry vermouth
1-2 dashes grenadine

Combine with ice; shake. Strain and add ice.

EL YUNQUE

1½ oz. white rum
2 tsp. lemon juice
A few drops of green creme de menthe
Pineapple juice

Combine everything except the pineapple juice with ice; shake well. Strain over ice and fill with juice.

ELK

1 oz. dry gin
1 oz. Prunelle
A few drops dry vermouth

Combine with ice; shake well. Strain and add ice.

ELK'S OWN

1½ oz. rye
¾ oz. port
1 tbs. lemon juice
1 egg white
1 tsp. powdered sugar
1 pineapple stick

Combine (except the pineapple stick) with ice; shake well. Strain and add ice; decorate with the pineapple.

EMERALD ISLE

2 oz. dry gin
1 tsp. green creme de menthe
A few dashes of Angostura bitters

Combine with ice; shake. Strain and add ice.

EMPIRE PEACH

3 bottles chilled Moselle, one sparkling
2 large peaches
2 tbs. powdered sugar

Place peeled peaches on the bottom of a pitcher. Add one bottle of plain Moselle and sugar; stir and refrigerate for at least a half-hour. Just before serving, add the other two bottles of Moselle.

ENGLISH BOLO

4 oz. sherry
1½ oz. lemon juice
1 tsp. sugar
A cinnamon stick

Muddle the sugar and the lemon juice with a cinnamon stick in a small tumbler. Add the sherry and stir. Serve straight up—stick and all.

ENGLISH CHRISTMAS PUNCH

2 bottles red wine
1 quart dark tea
3 oz. orange juice
3 tsp. lemon juice
2 lb. sugar
1 bottle rum

Combine all but the sugar and rum in a large saucepan and heat thoroughly. Strain into a punch bowl. Place the sugar in a shallow pan and soak it in some of the rum. Ignite it over the punch, pour it in, and add the rest of the rum. Stir well.

ENGLISH HOT PUNCH

1 pint rum
½ pint brandy
2 large lemons
1 orange
Several sugar cubes

Peel the fruit; rub the sugar cubes in the rinds until the cubes take no more color. Combine the colored cubes with 2 or 3 more oz. cane sugar in a large punch bowl; squeeze in the juice of the fruit meats and add 1½ pints of boiling water. Stir until all the sugar is dissolved. Pour in the rum and the brandy. Serve while warm.

ENGLISH MULE

1½ oz. gin
3 oz. green ginger wine
2½ oz. orange juice
Club soda
A chunk of preserved ginger

Combine (except soda and ginger) with ice; shake well. Strain into glass; add ice and club soda. Stir gently. Decorate with ginger.

ENGLISH ROYAL PUNCH

1 pint cognac
1 pint dark tea
½ pint Jamaican rum
3 oz. curacao
3 oz. Arrack
3 oz. lime juice
4 oz. sugar
1 lemon, sliced
4 egg whites

Combine all but the egg whites in a large saucepan and heat well (don't boil). Beat the egg whites until stiff and fold into the punch. Serve hot.

EVE

Pink champagne
1 tbs. cognac
2 tsp. sugar
2 tsp. curacao
Several drops of Pernod

Pour the Pernod drops into a wide champagne glass; turn the glass to coat its sides. Pour in the cognac; soak the sugar with the curacao until the sugar has dissolved and add to the cognac; stir gently. Fill the glass with champagne.

EVERGLADES SPECIAL

1 oz. white rum
1 oz. white creme de cacao
1 oz. light cream
2 tsp. coffee liqueur

Combine with ice; shake. Strain. Fill with ice.

EVERYBODY'S RUSH

1½ oz. Irish whiskey
1 tsp. green chartreuse
A few dashes creme de menthe

Combine with ice; shake well. Strain and add ice.

EWING

A straight shot of rye with a dash or two of Angostura bitters on top.

EYE-OPENER

1½ oz. white rum
1 tsp. curacao
1 tsp. white creme de cacao
Several drops Pernod
1 tsp. sugar syrup
1 egg yolk

Combine with ice; shake extremely well. Strain and add ice.

"BLACK JACK" Leather Bottle 1646 (English)

136

YOUR OWN RECIPE

YOUR OWN RECIPE

Use a bartender's mixing glass whenever the instructions state "combine" ingredients. Strain the drink from the mixing glass into the drinking glass suggested by the illustration alongside the ingredients.

NOTE: The number of glasses or cups shown alongside a recipe do not necessarily indicate the quantity of drinks the recipe will produce.

F

FAIR AND WARMER

1½ oz. white rum
1 tbs. sweet vermouth
1-2 dashes curacao

Combine with ice; shake well. Strain, add ice and a twist of lemon; drop in the peel.

FAIRY BELLE

2 oz. gin
2 tsp. apricot brandy
1 tsp. grenadine
1 egg white

Combine with ice; shake well. Strain and add ice.

FALLEN ANGEL

3 oz. gin
3 oz. lime juice
1-2 dashes green creme de menthe
A few dashes of Angostura bitters

Combine with ice; shake well. Strain and add ice. Decorate with a cherry.

FANCIULLI

1½ oz. bourbon
1 tbs. sweet vermouth
1 tbs. Fernet Branca

Combine with ice; shake well. Strain over crushed ice.

FANCY BRANDY

2 oz. brandy
A few drops curacao
½ tsp. sugar syrup
A few dashes of Angostura bitters

Combine with ice; shake well. Strain, add ice and a twist of lemon; drop in the peel. Whiskey or gin can be substituted for the brandy.

FANTASIO

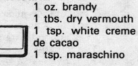

1 oz. brandy
1 tbs. dry vermouth
1 tsp. white creme de cacao
1 tsp. maraschino

Combine with ice; shake well. Strain and add ice.

FARMER'S COCKTAIL

1 oz. dry gin
2 tsp. dry vermouth
2 tsp. sweet vermouth
A few dashes of Angostura bitters

Combine with ice; shake well. Strain and add ice.

FAVORITE

¾ oz. gin
¾ oz. dry vermouth
¾ oz. apricot brandy
A few drops lemon juice

Combine with ice; shake well. Strain and add ice.

FEMINA

1½ oz. brandy
2 tsp. Benedictine
2 tsp. orange juice

Combine with ice; shake well. Strain and add ice. Decorate with an orange slice.

FERN GULLY

1 oz. Jamaican rum
1 oz. white rum
2 tsp. cream of coconut
2 tsp. orange juice
2 tsp. lime juice
1 tsp. almond extract
3 oz. crushed ice

Combine in a blender at a low speed for no more than 15 seconds. Strain and serve straight up.

FERN GULLY FIZZ

1 oz. Jamaican rum
1 oz. white rum
1 oz. pineapple juice
1 tbs. lime juice
1 fresh pineapple slice
Club soda

Combine the rums and juices with ice; shake well. Strain, add ice, and fill with soda. Decorate with pineapple.

FERNET BRANCA

2 oz. gin
2 tsp. sweet vermouth
2 tsp. Fernet Branca

Combine with ice; shake well. Strain and add ice.
*For a **FIFTH AVENUE,** add more vermouth and Fernet Branca at the expense of the gin.*

FESTIVAL

¾ oz. dark creme de cacao
¾ oz. heavy cream
1 tbs. apricot brandy
1 tsp. grenadine

Combine with ice; shake well. Strain and add ice.

FESTIVE WINE CUP

1 bottle white wine
2 oz. brandy
1 oz. sugar
1 pint club soda
Slices of peaches and strawberries
Mint sprigs

Combine the wine, brandy, and sugar. Stir until the sugar has dissolved. Add the club soda before serving. Top with fruit slices and mint.

FESTOONERS' HIGH TEA

1 bottle whiskey
1 bottle Angelica wine
1 bottle champagne
4 oz. curaçao
5 oz. lemon juice
2 quarts lemon juice
2 quarts iced, green tea

Combine and add chunks of ice. Decorate with lemon rinds and fruit slices.

FIFTY-FIFTY

1½ oz. gin
1½ oz. dry vermouth

Combine with ice; shake well. Strain. Decorate with an olive, and serve straight up.

FIG LEAF FLIP

1½ oz. sweet vermouth
1 oz. white rum
1½ tbs. lime juice
A few dashes of Angostura bitters

Combine with ice; shake well. Strain and add ice. Top with a cherry.

FINO

1½ oz. fino sherry
1½ oz. sweet vermouth

Combine with ice; shake well. Strain. Decorate with a lemon slice.

FINO MARTINI

2 oz. gin
2 tsp. fino sherry

Combine with ice; shake well. Strain. Add ice and a twist of lemon.

FINO RICKEY

1 oz. gin
1 oz. sherry
Club soda

Combine the sherry and gin. Add ice, fill with club soda, and stir. Add a twist of lime; drop in the peel.

FIORD

1 oz. brandy
2 tsp. aquavit
2 tsp. orange juice
2 tsp. lime juice
1 tsp. grenadine

Combine with ice; shake well. Strain and add ice.

FISH HOUSE PUNCH

1½ quarts brandy
1 pint peach brandy
1 pint rum
1 quart dark iced tea
1 quart club soda
8 oz. powdered sugar
1½ pints lemon juice

In a large punch bowl, dissolve the sugar in the lemon juice; add ice and combine the remaining ingredients. Decorate with slices of fruit. There are many variations of **FISH HOUSE PUNCHES.** You could use white and gold rums in place of half the brandy, and 9 oz. of frozen lemonade concentrate instead of the lemon juice (eliminating the sugar and adding a quart of water). Or use white wine and a cup of water instead of the tea.

FISH HOUSE PUNCH AU NATUREL

Follow your favorite **FISH HOUSE PUNCH** recipe, substituting bottled mineral or spring water for the tea.

FISH HOUSE PUNCH NO. 2

2 bottles Jamaican rum
1 bottle lemon juice
1 bottle cognac
4 oz. peach brandy
12 oz. sugar

Dissolve the sugar in enough water to make syrup; combine with the lemon juice in a large punch bowl and stir. Add the rum, cognac, and brandy; allow to stand an hour or two.

FIREMAN'S SOUR

1½ oz. white rum
2 oz. lime juice
2 tsp. grenadine
1 tsp. sugar syrup
Club soda

Combine everything except the club soda with ice; shake well. Strain and spritz it with soda. Serve straight up.

FLAG

1½ oz. apricot brandy
1 oz. claret
1 tsp. Creme Yvette
A few dashes of curacao

Combine the brandy and curacao with ice; shake well. Over the Creme Yvette carefully strain in the brandy and curacao so that it floats on top of the Creme Yvette. Top with the claret.

FLAMES OVER NEW JERSEY

1 quart apple brandy
A few dashes of Angostura bitters
8 oz. sugar

Warm the brandy and combine it with the bitters and the sugar in a punch bowl. Stir until the sugar is dissolved. Ignite at the table. Extinguish with a quart of boiling water; stir and serve hot.

FLAMING GLOGG

1 bottle red wine
1½ pints aquavit
1 cup orange juice
Cardamon seeds, whole cloves, cinnamon sticks
Blanched almonds, raisins, dried figs
Grated orange rinds
Sugar (to taste)

Combine everything except ¾ cup of the aquavit in a large pot; heat but do not allow to boil. Simmer several minutes. Serve unstrained over a chafing dish or similar warmer. Add the remaining aquavit and stir.

FLOATING TORCH for the FLAMING GLOGG

½ large grapefruit
6 oz. aquavit
Sugar

Carefully pare the meat of the fruit; do not puncture the skin. Line the rim of the fruit with a few drops of aquavit; press it in sugar. Warm the remaining aquavit. Float the grapefruit in the FLAMING GLOGG; pour in the aquavit (even if it overflows) and ignite. When flame subsides, overturn the grapefruit shell. Do not allow the aquavit to burn too long.

FLAMING HOT BUTTERED RUM

Follow the recipe for HOT BUTTERED RUM. Just before serving, tip a few drops of 151-proof rum over a few pinches of sugar in a ladle. Warm the ladle over the hot buttered rum; then ignite the rum and sugar and infuse into the drink. Drink at once.

FLAMING PETER

1 oz. vodka
1 oz. Cherry Herring
2 tsp. dry vermouth
2 tsp. orange juice

Combine with ice; shake well. Strain and add ice.

FLAMINGO COCKTAIL

1¼ oz. dry gin
½ oz. apricot brandy
1½ tsp. lime juice
1 tsp. grenadine

Combine with ice; shake well. Strain and add ice.

FLINTLOCK

1½ oz. bourbon
½ oz. apple brandy
1 tsp. lemon juice
Several drops grenadine
1-2 dashes white creme de menthe

Combine with ice; shake well. Strain and add ice.

FLORADORA

2 oz. gin
2 oz. lime juice
1 tsp. sugar syrup
1 tbs. grenadine
1 tsp. sugar syrup
Club soda

Combine (except the soda) with ice. Strain over crushed ice and fill with soda.

FLORIDA

1¼ oz. orange juice
½ oz. gin
1 tsp. kirschwasser
1 tsp. Triple Sec
1 tsp. lemon juice

Combine with ice; shake well. Strain and add ice.

FLORIDA PUNCH

1½ oz. rum
1½ oz. orange juice
1½ oz. grapefruit juice
¾ oz. brandy

Combine with ice; shake well. Strain and add ice.

FLORIDIAN

1½ oz. dry vermouth
2 oz. grapefruit juice
2 tsp. Forbidden Fruit
1 tsp. Falernum
1-2 dashes orange bitters

Combine with ice; shake well. Strain and add ice. Top with a lemon slice.

FLORIDIAN COCKTAIL

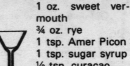

1 oz. sweet vermouth
¾ oz. rye
1 tsp. Amer Picon
1 tsp. sugar syrup
½ tsp. curacao
1-2 dashes orange bitters

Combine with ice; shake well. Strain and add ice.

FLYING DUTCHMAN

Pour just enough curacao into a glass to coat its side. Add 2 oz. cold gin.

FLYING GRASSHOPPER

1 oz. vodka
2 tsp. green creme de menthe
2 tsp. white creme de menthe

Combine with ice; shake well. Strain and add ice.

FLYING SCOTCHMAN

1 oz. Scotch
1 oz. sweet vermouth
A few drops sugar syrup
A few dashes of Angostura bitters

Combine with ice; shake well. Strain and add ice.

FOGGY DAY

1½ oz. gin
1 tsp. Pernod
1 lemon slice

Combine the gin and Pernod with ice; shake well. Rub the lemon slice around the rim of a glass, then drop it in. Strain in the drink and add ice.

FOGHORN

3 oz. gin
Ginger beer

Pour the gin into a glass, add ice and fill with beer. Decorate with a lemon slice.

FORESTER

1 oz. bourbon
1 tsp. cherry juice
1 tsp. lemon juice

Combine with ice; shake well. Strain and add ice. Decorate with a cherry.

FORT LAUDERDALE

1½ oz. gold rum
½ oz. sweet ver-
mouth
1 tsp. orange juice
1 tsp. lime juice

Combine with ice; shake well. Strain and add ice. Decorate with a slice of orange.

FOUR SECTORS

1 oz. bourbon
1 oz. vodka
1 oz. Grand Marnier
1 oz. unsweetened
lime juice
A few dashes of
Angostura bitters

Combine with ice; shake well. Strain and add ice. Garnish with slices of fruit, a slice of cucumber, and a cherry.

FOX RIVER

1½ oz. rye
2 tsp. dark creme de
cacao
A few drops peach
bitters

Combine with ice; shake well. Strain. Add ice and a twist of lemon; drop in the peel.

FOXHOUND

1½ oz. brandy
2 tsp. cranberry
juice
1 tsp. kummel
1 tsp. lemon juice

Combine with ice; shake well. Strain and add ice. Decorate with a lemon slice.

FRAISE FIZZ

1½ oz. gin
1 oz. Chambery
fraise
2 tsp. lemon juice
1½ tsp. sugar syrup
1 large strawberry
Club soda

Combine (except the strawberry and the soda) with ice; shake well. Strain, add ice and fill with soda. Add a twist of lemon and drop in the peel. Top with a strawberry.

FRANCES ANN

1 oz. Scotch
½ oz. Cherry Herring
1 tsp. dry vermouth

Combine with ice; shake well. Strain and add ice.

FRANKENJACK COCKTAIL

1 oz. dry gin
½ oz. apricot brandy
1 tbs. dry vermouth
1 tsp. Triple Sec

Combine with ice; shake well. Strain and add ice. Decorate with a cherry. Cointreau can be substituted for the Triple Sec.

FRAPPES

Any liqueur can be prepared as a FRAPPE. Simply pour 1½ oz. of your favorite — Pernod, white or green creme de menthe, creme de noyaux — into a glass filled with crushed ice.

FREE SILVER

1½ oz. Old Tom gin
¾ oz. Jamaican rum
1 tbs. lemon juice
1 tsp. sugar syrup
1 oz. milk
Club soda

Combine all but the club soda with ice; shake well. Strain; add ice and fill with soda.

FRENCH APPETIZER

1 tsp. dry vermouth
A few drops Pernod
1-2 dashes pepsin
Club soda

Combine the vermouth, Pernod, and pepsin with a few ice cubes; stir well. Strain over crushed ice; fill the tumbler with soda and stir.

FRENCH CHAMPAGNE PUNCH

1 bottle imported French champagne
1 bottle white wine
1 pint cognac
1 bottle club soda

Combine; add large chunks of ice before serving. Garnish with fruit slices.

FRENCH CIDER CUP

1 quart hard cider
2 oz. cognac
2 oz. curacao
2 oz. powdered sugar
12 oz. club soda
Orange slices
Mint sprigs

Combine everything except the soda and garnishes. Stir well. Add plenty of ice and the soda before serving. Top with the orange slices and mint.

FRENCH FOAM

¼ oz. brandy
¼ oz. kirschwasser
1½ tsp. sugar syrup
A few dashes of Angostura bitters
Champagne
Lemon sherbet

Combine all but the champagne and the sherbet in a glass; stir well. Fill the glass part way with champagne. Float a small scoop of sherbet on top. Pour more champagne over it until the glass is full.

FRENCH GREEN DRAGON

1½ oz. cognac
1½ oz. green char-
treuse

Combine with ice; shake well. Strain and add ice.

FRENCH PUNCH

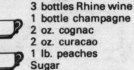

3 bottles Rhine wine
1 bottle champagne
2 oz. cognac
2 oz. curacao
1 lb. peaches
Sugar

Peel and slice the peaches; combine with enough sugar to barely cover them in a large punch bowl. Add the Rhine wine and allow to stand for at least one hour. Add the remaining ingredients plus chunks of ice.

FRENCH RIVIERA

2 oz. rye
1 oz. apricot brandy
1 tsp. lemon juice

Combine with ice; shake well. Strain and add ice. Top with a cherry.

FRENCH 75

1½ oz. cognac
1½ tsp. lemon juice
½ tsp. powdered
sugar
Champagne

Combine (except the champagne) with ice; shake well. Strain; add ice and fill with champagne. Add a twist of lemon.

FRENCH VERMOUTH AND CURACAO

3 oz. dry vermouth
1½ oz. curacao
Club soda

Into the vermouth and the curacao, add ice; fill with club soda, and stir gently.

FRISCO

2 oz. Benedictine
1 oz. lemon juice
Rye

Combine the Benedictine and lemon juice; add plenty of ice and fill with rye. Stir well. For more delicate palates, a FRISCO can be made of equal parts Benedictine and bourbon, adding a twist of lemon instead of the juice.

FRISCO SOUR

2 oz. whiskey
1 tbs. lemon juice
1 tbs. lime juice
2 tsp. grenadine
Club soda

Combine all but the soda with ice; shake well. Strain. Fill with club soda and decorate with fruit slices. Serve straight up.

FROBISHER

2 oz. gin
A few dashes of
Angostura bitters
Champagne

Combine the gin and the bitters; add ice and fill with champagne. Add a twist of lemon.

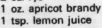

FROSTBITE

1 oz. tequila
2 oz. heavy cream
2 tsp. white creme de cacao
3 oz. crushed ice

Combine in a blender at a low speed no more than 15 seconds. Strain and serve straight up.

FROSTED COFFEE PUNCH

3 pints strong, iced coffee
8 oz. Jamaican rum
4 oz. sugar
5 pints vanilla ice cream
2 cups whipped cream

Dissolve the sugar with the coffee. Add the rum and ice cream and stir until smooth. Top with whipped cream.

FROSTED MINT COCOA

4 oz. cocoa
6 oz. sugar
5 cups milk
1½ pints vanilla ice cream
Several drops white creme de menthe

Combine the cocoa and sugar with a cup of boiling water in a saucepan; simmer for several minutes. Warm the milk in a double boiler; add the cocoa and creme de menthe. Stir well and allow to cool. Combine the cocoa with the ice cream; blend until smooth.

FROSTY VINE

2 oz. vanilla ice cream
1 oz. brandy
1 oz. port

Combine in a blender at high speed until smooth. Serve straight up.

FROTH BLOWER COCKTAIL

2 oz. dry gin
1 egg white
1 tsp. grenadine

Combine with ice; shake well. Strain and add ice.

FROTHY DAWN COCKTAIL

1½ oz. white rum
1 oz. orange juice
2 tsp. Falernum
1 tsp. maraschino

Combine with ice; shake well. Strain and add ice.

FROUPE

1½ oz. brandy
1½ oz. sweet vermouth
1 tsp. Benedictine

Combine with ice; shake well. Strain and add ice.

FROZEN DRINKS

All frozen are made basically the same way: Combine the ingredients in an electric blender, add 3 oz. of crushed ice, and blend at a low speed for no more than 15 seconds. Strain the drink into a wide champagne glass and serve straight up.

FROZEN APPLE

1½ oz. apple brandy
2 tsp. lime juice
1½ tsp. sugar syrup
½ egg white

FROZEN APPLE AND BANANA

1½ oz. apple brandy
½ oz. banana liqueur
2 tsp. lime juice

Garnish with a slice of banana.

FROZEN APPLE DAIQUIRI

1½ oz. white rum
2 tsp. apple juice
2 tsp. lemon juice
1½ tsp. sugar syrup

Garnish with an apple wedge.

FROZEN AQUAVIT

1½ oz. aquavit
2 tsp. lime juice
1½ tsp. sugar syrup
1 tsp. kirschwasser
½ egg white

Add one extra oz. of crushed ice.

FROZEN BERKELEY

1½ oz. white rum
½ oz. California brandy
2 tsp. passion fruit juice

FROZEN BLACK CURRENT

1 oz. creme de cassis
1 oz. pineapple juice
2 tsp. brandy

Garnish with a slice of orange.

FROZEN BLACKBERRY TEQUILA

1½ oz. tequila
1 oz. blackberry liqueur
2 tsp. lemon juice

Garnish with a slice of lemon.

FROZEN BRANDY AND PORT

1 oz. brandy
¾ oz. port
1 egg
1 tsp. powdered sugar

Garnish with nutmeg.

FROZEN BRANDY AND RUM

1½ oz. brandy
1 oz. rum
2 tsp. lemon juice
2 tsp. sugar syrup
1 egg yolk

FROZEN DAIQUIRI

1½ oz. white rum
2 tsp. lime juice
1 tsp. sugar syrup

Add an extra oz. of crushed ice. Serve with a straw and top with a teaspoon of 151-proof rum.

FROZEN GUAVA DAIQUIRI

1½ oz. white rum
1 oz. guava nectar
2 tsp. lime juice
1 tsp. banana liqueur

FROZEN GUAVA-ORANGE DAIQUIRI

1½ oz. white rum
¾ oz. guava syrup
2 tsp. orange juice
2 tsp. lime juice

FROZEN JULEP

2 oz. bourbon
1 oz. lemon juice
1 oz. sugar syrup
Several mint sprigs, crushed
6 oz. crushed ice

Combine in a blender at high speed for 20 seconds. Serve straight up. Top with a cherry and a mint sprig.

FROZEN LIME DAIQUIRI

2 oz. white rum
2 tsp. lime liqueur
2 tsp. lime juice

Add a twist of lime in the glass and drop in the peel.

FROZEN MANGO-LIME DAIQUIRI

1½ oz. white rum
1 oz. mango nectar
2 tsp. lime liqueur
2 tsp. lime juice

Garnish with a slice of mango.

FROZEN MATADOR

1 oz. tequila
2 oz. pineapple juice
2 tsp. lime juice

Garnish with a pineapple stick

FROZEN MINT DAIQUIRI

2 oz. white rum
2 tsp. lime juice
1½ tsp. sugar syrup
½ doz. mint leaves

Add an extra oz. of crushed ice

FROZEN PASSION FRUIT DAIQUIRI

1½ oz. white rum
½ oz. passion fruit syrup
2 tsp. lime juice
2 tsp. orange juice
1 tsp. lemon juice

FROZEN PEACH DAIQUIRI

1½ oz. white rum
2 oz. frozen peaches, thawed and sliced.

Save the syrup from the frozen peaches and add 2 teaspoons into the blender.

FROZEN PINEAPPLE DAIQUIRI

1½ oz. white rum
2 tsp. lime juice
1 tsp sugar syrup
2 canned pineapple rings, sliced and drained

FROZEN RUM HONEY

2 oz. 151-proof rum
½ oz. honey
2 tsp. lemon juice

Combine in a blender at a high speed for no more than 15 seconds. Strain. Add ice.

FROZEN RUSSIAN APPLE

1½ oz. vodka
¼ oz. calvados
2 tsp. lime juice
1 tsp. sugar syrup
2 oz. chopped apples

Put one less oz. of chopped ice in the blender.

FROZEN SESAME DAIQUIRI

1½ oz. rum
½ oz. sesame syrup
2 tsp. lime juice
2 tsp. dry vermouth
2 tsp. orange juice

FROZEN SOURSOP DAIQUIRI

1½ oz. white rum
¼ oz. Jamaican rum
1 oz. soursop (guanabana) nectar
1 tsp. lime juice
2 oz. bananas

FROZEN STEPPES

2 oz. vanilla ice cream
2 tbs. vodka
1 tbs. dark creme de cacao

Combine in a blender at a high speed until smooth. Serve straight up.

FULL HOUSE

¾ oz. apple whiskey
¾ oz. Benedictine
¾ oz. yellow chartreuse
A few dashes of Angostura bitters

Combine with ice; shake well. Strain and add ice.

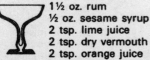

U.S. COLONIAL "Stone Jugg" or "Fflander"

YOUR OWN RECIPE

Use a bartender's mixing glass whenever the instructions state "combine" ingredients. Strain the drink from the mixing glass into the drinking glass suggested by the illustration alongside the ingredients.

The glass pictured for each drink is our suggestion; other drinking cups may be used as well.

GASLIGHT

1½ oz. Scotch
2 tsp. sweet vermouth
1-2 dashes orange curacao
A few drops Drambuie

Combine (except the Drambuie) with ice; shake well. Strain, add ice and a twist of orange, and pour the Drambuie on top.

GAUGUIN

2 oz. white rum
2 tsp. passion fruit syrup
2 tsp. lemon juice
1 tsp. lime juice
3 oz. crushed ice

Combine in a blender at a low speed for 15 seconds. Strain straight up and add a cherry.

GAZETTE

1½ oz. brandy
1 oz. sweet vermouth
1 tsp. lemon juice
1 tsp. sugar syrup

Combine with ice; shake. Strain and add ice.

GEISHA

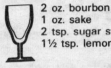

2 oz. bourbon
1 oz. sake
2 tsp. sugar syrup
1½ tsp. lemon juice

Combine with ice; shake well. Strain; add ice. Decorate with a cherry.

GENERAL HARRISON'S EGGNOG

1 egg
1 tsp. powdered sugar
Claret

Combine the egg and sugar with ice; shake extremely well. Strain. Add claret. Dust with nutmeg.

GENOA

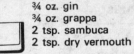

¾ oz. gin
¾ oz. grappa
2 tsp. sambuca
2 tsp. dry vermouth

Combine with ice; shake well. Strain and add ice and an olive.

GENTLE BULL

1½ oz. tequila
¾ oz. Kahlua
1 tbs. heavy cream

Combine with ice; shake well. Strain and add ice.

GENTLE JOHN

1¼ oz. Scotch
A few drops dry vermouth
A few drops Cointreau
1-2 dashes orange bitters

Combine with ice; shake well. Strain and add ice.

GEORGIA RUM COOLER

2½ oz. white rum
2 tsp. lemon juice
1 tsp. grenadine
1 tsp. Falernum
1 tsp. salted peanuts
4 oz. crushed ice
Club soda

Combine (except the soda) in a blender at a high speed for 30 seconds. Strain, add ice, and soda. Dust with cinnamon.

GIBSON

2½ oz. gin
A few drops dry vermouth
1 cocktail onion

Combine the gin and vermouth and stir well. Top with the onion.

GILDED ORANGE

2 oz. gin
3 tbs. orange juice
2 tsp. dark rum
2 tsp. sugar syrup
A few drops lemon juice
1-2 dashes almond extract

Combine with ice; shake well. Strain and add ice.

GILROY

¾ oz. gin
¾ oz. cherry brandy
2 tsp. dry vermouth
2 tsp. lemon juice
1-2 dashes orange bitters

Combine with ice; shake well. Strain and add ice.

GIMLET

2 oz. gin
2 tsp. Rose's lime juice

Combine with ice; shake well. Strain and add ice.

GIN ALOHA

1½ oz. gin
½ oz. unsweetened
pineapple juice
1 tsp. curacao
A few dashes
orange bitters

*Combine with ice; shake well.
Strain; add ice and a cherry.*

GIN AND CAMPARI

1½ oz. gin
1½ oz. Campari

*Combine with ice; shake.
Strain. Add ice and a twist of
orange.*

GIN AND LIME

1½ oz. gin
½ lime
2 tsp. orange juice
1 tsp. Rose's lime
juice

*Pour lime juice over ice; add
the gin and juices and shake
well. Strain. Add ice and a
twist of lime.*

GIN AND SIN

2 oz. gin
1 tbs. Cinzano

*Combine and stir. Serve
straight up.*

GIN AND TONIC

2½ oz. gin
Tonic water

*Pour the gin; add ice, tonic
and a twist of lemon. Or use
sherry instead of gin.*

GIN AQUAVIT

1½ oz. gin
½ oz. aquavit
2 tsp. lemon juice
1½ tsp. sugar syrup
1 tsp. heavy cream
½ egg white

*Combine with ice; shake ex-
tremely well. Strain and add
ice.*

GIN BENEDICTINE
SANGAREE

1¼ oz. gin
¼ oz. Benedictine
2 tsp. grapefruit
juice

*Combine with ice; shake well.
Strain, add ice and a slice of
lemon and garnish with
nutmeg.*

GIN BOWL

1 gallon dry white
wine
1 bottle gin
8 oz. iced green tea
Lemon slices

*Combine and stir well. Add
chunks of ice before serving.
To strengthen, add a cup of
Jamaican rum.*

GIN CASSIS

1½ oz. gin
2 tsp. lemon juice
2 tsp. creme de cassis

Combine with ice; shake well. Strain and add ice.

GIN COCO

Gin
1 coconut

Open the coconut and save the juice. Add one part gin for every two parts coconut juice; stir and serve over ice.

GIN DAIQUIRI

1½ oz. gin
½ oz. white rum
2 tsp. lime juice
1 tsp. sugar syrup

Combine with ice; shake well. Strain and add ice.

GIN DAISY

1½ oz. gin
2 tsp. lemon juice
1½ tsp. raspberry syrup
Club soda
Mint sprigs

Combine the gin, juice, and syrup with ice; shake well. Strain; add ice and club soda. Top with the mint or a lemon slice.

GIN FIZZ

3 oz. gin
1½ oz. lemon juice
¾ oz. lime juice
1 tbs. powdered sugar
Club soda

Combine (except the soda) with ice; shake well. Strain; add ice and soda.

GIN MINT FIZZ

2 oz. gin
2 tsp. lemon juice
1½ tsp. sugar syrup
1 tsp. white creme de menthe
Mint leaves

Combine (except the mint leaves) with ice; shake well. Strain over crushed ice and top with mint leaves, partially torn.

GIN OLD-FASHIONED

1½ oz. gin
½ tsp. sugar syrup
A few dashes of Angostura bitters

Combine and stir. Add ice and a twist of lemon.

GIN PUNCH

8 oz. gin
4 oz. maraschino
2 oz. lemon juice
Grated lemon rind
2 oz. sugar syrup
1 bottle ginger ale

Combine everything except the ale. Stir well. Add the ale plus chunks of ice before serving.

GIN RICKEY

1½ oz. gin
½ lime
Club soda

Pour the gin; add ice and club soda. Squeeze in the lime; include the rind and stir.

GIN RISQUE

2 oz. gin
3 tsp. lime juice

Combine with ice; shake. Strain; add plenty of ice and fill the glass with cold water. Touch it up with a twist of lime.

GIN SIDECAR

1½ oz. high-proof gin
1 oz. Triple Sec
1 oz. lemon juice

Combine with ice; shake. Strain and add ice.

GIN SOUTHERN

1½ oz. gin
½ oz. Southern Comfort
1 tsp. lemon juice
1 tsp. grapefruit juice

Combine with ice; shake well. Strain and add ice.

GIN SWIZZLE

2 oz. gin
2 tsp. lime juice
1½ tsp. sugar syrup
A few dashes of Angostura bitters
Club soda

Combine (except the soda) with ice; shake well. Strain; add ice and club soda.

GIN WITH A WEDGE

Pour 2 oz. gin into an old-fashioned glass; fill the glass with ice. Drop a thick orange slice into the glass; stir it well with the gin and ice to flavor the drink and frost the glass.

GINGER BEER

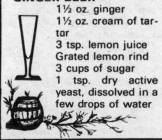

1½ oz. ginger
1½ oz. cream of tartar
3 tsp. lemon juice
Grated lemon rind
3 cups of sugar
1 tsp. dry active yeast, dissolved in a few drops of water

Pound the ginger into a powder; combine with a gallon of boiling water. Add the lemon juice and rind, cream of tartar, and sugar, stirring constantly. Remove from heat; add yeast when lukewarm. Close tightly and allow to stand for several hours. Strain and seal tightly in bottles. Store in a cool, dark place.

GINGER HIGHBALL

1½ oz. whiskey
A large chunk fresh
ginger root
Club soda

Pour the whiskey into a highball glass; squeeze the ginger root through a garlic press above it. Add ice and fill with soda; stir.

GINGER MARTINI

Fix your favorite martini in a mixing glass; add a sliver of dried ginger root and let it sit a few minutes. Add ice, shake, and strain straight up.

GINGER RUM TEA

1½ oz. rum
A chunk of preserv-
ed ginger
A cup of hot tea

Pour the rum into the tea; add the ginger and stir. This drink can be served iced.

GINGERSNAP

3 oz. vodka
1 oz. ginger wine
Club soda

Combine the vodka and wine, add ice and stir gently. Add soda.

GLACIER

1 oz. brandy
2 tsp. Parfait Amour
1½ tsp. lemon juice
1½ tsp. lime juice
A few drops of rock
candy syrup

Combine with ice; shake. Strain and add ice.

GLAD EYE

1½ oz. Pernod
¾ oz. peppermint

Combine with ice; shake well. Strain and add ice.

GLASGOW

1½ oz. Scotch
1 tbs. lemon juice
1 tsp. dry vermouth
1 tsp. almond extract

Combine with ice; shake well. Strain and add ice.

GLOGG

1 bottle port
1 bottle Madeira
1 bottle medium dry
sherry
½ bottle dry red
wine
4 oz. warm brandy
8 oz. sugar cubes
1 cup raisins
1
almonds
1 doz. cloves
1 cinnamon stick
A few cardamom
seeds

Combine everything except the sugar, brandy, raisins, and nuts in a large saucepan and heat. Place the sugar cubes in a shallow pan above the glogg; pour the brandy over the cubes and ignite. Extinguish the brandy by dipping the contents of the pan into the glogg. Stir until the sugar is completely dissolved. Serve in mugs; garnish each with a few of the almonds and raisins.

GLOOM CHASER

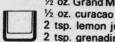

½ oz. Grand Marnier
½ oz. curacao
2 tsp. lemon juice
2 tsp. grenadine

Combine with ice; shake well. Strain and add ice.

GLOOM LIFTER

1¼ oz. whiskey
2 tsp. raspberry syrup
1½ tsp. lemon juice
1 tsp. sugar syrup
½ tsp. brandy
A small portion of egg white

Combine with ice; shake extremely well. Strain and add ice.

GLOW WINE

2 bottles claret
8 oz. sugar
½ doz. cloves
The peels of ½ lemon, sliced
A few dashes cinnamon

Combine in a large saucepan and boil. Serve immediately. Top with an orange slice.

GLUEWEIN

6 oz. claret
3 cubes sugar
1 cinnamon stick
1 clove

Combine in a small saucepan and bring to a boil. Serve in a large mug steaming hot. Cider can be used instead of claret; add a dash of rum or apple brandy.

GOLD CADILLAC

¾ oz. white creme de cacao
¾ oz. heavy cream
¾ oz. Galliano
3 oz. crushed ice

Combine in a blender at a low speed for 15 seconds. Strain straight up.

GOLDEN DAWN

1 oz. apple brandy
1 oz. apricot brandy
1 oz. dry gin
A few drops orange juice
A few drops grenadine

Combine (except the grenadine) with ice; shake well. Strain. Add ice and then the grenadine; do not stir.

GOLDEN DAZE

1½ oz. dry gin
1 oz. orange juice
¾ oz. apricot brandy

Combine with ice; shake well. Strain and add ice.

GOLDEN DRAGON

1 tbs. yellow char-
treuse
1 tsp. brandy

Float the brandy over the
chartreuse.

GOLDEN FROG

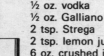

½ oz. vodka
½ oz. Galliano
2 tsp. Strega
2 tsp. lemon juice
6 oz. crushed ice

Combine in a blender at a
high speed for 15 seconds.
Strain and add ice.

GOLDEN GATE

¾ oz. white rum
¾ oz. gin
2 tsp. lemon juice
2 tsp. white creme
de cacao
1 tsp. 151-proof rum
A few drops Faler-
num

Combine with ice; shake well.
Strain and add ice. Top with
an orange slice.

GOLDEN GIN FIZZ

2½ oz. gin
1½ tbs. lemon juice
2½ tsp. sugar syrup
1 egg yolk
Club soda

Combine (except the soda)
with ice; shake well. Strain;
add ice and soda. Top with a
lemon slice and nutmeg.

GOLDEN GLOW

1¼ oz. bourbon
2 tbs. orange juice
2 tsp. lemon juice
1½ tsp. sugar syrup
A few drops
Jamaican rum
Grenadine

Combine (except the
grenadine) with ice; shake.
Strain straight up over a few
drops of grenadine.

GOLDEN HORNET

1½ oz. gin
½ oz. amontillado
2 tsp. Scotch

Combine the gin and amon-
tillado with ice; shake. Strain.
Add ice and a twist of lemon;
float the Scotch on top.

GOLDEN RETRIEVER PUNCH

1 pint apricot syrup
1 pint lime juice
3 pints orange juice
3 quarts club soda

Combine in a large punch
bowl. Add chunks of ice immediately before serving.

GOLDEN SCREW

1 oz. gin
2 oz. orange juice
A few dashes of
Angostura bitters

Combine, add ice, and stir
well.
For a SCREWDRIVER, use
vodka instead of gin and no
bitters.

GOLDEN SLIPPER

1 oz. yellow char-
treuse
1 oz. apricot brandy
1 egg yolk

*Combine with ice; shake well.
Strain and add ice.*

GOLF MARTINI

1½ oz. gin
2 tsp. dry vermouth
A few dashes of
Angostura bitters

*Combine straight up and
gently stir. Add an olive.*

GOOD NIGHT ALL

1 gallon beer
8 oz. honey
A few pinches
pepper and ground
cloves
1 pinch ground
ginger
2 cinnamon sticks

*Combine the beer and honey
in a saucepan; heat until the
honey is completely dissolved. Place the spices in an in-
fuser and steep them in the
beer overnight. Serve hot.*

GOSSIP'S CUP

12 oz. ale
1½ oz. cognac
1 tsp. brown sugar
Grated lemon rind
A pinch of ginger
and nutmeg

*Combine in a saucepan; heat
but do not allow to boil. Serve
in mugs. Add extra garnish if
you wish.*

GOURMET MARTINI

1½ oz. gin
2 tsp. dry vermouth
A few drops Campari

Combine straight up; stir.

GRANADA

1 oz. fino sherry
1 oz. brandy
2 tsp. curacao
Tonic water

*Combine (except the tonic)
with ice; shake. Strain; add
ice and tonic. Top with an
orange slice.*

GRAND CENTRAL

1½ oz. bourbon
1 tsp. sugar syrup
A few dashes of
Angostura bitters

*Combine with ice; shake well.
Strain and add ice.*

GRAND EGG NOG

4 oz. Grand Marnier
4 oz. each white
rum and brandy
4 oz. sugar
3 eggs, separated
1 quart milk
1 pint cream
Grated nutmeg

*Beat the sugar with the yolks.
Slowly add the rum, brandy,
and Grand Marnier, stirring
constantly. Cool in the
refrigerator for a few hours,
stirring occasionally. When
ready, slowly add the milk,
again stirring constantly.
Whip the cream; beat the
whites until stiff. Fold them
into the nog. Garnish with
nutmeg.*

GRAND MARNIER QUETSCH

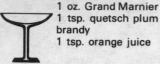

1 oz. Grand Marnier
1 tsp. quetsch plum brandy
1 tsp. orange juice

Combine without ice; stir well. Pour over crushed ice. Add a lemon slice.

GRAND ORANGE BLOSSOM

1½ oz. gin
2 tbs. orange juice
1 tbs. Grand Marnier
1 tsp. sugar syrup

Combine with ice; shake well. Strain and add ice.

GRAND PASSION

2 oz. gin
1 oz. passion fruit nectar
1-2 dashes Angostura bitters

Combine with ice; shake well. Strain and add ice.

GRAND ROYAL FIZZ

2 oz. gin
1 oz. orange juice
1 oz. lemon juice
2 tsp. heavy cream
1 tsp. powdered sugar
A few drops of maraschino
Club soda

Combine (except soda) with ice. Strain; add ice and soda.

GRAND SLAM

2 oz. Swedish Punch
2 tsp. sweet vermouth
2 tsp. dry vermouth

Combine with ice; shake. Strain and add ice.

GRANVILLE

1½ oz. gin
1 tsp. Grand Marnier
1 tsp. calvados
1 tsp. lemon juice

Combine with ice; shake. Strain and add ice.

GRAPEFRUIT BEER

½ doz. grapefruit
12 oz. dry active yeast

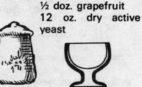

Peel and slice the grapefruit; combine with 3 gals. of hot water in a large crock pot. Allow to cool; add the yeast. Seal and allow to ferment. Bottle immediately after fermentation.

GRAPEFRUIT COCKTAIL

1½ oz. dry gin
1½ oz. grapefruit juice
1 tsp. maraschino

Combine with ice; shake. Strain and add ice. Add a cherry.

GRAPEFRUIT COOLER

2 oz. whiskey
4 oz. unsweetened grapefruit juice
2 tsp. red currant syrup
1 tsp. lemon juice

Combine with ice; shake. Strain; add plenty of ice and a slice of lemon or orange.

GRAPEFRUIT HIGHBALL

1½ oz. Puerto Rican rum
Grapefruit juice

Pour the rum into a highball glass; add ice and fill with grapefruit juice. Stir well.

GRAPEFRUIT NOG

1½ oz. brandy
4 oz. unsweetened grapefruit juice
1 tbs. lemon juice
1 tbs. honey
1 egg
4 oz. crushed ice

Combine in a blender at a low speed for 20 seconds. Strain and add lots of ice.

GRAPPA STREGA

1 oz. grappa
1 oz. Strega
1 tsp. lemon juice
1 tsp. orange juice

Combine with ice; shake. Strain. Add ice and a twist of lemon.

GRASSHOPPER

1 oz. green creme de menthe
1 oz. white creme de cacao
1 oz. heavy cream

Combine with ice; shake well. Strain straight up. For a **MEXICAN GRASSHOPPER** *use Kahlua instead of creme de cacao.*

GREAT SECRET

1½ oz. gin
2 tsp. Lillot
1-2 dashes Angostura bitters

Combine with ice; shake. Strain. Add ice and a twist of orange.

GREEK BUCK

1½ oz. Metaxa brandy
2 tsp. lemon juice
1 tsp. ouzo
Ginger ale

Combine the brandy and lemon juice with ice; shake. Strain; add ice, ginger ale, and a slice of lemon. Float the ouzo on top.

GREENBACK

2 oz. gin
2 tsp. lime juice
1 tsp. green creme de menthe

Combine with ice; shake. Strain and add ice.

GREEN DEVIL

1½ oz. gin
1 tsp. green creme de menthe
2 tsp. lime juice
Mint sprigs

Combine (except mint) with ice; shake well. Strain, add ice and mint.

GREEN DRAGON

1½ oz. dry gin
1 oz. green creme de menthe
2 tsp. lemon juice
2 tsp. kummel
A few dashes peach bitters

Combine with ice; shake. Strain and add ice.

GREEN FIRE

1½ oz. gin
2 tsp. green creme de menthe
2 tsp. kummel

Combine with ice; shake well. Strain and add ice.

GREEN ROOM

1½ oz. dry vermouth
2 tsp. brandy
A few drops curacao

Combine with ice; shake. Strain and add ice.

GRENADINE RICKEY

1½ oz. grenadine
½ lime
Club soda

Squeeze the lime into a glass; add the rind, the grenadine and a few cubes of ice. Add club soda and stir.

GROG

2 oz. Jamaican rum
1 tbs. lemon juice
1 cube sugar
A few cloves
1 cinnamon stick

Combine in a mug; fill with boiling water and stir until the sugar is completely dissolved. Add a twist of lemon. Serve hot.

GUANABANA

1½ oz. white rum
1½ tbs. soursop (guanabana) nectar
1 tsp. lime juice

Combine with ice; shake. Strain and add ice.

GUARDSMAN'S PUNCH

1 bottle Scotch
1 pint green tea
6 oz. brandy
½ cup sugar
1 oz. port
The peels of 1 lemon, sliced

Combine in a large saucepan. Heat, but do not boil; serve steaming hot.

GUARDSMAN'S PUNCH II

1 bottle Scotch
1 quart green tea
8 oz. cognac
8 oz. brown sugar
2 oz. port
Grated lemon peels

Combine the tea, sugar, and grated peels in a large pot; heat and stir until the sugar has dissolved. Add the port and Scotch; stir well. Heat a ladle-full of the cognac over low heat; ignite and infuse the punch. Add the rest of the cognac and serve immediately.

GUAVA COOLER

2 oz. vodka
2 tbs. guava nectar
2 tsp. sugar syrup

Combine with ice; shake well. Strain and add ice.

GUAVA WATER

1½ oz. rum
1½ oz. guava nectar
2 tsp. lemon juice
2 tsp. pineapple juice
2 tsp. maraschino
1 tsp. sugar syrup
1 guava shell
Club soda

Combine (except the shell and the soda) with ice; shake. Strain; add ice and club soda. Top with the guava shell or a slice of lemon.

GYPSY

2 oz. vodka
2 tsp. Benedictine
1 tsp. lemon juice
1 tsp. orange juice

Combine with ice; shake. Strain and add ice. Top with a slice of orange.

Ale Jug
1800
(United states)

YOUR OWN RECIPE

YOUR OWN RECIPE

Use a bartender's mixing glass whenever the instructions state "combine" ingredients. Strain the drink from the mixing glass into the drinking glass suggested by the illustration alongside the ingredients.

The glass pictured for each drink is our suggestion; other drinking cups may be used as well.

HABITANT COCKTAIL

1½ oz. Canadian whiskey
1 oz. lemon juice
1 tsp. maple syrup

Combine with ice; shake. Strain and add ice. Top with a slice of orange and a cherry.

HABIT ROUGE

1½ oz. gin
2 tbs. grapefruit juice
2 oz. cranberry juice
1 tsp. honey
2 oz. crushed ice

Combine in blender at a high speed until the consistency of snow. Serve unstrained.

HAPA TIQI

1 oz. white rum
1 oz. orange juice
1 tbs. lemon juice
2 tsp. brandy
1 tsp. almond extract
Gardenia blossoms

Combine everything except the blossoms with ice; shake well. Strain over plenty of ice. Garnish with gardenia.

HAPPY APPLE RUM TWIST

1½ oz. white rum
3 oz. coder
1 oz. lemon juice
Combine with ice; shake. Strain. Add ice and a twist of lime with its peel.

HAPPY HOUR PUNCH

1 fifth Southern Comfort
8 oz. pineapple juice
8 oz. grapefruit juice
4 oz. lemon juice
4 bottles champagne
Orange slices

Combine (except the champagne) in a large punch bowl; decorate with slices of orange. Add the champagne and chunks of ice immediately before serving.

HARBORMASTER SWIZZLE

2½ oz. Jamaican rum
1½ tsp. lime juice
1½ tsp. sugar syrup
Several dashes of Demarara bitters
Combine with ice; shake well. Strain over crushed ice; add cold water to fill. Stir gently until the glass begins to frost.

HARLEM

1½ oz. dry gin
1 tbs. pineapple juice
A few chunks canned pineapple
A few drops maraschino

Combine with ice; shake well. Strain and add ice.

HARRITY

1¼ oz. whiskey
A few drops gin
A few dashes of Angostura bitters

Pour the whiskey into a glass; add the gin and bitters. Stir well and add ice.

HARRY LAUDER

1¼ oz. Scotch
1¼ oz. sweet vermmouth
½ tsp. sugar syrup

Combine with ice; shake well. Strain and add ice.

HARVARD

1½ oz. brandy
1 tbs. sweet vermouth
2 tsp. lemon juice
1 tsp. grenadine
A few dashes of Angostura bitters

Combine with ice; shake well. Strain and add ice.

HARVARD COOLER

3 oz. apple brandy
1½ oz. lemon juice
1 tbs. sugar syrup
Club soda

Combine (except the soda) with ice; shake. Strain; add ice and club soda.

HARVARD WINE

1 oz. dry vermouth
1 tbs. brandy
1-2 dashes orange bitters
Club soda

Combine (except the soda) with ice; shake. Strain; add ice and soda.

HARVEY WALLBANGER

1 oz. vodka
2 tsp. Galliano
Orange juice

Pour the vodka into a tall glass; add ice and almost fill the glass with orange juice. Float the Galliano on top.

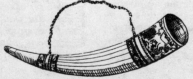

HASTY COCKTAIL

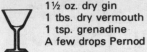

1½ oz. dry gin
1 tbs. dry vermouth
1 tsp. grenadine
A few drops Pernod

Combine with ice; shake. Strain and add ice.

HAVANA

1 oz. apricot brandy
½ oz. gin
2 tsp. Swedish Punch
A few drops lemon juice

Combine with ice; shake. Strain and add ice.

HAVANA CLUB

1½ oz. white rum
1 tbs. dry vermouth

Combine with ice; shake. Strain and add ice.

HAVANA DAIQUIRI

2 oz. white rum
1 oz. lemon juice
1 tbs. banana liqueur
1 tsp. sugar syrup

Combine with ice; shake well. Strain and add ice.

HAWAIIAN

1½ oz. gin
1 tbs. pineapple juice
1 egg white
1-2 dashes orange bitters

Combine with ice; shake well. Strain and add ice. This can also be made with a tablespoon of curacao and a tablespoon of orange juice instead of the pineapple juice and the egg white.

HAWAIIAN CHAMPAGNE PUNCH

1 pint rum
1 pint brandy
1 pint lemon juice
4 oz. curacao
4 oz. marashino
3 cups powdered sugar
3 large pineapples
4 bottles champagne

Pare the meat out of the pineapples; crush and combine with the powdered sugar in a bowl. Allow to stand for a few hours. Turn out into a large punch bowl; add everything except the champagne. Stir well and allow to stand overnight. Add the champagne plus chunks of ice immediately before serving.

HAWAIIAN COFFEE

1 cup iced coffee
8 oz. coffee ice cream
4 oz. pineapple juice
2 oz. white rum

Combine in blender at a high speed until smooth. Split between two tall glasses.

HAWAIIAN DAISY

1½ oz. white rum
2 tsp. pineapple juice
1 tsp. lime juice
1 tsp. grenadine
1 tsp. 151-proof rum
1 chunk papaya
Club soda

Combine (except the rum, papaya, and the soda) with ice; shake. Strain; add ice and club soda. Decorate with the papaya and float the rum on top.

HAWAIIAN EYE

1½ oz. bourbon
1 oz. each of vodka, Kahlua, and heavy cream
2 tsp. Pernod
1 egg white
2 oz. cherry juice
3 oz. crushed ice

Combine in a blender at a high speed for 15 seconds. Strain straight up. Decorate with slices of pineapple and a cherry.

HAWAIIAN HIGHBALL

3 oz. Irish whiskey
2 tsp. pineapple juice
1 tsp. lemon juice
club soda

Combine the whiskey with the juices; add ice and fill with soda. Stir gently.

HAYMAKER'S SWITCHEL

1 pint brandy
2 quarts water
6 oz. vinegar
4 oz. molasses
8 oz. brown sugar
1 pinch of ginger

Combine; stir until the sugar is dissolved and the vinegar is dispersed. Add ice before serving.

HEARNS

¾ oz. bourbon
¾ oz. sweet vermouth
¾ oz. Pernod
A few dashes of Angostura bitters

Combine with ice; shake. Strain and add ice.

HEART WARMER

3 oz. cognac
1 egg yolk
A pinch of paprika

Combine with ice; shake extremely well. Strain over ice.

HEATHER

1½ oz. Scotch
Several drops dry vermouth
A few dashes of Angostura bitters

Combine with ice; shake well. Strain and add ice.

HESITATION

1½ oz. Swedish Punch
2 tsp. rye
A few drops lemon juice

Combine with ice; shake. Strain and add ice.

HET PINT

2 quarts ale
8 oz. Scotch
2 eggs + 1 yolk
Grated nutmeg
Powdered sugar

Combine the ale and nutmeg in a saucepan; add sugar to taste and bring to a boil. Lower the heat. Beat the eggs; add the yolk and combine with the hot ale; stir constantly. Add the Scotch. Pour the brew mug-to-mug to build up a head; serve while still foamy and hot.

HIBISCUS CUG

2 oz. white rum
1 oz. Cointreau
1½ tsp. lime juice
1 tsp. Pernod
3 oz. crushed ice
Hibiscus blossoms

Combine in a blender at high speed for 15 seconds. Turn out straight up; serve with a straw. Decorate with hibiscus.

HIGH HAT

1 oz. Cherry Herring
4 oz. rye
3 tbs lemon juice

Combine with ice; shake. Strain and add ice.

HIGHLAND BITTERS

2 tbs. gentian root
2 tsp. orange peels
1 tsp. camomile flowers
1 tsp. cinnamon
2 cloves
1 oz. coriander seeds
2 bottles Scotch

Pound the spices until fine and mix well; add them to the Scotch. Store in tightly sealed pots or bottles for two weeks before drinking.

HIGHLAND FLING

1½ oz. Scotch
3 oz. milk
1 tsp. powdered sugar

Combine with ice; shake well. Strain and add ice. Dust with nutmeg.

HIGHLAND FLING NO 2.

1½ oz. Scotch
1 tbs. sweet vermouth
1-2 dashes orange bitters

Combine with ice; shake. Strain and add ice plus an olive.

HIPPOCRAS

2 bottles Vouvray (or any semi-sweet Alsation wine)
12 oz. sugar
2 lemons, quartered
1 tsp. mace
A few pinches freshly ground white pepper
2 cinnamon sticks

Combine the wine and the sugar in a punch bowl and stir until the sugar is completely dissolved. Squeeze in the lemons and drop in the rinds. Add the spices and chunks of ice; allow them some time to blend before serving.

HIT AND RUN

2 oz. gin
1 tbs. port
A few drops of anisette

Combine with ice; shake. Strain and add ice.

HOFFMAN HOUSE

1½ oz. dry gin
1 tbs. dry vermouth
1-2 dashes orange bitters

Combine with ice; shake. Strain straight up and add an olive.

HOLIDAY

1½ oz. tequila
2 tsp. lemon juice
A few drops grenadine
1 green cherry

Combine (except the cherry) with ice; shake well. Strain straight up and add a cherry.

HOLIDAY EGGNOG

1 pint rye
1 oz. Jamaican rum
6 eggs
6 oz. sugar
1 pint heavy cream
1 pint milk

Separate the eggs; beat 4 oz. of sugar with the yolks and save the rest for the whites. In a large bowl, combine the milk and the cream with the yolks. Add the rye; allow it to stand for a few hours. Just before serving, beat the egg whites, add the remaining sugar, and fold this into the nog. Dust with nutmeg.

HOLLAND HOUSE

1½ oz. gin
2 tsp. dry vermouth
1 tbs. lemon juice
A few drops maraschino
1 pineapple slice, chopped

Combine with ice; shake well. Strain and add ice.

HONEYBEE

2 oz. white rum
2 tsp. lemon juice
1 tbs. honey

Combine with ice; shake well. Strain and add ice.

HONEYDEW COOLER

1½ oz. gin
1 tbs. lemon juice
1 tbs. heavy cream
1 tsp. sugar syrup
A few drops Pernod
3 oz. honeydew, diced
4 oz. crushed ice
Club soda

Combine (except the soda) in a blender at a low speed for 20 seconds. Strain; add ice and a splash of soda.

HONEYMOON

1½ oz. apple brandy
1½ oz. lemon juice
3 tsp. Benedictine
A few drops curacao

Combine with ice; shake. Strain and add ice.

HONEYSUCKLE

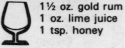

1½ oz. gold rum
1 oz. lime juice
1 tsp. honey

Combine with ice; shake. Strain and add ice.

HONOLULU

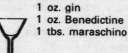

1 oz. gin
1 oz. Benedictine
1 tbs. maraschino

Combine with ice; shake. Strain and add ice.

HONOLULU PUNCH

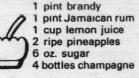

1 pint brandy
1 pint Jamaican rum
1 cup lemon juice
2 ripe pineapples
6 oz. sugar
4 bottles champagne

Peel and grate the pineapples; place in a large punch bowl, sprinkle with the sugar, and allow to stand for at least one hour. Add the juice, brandy, and rum and refrigerate overnight. Just before serving, add the champagne and chunks of ice.

HONORABLE

¾ oz. bourbon
¾ oz. sweet vermouth
¾ oz. dry vermouth

Combine with ice; shake. Strain and add ice.

HOOPLA

½ oz. Cointreau
½ oz. Lillet
2 tsp. lemon juice
2 tsp. brandy

Combine with ice; shake. Strain and add ice.

HOOT MON

1 oz. Scotch
½ oz. Lillet
2 tsp. sweet vermouth

Combine with ice; shake. Strain and add ice.

HOP FROG

1 oz. brandy
2 oz. lime juice

Combine with ice; shake. Strain and add ice.

HOP TOAD

¾ oz. white rum
¾ oz. apricot brandy
1 tbs. lime juice

Combine with ice; shake well. Strain and add ice.

HOPPEL POPPEL

8 oz. dark rum
5 oz. sugar
4 egg yolks
1 tsp. vanilla extract
1 quart milk

Combine the yolks and the sugar; beat until creamy. Heat but do not scald the milk in a separate saucepan. Add the egg mixture plus the vanilla; stir constantly. Pour in the rum. Serve warm in mugs. Garnish with nutmeg.

HORSECAR

1 oz. rye
1½ tbs. sweet vermouth
1½ tbs. dry vermouth
1-2 dashes Angostura bitters

Combine with ice; shake. Strain and add ice. Top with a cherry.

HORSE MARY

1½ oz. vodka
5 oz. tomato juice
1½ tsp. lemon juice
2 tsp. grated horseradish
1 egg white
A few drops of Worchestershire sauce
A few drops of Tabasco sauce
Salt and pepper to taste

Combine; shake with ice. Strain straight up.

HORSE'S NECK

2½ oz. whiskey
1 lemon
Ginger ale

Carefully peel the lemon so that the peel turns out one long spiral strip. Pour out the whiskey; drop in the spiral peel. Add ice and ginger ale. Squeeze in a few drops of the lemon's juice and gently stir. Gin can be used instead of whiskey.

HOT APPLE TODDY

2 oz. apple brandy
2 oz. hot baked apple
2 tsp. cider

Combine in a heated mug; fill with very hot water and stir. Dust with nutmeg.

HOT BRANDY

4 oz. brandy
1 tsp. sugar

Dissolve the sugar in a mug with a few drops of hot water. Pour in the brandy and fill with boiling water. Top with nutmeg.

HOT BRICK TODDY

2 oz. whiskey
1 tsp. sweet butter
1 tsp. powdered sugar
1 tbs. hot water
1 dash cinnamon

Combine (except the whiskey) and stir until well-blended. Add the whiskey and boiling water.

HOT BUTTERED COMFORT

1¼ oz. Southern Comfort
1 cinnamon stick
1 lemon slice
1 pat butter

Combine (except the butter) with boiling water and stir with the cinnamon stick. Float the butter on top.

HOT BUTTERED RUM

2½ oz. Jamaican rum
1 tbs. sweet butter
6-8 oz. cider
1 lemon slice
1 cinnamon stick
Cloves

Combine (except the cider and butter) in a warmed mug. Add hot cider to the spiced rum. Top with butter and nutmeg.

HOT BUTTERED APPLE-JACK

1 quart cider
4 oz. apple brandy
4 oz. powdered sugar
Cinnamon sticks
Butter

Heat the cider but do not boil. Serve into four mugs; add an oz. of apple brandy, an oz. of sugar, a cinnamon stick, and a pat of butter. Top with nutmeg, add a twist of lemon, and stir.

HOT BUTTERED RUM DE CACAO

2 oz. Jamaican rum
1 oz. dark creme de cacao
2 tsp. brown sugar
Whole cloves, a cinnamon stick, nutmeg
Butter

Combine the spices and sugar in a warm mug; add a little boiling water and allow to steep a minute or two. Add the rum and creme de cacao; fill the mug with boiling water and stir well. Touch it up with a twist of lemons. Top it with a spot of butter.

HOT BUTTERED TODDY

1¼ oz. whiskey
1 oz. orange juice
1 tsp. sugar
1 pat butter

Combine (except the butter) with hot water and stir well. Top it off with the butter.

HOT CREOLE

1½ oz. white rum
1 tsp. lemon juice
1-2 dashes Tabasco sauce
Cold beef bouillon

Combine (except the bouillon), then add ice and bouillon. Stir well. Top with salt and pepper to taste.

HOT GIN TODDY

2½ oz. gin
1½ oz. lemon juice
2 cubes sugar

Combine the sugar and the lemon juice; stir until the sugar is completely dissolved. Add the gin and boiling water. Top with a lemon slice.

HOT IRISH PUNCH

4 oz. Irish whiskey
2 cubes sugar
A few drops lemon juice

Combine the sugar with a few drops of hot water; stir until the sugar is completely dissolved. Add the whiskey and lemon juice to the hot water and stir. Top with a lemon slice and nutmeg.

HOT JAMAICAN GROG

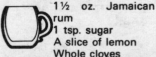

1½ oz. Jamaican rum
1 tsp. sugar
A slice of lemon
Whole cloves

Place the sugar, lemon slice, and cloves in a mug; add the rum and fill the mug with boiling water. Stir and allow to steep for a few minutes. Drink piping hot.

HOT LOCOMOTIVE

6 oz. Burgundy
2 tbs. honey
1 tbs. sugar syrup
1 tbs. curacao
1 egg yolk

Combine the egg yolk, sugar, and honey without ice; stir well. Pour the curacao and the Burgundy into a saucepan; add the honey/egg mixture and heat until boiling, stirring constantly. Serve steaming hot. Top with lemon slice and cinnamon.

HOT MILK PUNCH

2 oz. rum
2 oz. brandy
1 tsp. powdered sugar
Hot milk

Combine and stir very well. Top with nutmeg.

HOT MINT BURGUNDY DELIGHT

3 oz. hot Burgundy
6 fresh mint leaves
1½ tbs. sugar syrup
1 lemon peel
A few drops maraschino
1 cinnamon stick

Muddle the mint leaves with the sugar syrup. Add the lemon peel, maraschino, cinnamon stick, and Burgundy; stir well. Add boiling water.

HOT POT

1 pint bourbon
1 pint rum
8 oz. brandy
2 quarts milk
2 quarts heavy cream
2 cups sugar
1 dozen egg yolks
Ginger, cinnamon, nutmeg and salt
Whole cloves, brown sugar

Combine the yolk and the sugar in a large bowl; beat until creamy. Add the milk and the cream plus the spices and stir to blend. Turn out into a large pot or cauldron; add the liquors and heat until thick. Do not allow to boil; stir constantly. Serve hot in mugs.

HOT PUNCH

1 bottle whiskey
1 bottle dark rum
1 bottle Benedictine
1 bottle cherry brandy
1 pint light tea
Sliced bananas, grapes, apples, lemons

Simmer the sliced fruit with the sugar and spices in the tea for several hours. Add the liquors and keep warm until ready to serve.

HOT RUM

4 oz. Jamaican rum
1½ tsp. lemon juice
2 cubes sugar

Dissolve the sugar with a few drops of hot water. Add the rum and the lemon juice; fill with hot water and stir. Garnish with cinnamon.

HOT RUM PUNCH

1 pint gold rum
4 oz. cognac
4 oz. kummel
4 oz. Benedictine
1 orange, peeled and sliced
1 lemon, peeled and sliced.

Combine; add sugar to taste. Add 3 pints of boiling water; stir well.

HOT RYE

2½ oz. rye
1 cube sugar

Dissolve the sugar with a few drops of hot water; add the rye and top with cinnamon. Serve with a small pitcher of hot water and a slice of lemon on the side.

HOT SCOTCH

4 oz. Scotch
1-2 cubes sugar

Dissolve the sugar with a few drops of hot water; add the Scotch and hot water. Add twist of lemon slice and the peel; top with nutmeg.

HOT SPICED PORT

1½ oz. port
1 sugar cube
Whole cloves, allspice
A pinch nutmeg
Grated lemon rind

Dissolve the sugar with a few drops of warm water in a mug; add the spices and port and fill the mug with boiling water. Stir well. Garnish with the grated rind plus extra nutmeg if you like. Sherry Madeira, brandy, rum, or claret can be used instead of the port.

HOT SPICED RUM

1¼ oz. Jamaican rum
2 tsp. sugar
2 tsp. butter
A few dashes ground cloves and cinnamon

Combine with boiling water and stir well.

HOT SPICED WINE

1 bottle Burgundy
4 oz. hot sugar syrup
Ground cloves and cinnamon
Cinnamon sticks

Heat the bottle of Burgundy in a pot of water, but do not boil. Pour it into a pitcher with the hot sugar syrup; add the powdered spices and stir. Serve with a cinnamon stick or slices of fruit.

HOT TEA PUNCH

1 pint gold gum
1 pint brandy
3 pints hot tea
2 oranges, sliced
1 lemon, sliced

Combine in a large saucepan; add sugar to taste and heat. Serve steaming hot.

HOT WHISKEY TODDY

2 oz. whiskey
1 cube sugar

Dissolve the sugar with a few drops of hot water. Pour in the whiskey and boiling water; stir well. Top with lemon slice and nutmeg.

HOT WINE PUNCH

1 bottle red wine
3 tsp. sugar
Cloves
Cinnamon sticks
1 lemon rind, sliced

Combine the sugar with a cup of boiling water in a saucepan and stir until completely dissolved. Add the spices, rind, and wine; bring to a second boil. Serve hot.

HOTEL PLAZA

¾ oz. dry gin
1 tbs. sweet vermouth
1 tbs. dry vermouth
1 slice pineapple, crushed

Combine with ice; shake. Strain and add ice.

HPW

1½ oz. gin
2 tsp. dry vermouth
2 tsp. sweet vermouth

Combine with ice; shake. Strain. Add ice and a twist of orange; add the peel.

HUDSON BAY

1 oz. gin
½ oz. cherry liqueur
2 tsp. orange juice
1 tsp. lime juice
1 tsp. 151-proof rum

Combine with ice; shake. Strain and add ice. Top with lime slice.

HOT ZOMBIE

2 oz. gold rum
1 oz. apiece dark rum, 151-proof rum, and orange curacao
1 oz. apiece orange and lemon juice
A few drops grenadine
A few drops Pernod
Hot tea

Combine the fruit juices and grenadine; add a little tea and mix well. Add the gold and dark rums, curacao, and Pernod. Heat the 151-proof rum in a ladle; ignite and infuse in the mug. Extinquish, stir well, and serve hot.

HUNDRED PERCENT

1½ oz. Swedish Punch
1 tsp. lemon juice
1 tsp. orange juice
1-2 dashes grenadine

Combine with ice; shake. Strain and add ice.

HUNTER'S COCKTAIL

1½ oz. rye
1 tbs. cherry brandy

Combine straight up; stir to blend. Decorate with a cherry.

HUNTINGTON SPECIAL

1½ oz. gin
2 tsp. lemon juice
1 tsp. grenadine

Combine with ice; shake. Strain and add ice.

HUNTSMAN

1½ oz. Vodka
2 tsp. Jamaican rum
1½ tsp. lime juice
1-2 pinches powdered sugar

Combine with ice; shake well. Strain and add ice.

HURRICANE

1 oz. white rum
1 oz. gold rum
2 tsp. passion fruit syrup
2 tsp. lime juice.

Combine with ice; shake. Strain and add ice.

HURRICANE COOLER

1 oz. white rum
1 oz. Jamaican rum
1 oz. ljme juice
1 pineapple stick
2 oz. orange juice
1 tbs. sugar syrup
2 tsp. orange bitters
A few drops of Pernod

Combine with ice; shake well. Strain over crushed ice. Decorate with the pineapple stick and a cherry.

HUSTLER

2 oz. bourbon
1 oz. orange curacao
1 oz. sweet vermouth
2 tsp. lime juice

Combine with ice; shake well. Strain and add ice.

Swiss Hand-Carved Wooden Tankard

YOUR OWN RECIPE

YOUR OWN RECIPE

Use a bartender's mixing glass whenever the instructions state "combine" ingredients. Strain the drink from the mixing glass into the drinking glass suggested by the illustration alongside the ingredients.

ICEBERG

2 oz. orange sherbet
1 oz. Galliano
2 tsp. Cointreau

Combine in a blender until smooth. Serve straight up.

ICEBREAKER

2 oz. tequila
2 oz. grapefruit juice
1 tbs. grenadine
2 tsp. Cointreau
4 oz. crushed ice

Combine in a blender at a low speed for 15 seconds. Strain straight up.

ICED COFFEE COCKTAIL

1½ oz. Jamaican rum
1½ oz. iced coffee
2 tsp. dark creme de cacao
1 tsp. sugar

Combine with ice; shake well. Strain and add ice. Decorate with a cherry.

ICED COFFEE FILLIP

1-2 tsp. Tia Maria
8 oz. iced black coffee

ICED COFFEE PUNCH

1 gallon iced coffee
1 quart vanilla ice cream
2 quarts light cream
8 oz. sugar
2 oz. Jamaican rum

Combine the sugar with the coffee; refrigerate until very cold. When ready to serve, place the ice cream in the center of a large punch bowl; pour in the coffee, rum and cream. Stir until smooth and well blended.

ICED RUM COFFEE

1½ oz. white rum
1 tsp. Jamaican rum
2 tbs. whipped cream
6 oz. iced black coffee
Sugar

Combine the rums and the coffee; sugar to taste. Fill the glass with ice and top with the whipped cream.

Pour the coffee. Add ice and the Tia Maria; stir well.

ICED RUM TEA

1½ oz. white rum
2 tsp. 151-proof rum
1 tsp. Falernum
1 tsp. lemon juice
1 tsp. sugar
6 oz. iced dark tea
Mint leaves

Combine (except the mint leaves); allow to stand a few minutes before filling the glass with ice. Stir well. Garnish with mint leaves, partially torn, and a slice of lemon.

IL MAGNIFICO

¾ oz. Tuaca
¾ oz. curacao
1 tbs. heavy cream
3 oz. crushed ice

Combine in a blender at a low speed for 15 seconds. Strain straight up.

IMPERIAL

1½ oz. dry gin
1½ oz. dry vermouth
A few dashes of maraschino
A few dashes of Angostura bitters

Combine with ice; shake. Strain and add ice and top with an olive.

INCOME TAX COCKTAIL

1 oz. dry gin
1 tbs. orange juice
1 tsp. dry vermouth
1 tsp. sweet vermouth
A few dashes of Angostura bitters

Combine with ice; shake. Strain and add ice.

INDEPENDENCE DAY PUNCH

2 quarts bourbon
1 pint pineapple juice
8 oz. lime juice
4 bottles club soda

Combine everything except the soda; stir until well blended. Add the soda plus chunks of ice.

INDEPENDENCE SWIZZLE

2 oz. Trinidad rum
2 tsp. lime juice
A few dashes Angostura bitters
1 tsp. honey
1 tsp. sugar

Combine; stir until the sugar and honey are blended well. Add ice and twirl to partially melt the ice. Repeat and keep adding ice until the glass is full.

INDIAN RIVER

1½ oz. whiskey
2 tsp. unsweetened grapefruit juice
1 tsp. raspberry liqueur
1 tsp. sweet vermouth

Combine with ice; shake. Strain and add ice.

INSTANT EGG NOG

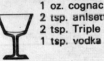

2 quarts vanilla ice cream
1 bottle bourbon
4 oz. Jamaican rum

Place the ice cream in a punch bowl; add the bourbon and rum and stir until the ice cream has melted and blended with the liquors. Dust with nutmeg.

INTERNATIONAL

1 oz. cognac
2 tsp. anisette
2 tsp. Triple Sec
1 tsp. vodka

Combine with ice; shake well. Strain straight up.

IQUIQUE COCKTAIL

4 oz. gin
1 oz. lemon juice
3 tsp. powdered sugar
Several drops of Angostura bitters

Combine with ice; shake. Strain and add ice.

IRISH

1¼ oz. Irish whiskey
A few drops Pernod
A few drops curacao
1-2 dashes maraschino
1-2 dashes Angostura bitters

Combine with ice; shake. Strain. Add ice and a twist of orange plus the peel.

IRISH-CANADIAN SANGAREE

1¼ oz. Canadian whiskey
2 tsp. Irish Mist
1 tsp. orange juice
1 tsp. lemon juice

Combine and stir well. Add ice and dust with nutmeg.

IRISH COFFEE

1½ oz. Irish whiskey
6 oz. freshly brewed coffee
Cream
Sugar

Sweeten the coffee to taste; add the whiskey and stir. Float cream on top.

IRISH COOLER

3 oz. Irish whiskey
Club soda

Pour; add ice, soda, and a twist of lemon plus the peel.

IRISH COW

1½ oz. Irish whiskey
8 oz. hot milk
1 tsp. sugar

Pour the milk into a glass; add the sugar and whiskey. Stir well.

IRISH CRESTA

1 oz. Irish whiskey
2 tsp. Irish Mist
2 tsp. orange juice
1 egg white

Combine with ice; shake well. Strain and add ice.

IRISH EYES

2 oz. green creme de menthe
2 oz. heavy cream
2 tbs. Irish whiskey

Combine with ice; shake. Strain straight up and decorate with a cherry.

IRISH FIX

2 oz. Irish whiskey
2 tsp. Irish Mist
2 tsp. lemon juice
1 tsp. sugar

Dissolve the sugar with a few drops of hot water in a glass. Add whiskey and lemon juice; fill with crushed ice and stir well. Add slices of orange and lemon and float the Irish Mist on top.

IRISH FIZZ

2½ oz. Irish whiskey
1½ tsp. lemon juice
1 tsp. curacao
½ tsp. sugar
Club soda

Combine (except the soda) with ice; shake. Strain; add ice and club soda.

IRISH SHILLELAGH

1½ oz. Irish whiskey
½ oz. sloe gin
1½ oz. lemon juice
2 tsp. white rum
1 tsp. sugar
2 peach slices, chopped
2 raspberries
1 strawberry
1 cherry

Combine (except the berries and cherry) with ice; shake. Strain and add ice. Add the fruit to decorate.

ISLE OF THE BLESSED COCONUT

1½ oz. white rum
2 tsp. cream of coconut
2 tsp. lime juice
1 tsp. lemon juice
1 tsp. orange juice
1 tsp. sugar syrup
3 oz. crushed ice
Coconut slices

Combine (except the coconut slices) in a blender at a low speed for 15 seconds. Strain straight up. Serve with the coconut slices on the side.

ITALIAN APERITIF

3 oz. Punt e Mes
A few drops sweet vermouth
A few drops Campari

Pour the Punt e Mes over ice into a small goblet. Add the vermouth and the Campari; stir gently. Touch it up with a squeeze of lemon plus the peel; garnish with slice of lemon.

YOUR OWN RECIPE

Use a bartender's mixing glass whenever the instructions state "combine" ingredients. Strain the drink from the mixing glass into the drinking glass suggested by the illustration alongside the ingredients.

The glass pictured for each drink is our suggestion; other drinking cups may be used as well.

JACKALOPE

1 bottle Bourbon
8 oz. sugar
1 doz. lemons

Slice the lemons in half; squeeze the juice into a large pot. Add the rinds plus the bourbon and sugar; stir until smooth. Close the pot and refrigerate overnight. Strain clean when ready to use; serve over ice.

JACKIE O. 'S ROSE

1 oz. white rum
2 tsp. orange Cointreau
2 tsp. lime juice
1 tsp. sugar syrup

Combine with ice; shake. Strain over crushed ice.

JACK-IN-THE-BOX

1¼ oz. apple brandy
2 tsp. pineapple juice
1½ tsp. lemon juice
A few dashes of Angostura bitters

Combine with ice; shake. Strain and add ice.

JACK THE GRIPPER

1 bottle apple brandy
8 oz. sugar
2 tbs. Angostura bitters
3 tsp. lemon juice
Cinnamon sticks
Grated lemon peel

Combine the brandy, sugar, and bitters in a large saucepan; heat and stir until the sugar has dissolved. Simmer with a few cinnamon sticks and lemon peels for several minutes. Just before serving; ignite. Extinguish the flames with a few spritzes of boiling water. Serve at once, piping hot, in mugs.

JADE

1¾ gold rum
1½ tsp. lime juice
1½ tsp. sugar syrup
Several drops green creme de menthe
Several drops curacao

Combine with ice; shake. Strain and add ice. Decorate with a lime slice.

JAMAICA GINGER

1½ oz. white rum
½ oz. Jamaican rum
2 tsp. 151-proof rum
2 tsp. Falernum
2 tsp. lime juice
Ginger beer
1 pineapple slice dipped into white creme de menthe
1 chunk ginger

Combine the rums, Falernum, and juice with ice; shake well. Strain add ice, and fill with ginger beer. Decorate with the pineapple and ginger.

JAMAICA GLOW

1½ oz. gin
½ oz. dry red wine
2 tsp. orange juice
1 tsp. Jamaican rum

Combine with ice; shake. Strain over ice. Top with a lime slice.

JAMAICAN ELEGANCE

1½ oz. Jamaican rum
½ oz. brandy
1 tbs. lime juice
2 tsp. pineapple juice
1 tsp. sugar syrup

Combine with ice; shake. Strain and add plenty of ice. Top with a lemon slice.

JAMAICAN GINGER BEER

5 oz. Jamaican ginger
2 oz. honey
2 oz. lime juice
1 egg white
24 oz. sugar
1 cake of yeast
2 quarts water
A few drops of Angostura bitters

Combine the ginger, sugar, honey, water, and lime juice in a large pot. Add the yeast and the egg white; stir to blend. Allow to stand in a cool, dark place for several days. When ready, strain through cheesecloth; add more sugar to taste, plus bitters. Bottle and refrigerate until ready to use.

JAMAICAN HOT TEA PUNCH

1 pint Jamaican rum
1 pint brandy
2 oranges, sliced
1 lime, sliced
3 pints hot tea
Sugar and spices

Combine in a saucepan, heat slowly and stir. Add sugar to taste; spices if you wish.

JAMAICAN SHANDY

1 bottle Red Stripe beer
1 pt. ginger beer, ice cold

Combine stir gently. Serve over ice.

JAMOCHA

1½ oz. Jamaican rum
½ tsp. sugar
A pinch of cinnamon
1 tbs. of whipped cream
Freshly brewed coffee

Combine the rum, sugar, and cinnamon in a mug; fill the mug with coffee and stir. Top with the whipped cream.

JAPALAC

1¼ oz. rye
1¼ oz. dry vermouth
1 tbs. orange juice
1-2 dashes raspberry syrup

Combine with ice; shake. Strain and add ice.

JAPANESE COCKTAIL

2 oz. brandy
1 tsp. lime juice
1 tsp. almond extract
A few dashes of Angostura bitters

Combine with ice; shake. Strain and add ice, a twist of lime, and the peel.

JAPANESE FIZZ

2¼ oz. whiskey
¾ oz. port
2 tsp. lemon juice
1½ tsp. sugar syrup
Club soda
1 pineapple stick

Combine (except the soda and pineapple stick) with ice; shake well. Strain, add ice and soda. Add the twist of orange, plus its peel. Top with the pineapple stick.

JAVA COOLER

1½ oz. gin
1½ tsp. lemon juice
A few dashes of Angostura bitters
Tonic water

Add the lime juice, bitters, and gin over ice; stir well. Fill with tonic.

JEFFERSON DAVIS PUNCH

12 bottles claret
2 bottles sherry
½ bottle brandy
½ pint Jamaican rum
1½ pints lemon juice
8 oz. maraschino
3 bottles ginger ale
6 bottles club soda
3 lb. sugar

Dissolve the sugar in some water to make it syrup; combine (except the ginger ale and soda) and stir. Top with slices of lemon and orange. Allow to stand overnight. Add the soda and ginger ale, plus ice, before serving.

JERSEY DEVIL

1½ oz. apple brandy
1 oz. cranberry juice
2 tbs. lime juice
2 tsp. Cointreau
1 tsp. sugar syrup
An apple slice

Combine with ice; shake well. Strain decorate with apple slice.

JERSEY LIGHTNING

2½ oz. apple brandy
A few dashes of
Angostura bitters
Sugar

Combine with ice. Sugar to taste. Strain and add ice.

JERSEY MUG

2½ oz. apple brandy
A few dashes of
Angostura bitters
A few whole cloves
A lemon peel

Combine with boiling water. Add a dash of the brandy and ignite and serve.

JERSEY SOUR

3 oz. apple brandy
1 tbs. lemon juice
2 tbs. sugar syrup

Combine with ice; shake. Strain and add ice. Top with a cherry.

JEWEL

1 oz. gin
1 oz. sweet vermouth
1 tbs. green chartreuse
1-2 dashes orange bitters

Combine with ice; shake. Strain and add ice and a twist of lemon plus the peel.

JOBURG

1½ oz. white rum
1½ oz. Dubonnet
Several dashes
orange bitters

Combine with ice; shake. Strain and add ice.

JOCKEY CLUB

2 oz. gin
A few drops creme
de noyeaux
A few drops lemon
juice
A few dashes of
Angostura and
orange bitters

Combine with ice; shake. Strain and add ice.

JOCOSE JULEP

2½ oz. bourbon
1 oz. lime juice
2 tsp. green creme
de menthe
1½ tsp. sugar syrup
Club soda
½ doz. mint leaves,
finely chopped
Mint sprigs

Combine (except the soda and mint sprigs) with ice; shake. Strain and add ice and club soda. Top with mint sprigs.

JOHN ALDEN

1 oz. gold rum
1 oz. coffee liqueur
1 oz. orange curacao

Combine with ice; shake well. Strain straight up.

JOHN McCLAIN

1¼ oz. Scotch
1 tsp. sugar syrup
A few dashes of
Angostura bitters

Combine with ice; shake. Strain and add ice.

JOHNNY COCKTAIL

1½ oz. sloe gin
1 tbs. curacao
1 tsp. anisette

Combine with ice; shake. Strain and add ice.

JOHNSON DELIGHT

1½ oz. Pernod
1 oz. Cointreau
1½ tsp. lime juice

Combine with ice; shake. Strain and add ice.

JOULOUVILLE

1 oz. gin
2 tsp. apple brandy
2 tsp. lemon juice
1 tsp. sweet vermouth
A few drops grenadine

Combine with ice; shake. Strain and add ice.

JOURNALIST

1½ oz. dry gin
1 tsp. dry vermouth
A few drops curacao
A few drops of lemon juice
A few dashes of Angostura bitters

Combine with ice; shake well. Strain and add ice.

JUBAL EARLY PUNCH

1 pint Jamaican rum
3 pints brandy
1½ gallons lemonade
1 lb. sugar
6 bottles champagne

Dissolve the sugar with the lemonade; add the remaining ingredients plus chunks of ice and stir well.

JUDGE, JR.

¾ oz. white rum
¾ oz. gin
1 tbs. lemon juice
1 tsp. grenadine

Combine with ice; shake. Strain and add ice.

JUDGETTE

¾ oz. peach brandy
¾ oz. dry gin
1 tbs. dry vermouth
1 tsp. lime juice

Combine with ice; shake. Strain and add ice. Top with a cherry.

JUJUBE CORDIAL

1 quart jujube fruit
Brown sugar
Whiskey

Combine the jujube fruit with a brown sugar syrup (three parts sugar to one parts water) in a large pot and allow to stand at room temperature for several days. Double the amount of fruit and syrup with whiskey; stir, strain, and bottle for future use.

JULEP

3 oz. bourbon
1 cube sugar
Mint sprigs

Dissolve the sugar with a few drops of water. Add a few sprigs of mint; fill the glass with ice and add the bourbon. Stir and add more mint (cut and bled) into the julep. Allow to stand a few minutes before serving.

JUNIOR

1½ oz. rye
2 tsp. lime juice
2 tsp. Benedictine
A few dashes of
Angostura bitters

Combine with ice; shake. Strain and add ice.

JUPITER MARTINI

1½ oz. gin
1 tbs. dry vermouth
1 tsp. Parfait Amour
1 tsp. orange juice

Combine with ice; shake well. Strain straight up.

JULGLOGG

1 bottle Burgundy
½ bottle aquavit
8 oz. sugar
Orange and lemon peels

Blanched almonds
Seedless raisins
Cinnamon
Whole cardamom seeds

Combine in a large saucepan; heat throughly but do not bring to a boil. Serve at once. Ignite when serving, scooping a bit of the fire as well as a few of the nuts and whole spices into each mug.

YOUR OWN RECIPE

YOUR OWN RECIPE

Use a bartender's mixing glass whenever the instructions state "combine" ingredients. Strain the drink from the mixing glass into the drinking glass suggested by the illustration alongside the ingredients.

The glass pictured for each drink is our suggestion; other drinking cups may be used as well.

K

KAHLUA JAVA

2 pints fresh, hot coffee
2 pints hot cocoa
3 tbs. Kahlua
Marshmallows

Combine the coffee, cocoa, and Kahlua in a chafing dish; stir gently to blend. Serve piping hot in mugs; garnish with a marshmallow.

KAHLUA TOREADOR

2 oz. brandy
1 oz. Kahlua
1 egg white

Combine with ice; shake. Strain and add ice.

KAISER SOUR PUNCH

1 bottle chilled Rhine wine
3 cups lemon juice
4 oz. powdered sugar

Combine the sugar with the lemon juice in a pitcher and stir until the sugar is completely dissolved. Add the wine, plenty of ice and stir well.

KAMEHAMEHA RUM PUNCH

1 oz. white rum
1 oz. Jamaican rum
2 oz. pineapple juice
1 tbs. lemon juice
1 tsp. blackberry brandy
1 tsp. lemon juice
1 tsp. powdered sugar
1 pineapple stick

Combine (except the Jamaican rum and pineapple stick) with ice; shake. Strain; add ice and float the Jamaican rum on top. Top with the pineapple stick and a cherry.

KANGAROO

1½ oz. vodka
¾ oz. dry vermouth

Combine with ice; shake. Strain; add ice and a twist of lemon.

KCB

1½ oz. gin
2 tsp. kirsch
A few drops apricot brandy
A few drops lemon juice

Combine with ice; shake. Strain. Add ice and a twist of lemon with its peel.

KE KALI NEI AU

1½ oz. white rum
1½ oz. passion fruit juice
1 oz. Jamaican rum
2 tbs. lemon juice
1½ tbs. sugar syrup
2 tsp. kirsch
1 green coconut
Red hibiscus

Slice off the top of the coconut and drain. Combine all the liquors and juices (except the Jamaican rum) with ice; shake. Strain into the coconut; float the Jamaican rum and the red hibiscus or fruit slices.

KENNY

2 oz. apple brandy
1 tbs. sweet vermouth
1½ tsp. lemon juice
A few dashes of Angostura bitters
A few drops of grenadine

Combine with ice; shake. Strain and add ice.

KENTUCKY

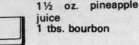

1½ oz. pineapple juice
1 tbs. bourbon

Combine with ice; shake. Strain and add ice.

KENTUCKY COLONEL

1½ oz. bourbon
2 tsp. Benedictine

Combine with ice; shake. Strain. Add ice and a twist of lemon; add the peel.

KENTUCKY TODDY

1½ oz. bourbon
1 tsp. sugar

Dissolve the sugar with a little water. Add the bourbon and ice; stir briskly. To make a HOT KENTUCKY TODDY, add 3 ozs. of boiling water to the mug.

KERRY COOLER

2 oz. Irish whiskey
1½ oz. sherry
1¼ tbs. almond extract
1¼ tbs. lemon juice
Club soda

Combine (except the soda) with ice; shake well. Strain; add ice and soda. Top with a lemon slice.

KEUKA CUP

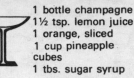

1 bottle champagne
1½ tsp. lemon juice
1 orange, sliced
1 cup pineapple
cubes
1 tbs. sugar syrup

*Combine and chill. Add ice
before serving.*

KEY COCKTAIL

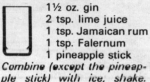

1½ oz. gin
2 tsp. lime juice
1 tsp. Jamaican rum
1 tsp. Falernum
1 pineapple stick

*Combine (except the pineapple stick) with ice, shake.
Strain and add ice. Top with
the pineapple stick.*

KIDDIE CAR

2 oz. apple brandy
2 tsp. lime juice
1 tsp. Triple Sec

*Combine with ice; shake.
Strain and add ice.*

KING COLE

2 oz. bourbon
½ tsp. sugar syrup
A few drops Fernet
Branca
1 orange slice
1 pineapple slice

*Muddle the fruit with the
sugar and Fernet Branca; add
the bourbon and stir.*

KING'S PEG

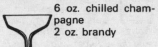

6 oz. chilled champagne
2 oz. brandy

*Combine with two cubes ice
and stir. For a QUEEN'S
PEG, use a tablespoon of dry
gin instead of the brandy.*

KINGSTON

1 oz. Jamaican rum
2 tsp. kummel
2 tsp. orange juice
1-2 dashes Pimento
Dram

*Combine with ice; shake and
strain. Serve over ice.*

KIPINSKI

1 oz. white rum
1 oz. Triple Sec
1 oz. grapefruit juice

*Combine with ice; shake well.
Strain and add ice.*

KIRSCH AND CASSIS

2 oz. creme de
cassis
1 oz. kirsch
Club soda

*Combine the cassis and the
kirsch with ice; shake. Strain.
Add ice and fill with soda.*

KIRSCH CUBA LIBRE

1½ oz. Kirschwasser
2 tsp. lime juice
Cola

Combine the kirschwasser and lime juice; add ice and cola. Stir.

KIRSCH RICKEY

1½ oz. Kirschwasser
2 tsp. lime juice
Club soda
2 black cherries

Combine kirschwasser and the lime juice; add ice and club soda. Stir. Top with cherries, pitted and speared.

KISS IN THE DARK

¾ oz. dry gin
¾ oz. cherry brandy
1 tbs. dry vermouth

Combine with ice; shake. Strain and add ice.

KISS ME QUICK

1½ oz. Pernod
Several drops curacao
A few dashes of Angostura bitters
Soda water

Combine (except the soda) with ice; shake. Strain; add ice and soda.

KISS THE BOYS GOODBYE

1 oz. sloe gin
1 oz. brandy
1½ tsp. lemon juice
½ egg white

Combine with ice. Shake. Strain and add ice.

KNICKERBOCKER

2 oz. gin
2 tsp. dry vermouth
1 tsp. sweet vermouth

Combine with ice; shake. Strain straight up.

KNOCK-OUT

¾ oz. dry gin
¾ oz. dry vermouth
2 tsp. Pernod
1 tsp. white creme de menthe

Combine with ice; shake. Strain and add ice.

KRAMBAMBULI PUNCH

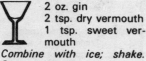

2 bottles red wine
1 pint arrack
1 pint dark rum
8 oz. sugar
A pair of oranges and lemons

Pour the wine into a large pot; heat thoroughly but do not allow to boil. Peel the fruit; squeeze in all the juice and grate a bit of the rind. Put the sugar into a king-sized ladle; soak in a little rum and arak. Ignite and infuse the punch; stir to dissolve the sugar. Add the rest of the rum and arak; stir. Serve hot.

KREMLIN COLONEL

2 oz. vodka
2 tsp. lime juice
1½ tsp. sugar syrup
Mint leaves, partially
torn

Combine (except the mint leaves) with ice; shake. Strain and add ice. Top with mint.

KRETCHMA

1 oz. vodka
1 oz. white creme de cacao
2 tsp. lemon juice
A few drops of grenadine

Combine with ice; shake well. Strain and add ice.

KRUPNIK

3 cups cooking alcohol
2 cups honey
1 tsp. vanilla extract
Whole cloves,
grated lemon rinds,
cinnamon, whole
peppercorns and
vanilla

Combine the honey with the spices and vanilla in a large saucepan; warm through. Add 2 cups of water and bring to a boil; stirring constantly. Remove from heat; add the alcohol and serve.

KUALA LAMPUR COOLER

2 oz. gin
1 oz. pineapple juice
2 tsp. lime juice
Club soda
A chunk of fresh pineapple

Combine the gin and juices; stir. Add ice and soda. Decorate with the pineapple chunk.

KUMMEL

1 oz. kummel oil
1 quart cooking alcohol
4 cups of sugar

Combine the sugar with 1 qt. of water; boil for at least twenty minutes. Remove from heat. When lukewarm, add the oil and the alcohol; stir. Bottle and store in a cool place for several months before using.

KUMMEL BLACKBERRY FRAPPE

½ oz. kummel
2 tsp. blackberry brandy
1 tsp. lemon juice

Combine without ice; stir well. Strain over crushed ice.

KVASS

1 oz. malt
3 tbs. honey
1 doz. slices sour pumpernickel bread

Tear the bread into tiny pieces and put it in a large crock pot. Add 5 cups of boiling water and the malt; seal and allow to stand at room temperature for a day or until fermented. Sweeten with the honey; bottle and store in your refrigerator.

YOUR OWN RECIPE

Use a bartender's mixing glass whenever the instructions state "combine" ingredients. Strain the drink from the mixing glass into the drinking glass suggested by the illustration alongside the ingredients.

The glass pictured for each drink is our suggestion; other drinking cups may be used as well.

LA BELLE CREME
        1 oz. vodka
        1 oz. heavy cream
        2 tsp. white creme
        de cacao
        2 tsp. Cointreau

Combine with ice; shake well. Strain straight up.

LA JOLLA
        1½ oz. brandy
        2 tsp. banana liqueur
        2 tsp. lemon juice
        1 tsp. orange juice

Combine with ice; shake. Strain and add ice.

LADDIES SUB-BOURBON
        2 oz. bourbon
        A few drops orange
        curacao
        A few dashes of
        Angostura bitters
        Soda water

Combine (except the soda) with ice; shake well. Strain. Add ice and soda.

LADIES' COCKTAIL
        1½ oz. whiskey
        Several drops anisette
        A few drops Pernod
        A few dashes of
        Angostura bitters
        1 pineapple stick

Combine (except the pineapple stick) with ice; shake. Strain and add ice. Top with the pineapple.

LADYFINGER
        1 oz. gin
        2 tsp. kirsch
        2 tsp. cherry brandy

Combine with ice; shake. Strain and add ice.

LAFAYETTE
        3 oz. rye
        2 tsp. dry vermouth
        2 tsp. Dubonnet
        A few dashes of
        Angostura bitters

Combine with ice; shake well. Strain and add ice.

LAFAYETTE PUNCH

1 bottle chilled Moselle
4 bottles champagne
8 oz. powdered sugar
½ doz. oranges

Peel the oranges and cut into thin slices. Combine with the sugar, add the wine, stir, and refrigerate. Before serving, combine the sweetened wine and the champagne and add chunks of ice.

LAKE KEUKA PUNCH

1 bottle dry champagne
1 bottle Burgundy
1 bottle Sauterne
1 pint strawberries
4 tsp. lime juice
Grated lemon rinds

Combine the strawberries, juice, and the rinds in a saucepan; simmer for serveral minutes. Strain and allow to cool. Before serving, combine the wines and fruit syrup. Stir and add chunks of ice.

LALLAH ROOKH COCKTAIL

1 ¼ oz. chilled cognac
1 tbs. Jamaican rum
2 tsp. sugar syrup
2 tsp. vanilla extract
1 tsp. heavy cream

Combine with ice; shake. Strain and add ice.

LAMB'S WOOL

1 quart hot ale
6 baked apples
Sugar

Pour the ale over the apples. Sugar to taste and dust with ginger and nutmeg. Serve piping hot.

LAS VEGAS JULEP

1 oz. bourbon
1 oz. lemon juice
2 tsp. Galliano
1 tsp. sugar syrup

Combine with ice; shake well. Strain over crushed ice. Decorate with mint.

LASKY

¾ oz. Swedish Punch
¾ oz. dry gin
1 tbs. grape juice

Combine with ice; shake. Strain and add ice.

LATIN BITTERS

1½ oz. Campari
1 tbs. sweet vermouth
Club soda

Combine the Campari and the vermouth; add ice and soda. Stir well. Touch it up with a twist of lemon and drop in the peel.

LATIN LOVER

1½ oz. Valentino
1 oz. tequila
2 tsp. lemon juice
A few dashes
grenadine

*Combine with ice; shake well.
Strain and add ice.*

LAWHILL

1½ oz. whiskey
1 tbs. dry vermouth
2 tsp. orange juice
A few drops Pernod
A few drops mar-
aschino
A few dashes of
Angostura bitters

*Combine with ice; shake.
Strain and add ice.*

LAYER CAKE

1 tbs. dark creme de
cacao
1 tbs. apricot brandy
1 tbs. heavy cream

*Carefully pour, floating the
above in order shown. Top
with a cherry and chill before
serving.*

LE COQ HARDY

Fernet Branca
Grand Marnier
Champagne
Cognac
Angostura bitters
1 sugar cube

*Place the sugar cube on the
bottom of a wide champagne
glass; top it with a drop of
Fernet Branca, Grand Mar-
nier, Cognac, and bitters. Fill
the glass with champagne;
stir gently until the sugar has
dissolved. Decorate with a
slice of orange and a cherry.*

LEAMINGTON BRANDY PUNCH

2 bottles Sauterne
1 small bottle
Cognac
1 quart lemon juice
12 oz. powdered
sugar

*Dissolve the sugar with the
lemon juice in a large punch
bowl. Add the cognac and the
wine and stir to blend. Keep
refrigerated until ready to
serve. Add chunks of ice.
Garnish with mint.*

LEAP YEAR

1½ oz. gin
1 tsp. sweet ver-
mouth
1 tsp. Grand Marnier
A few drops lemon
juice

*Combine with ice; shake well.
Strain. Add ice and a twist of
lemon with its peel.*

LEAPFROG

1½ oz. gin
1½ oz. lemon juice
Ginger ale

*Combine the gin and lemon
juice with ice; shake well.
Strain; add ice and fill with
ginger ale.*

LEAVE IT TO ME

2 oz. gin
¼ oz. lemon juice
1 tsp. raspberry
syrup
A few drops mar-
aschino

*Combine with ice; shake.
Strain and add ice.*

LEEWARD

1½ oz. white rum
2 tsp. calvados
2 tsp. sweet vermouth

Combine with ice; shake. Strain. Add ice and a twist of lemon with its peel.

LEMON BISHOP

Follow the recipe for **ARCHBISHOP'S PUNCH,** *using a lemon instead of an orange, and adding to the claret cinnamon, mace, allspice, and ginger before cooking.*

LEMON RUM COOLER

2 oz. white rum
2 oz. pineapple juice
2 tsp. lemon juice
2 fsp. Falernum
1 tsp. 151-proof rum
Lemon soda

Combine (except the soda) with ice; shake. Strain. Add ice and fill with soda. Top with a lemon slice.

LEMON WINE

2 tsp. citric acid
1 doz. drops of lemon essence
Several drops of cooking alcohol
1 lb. sugar
Saffron

Boil the sugar in a quart of water until the sugar has dissolved; add the citric acid and allow to cool. Stir in the lemon essence and alcohol; add saffron for color.

LEONINE EGG NOG

4 doz. eggs, separated
3 pints bourbon
1 quart milk
1 pint heavy cream
1 cup sugar

Combine the sugar with the egg yolks; stir until the sugar is dissolved. Pour in the whiskey; add the milk and cream, and stir. (Cream can be whipped.) Beat the egg whites until stiff and gently fold them into the nog. Top with nutmeg.

LEPRECHAUN

2 oz. Irish whiskey
Tonic Water

Pour the Irish whiskey into a glass; add ice and fill with tonic water. Touch up with a twist of lemon with its peel.

LIBERAL

1 oz. whiskey
1 oz. sweet vermouth
Several dashes Amer Picon
1-2 dashes orange bitters

Combine with ice; shake. Strain and add ice.

LIBERTY

1½ oz. apple brandy
1 tbs. white rum
A few drops sugar syrup

Combine with ice; shake. Strain and add ice.

LIEBFRAUMILCH

1¼ oz. white creme de cacao
1¼ oz. heavy cream
3 tsp. lime juice

Combine with ice; shake well. Strain straight up.

LIL NAUE

¾ oz. cognac
¾ oz. port
¾ oz. apricot brandy
1 egg yolk
1½ tsp. sugar syrup

Combine with ice; shake. Strain. Add ice and a twist of lemon with its peel. Top with cinnamon.

LILLET COCKTAIL

1½ oz. Lillet
1 tbs. gin

Combine with ice; shake. Strain. Add ice and a twist of lemon with its peel. For a **LILLET NOYAUX,** *follow the recipe for a* **LILLET COCKTAIL** *and add a teaspoon of creme de noyaux before shaking.*

LIME DAIQUIRI

1½ oz. white rum
2 tsp. lime liqueur
2 tsp. lime juice

Combine with ice; shake well. Strain. Add ice and a twist of lime with its peel.

LIME RUM PUNCH

1 bottle white rum
8 o z. lime juice
8 oz. sugar
8 oz. water

Combine the sugar with the water in a saucepan and heat until blended. Allow to cool before combining with the rum and juice. Add ice.

LIME RUM SHRUB

1 quart Jamaican rum
8 oz. lime juice
1½ cups of sugar dissolved in 2½ cups of water

Combine in a large bottle; mix, seal tightly, and allow to stand for a week. Serve straight up or over ice.

LIMEY

1 oz. white rum
1½ tbs. lime liqueur
2 tsp. Triple Sec
2 tsp. lime juice
3 oz. crushed ice

Combine in a blender at low speed for 15 seconds. Strain straight up. Add a twist of lime with its peel.

LINSTEAD

1½ oz. whiskey
1½ oz. pineapple juice
A few drops Pernod
Several drops lemon juice
½ tsp. sugar syrup
A few dashes of Angostura bitters

Combine with ice; shake. Strain. Add ice and a twist of lemon.

LITTLE DEVIL

¾ oz. dry gin
¾ oz. gold rum
1 tsp. Triple Sec
Several drops lemon juice

Combine with ice; shake. Strain and add ice.

LITTLE PRINCESS

1¼ oz. gold rum
1¼ oz. sweet vermouth

Combine with ice; shake. Strain and add ice.

LOCH LOMOND

1½ oz. Scotch
1½ tsp. sugar syrup
A few dashes Angostura bitters

Combine with ice; shake. Strain and add ice.

LOCOMOTIVE

1 quart hard cider
3 eggs
Sugar
Cinnamon sticks

Bring the cider almost to a boil. Beat the eggs in a large bowl; slowly pour the cider over the eggs, an oz. at a time. Stir constantly. Add sugar; stir until the sugar dissolves. Serve warm in mugs, using cinnamon sticks as swizzlers.

LOLITA

1½ oz. tequila
3 tsp. lime juice
1 tsp. honey
A few dashes of Angostura bitters

Combine with ice; shake. Strain and add ice.

LOLLIPOP

¾ oz. Cointreau
¾ oz. kirsch
1 tbs. green chartreuse
A few drops maraschino

Combine with ice; shake. Strain and add ice.

LOMA BONITA

1½ oz. tequila
3 oz. pineapple juice

Combine with ice; shake. Strain and add ice. Top with a cherry.

LONDON

1½ oz. dry gin
½ tsp. sugar syrup
1-2 dashes orange bitters
A few drops maraschino

Combine with ice; shake well. Strain, add ice and a twist of lemon plus peel.

LONDON DOCK

1½ oz. Burgundy
2 tbs. dark rum
2 tsp. sugar
A cinnamon stick, lemon peel, and nutmeg

Dissolve the sugar with a few drops of hot water in a mug; add everything else except the nutmeg. Fill with boiling water and stir. Garnish with nutmeg. Bordeaux wine can be used instead of the Burgundy.

LONDON FOG

1 tbs. white creme de menthe
1 tbs. anisette
A few dashes of Angostura bitters

Combine with ice; stir briskly to chill. Strain straight up.

LONDON SPECIAL

Champagne
1 cube sugar
A few dashes of Peychaud's bitters

Drop the sugar cube into a small goblet; add the bitters plus ice and fill with champagne. Top with a twist of orange; add the peel.

LONE TREE MARTINI

1½ oz. dry gin
1 tbs. sweet vermouth

Combine with ice; shake well. Strain straight up and top with an olive.

LOS ANGELES

1½ oz. whiskey
1½ tsp. lemon juice
1½ tsp. sugar syrup
A few drops sweet vermouth
1 egg

Combine with ice; shake. Strain and add ice.

LOS ANGELES LUV

1 oz. bourbon
1 oz. creme de banana
2 tsp. Triple Sec
2 tsp. lemon juice
2 oz. pineapple juice
3 oz. crushed ice

Combine in a blender at low speed for 15 seconds. Strain. Add ice. Decorate with pineapple.

LOUDSPEAKER

1 oz. brandy
1 tbs. gin
1 tsp. lime juice

Combine with ice; shake well. Strain and add ice.

LOUISIANA LULLABY

1½ ozs. Jamaican rum
2 tsp. Dubonnet
A few drops of Grand Marnier

Combine with ice; shake well. Strain straight up. Touch it up with a twist of lemon.

LOUISIANA PUNCH

2 bottles white Burgundy
1 pint apiece brandy, cognac, and curacao
1 pint lemon juice
1 lb. sugar
Cherries, whole strawberries, sliced pineapple
2 bottles club soda

Dissolve the sugar with the lemon juice; add the wine and liquors and stir. Add the soda plus chunks of ice; garnish with fruit.

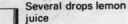

LOVE

2 oz. sloe gin
1 egg white
Several drops lemon juice
Several drops raspberry syrup

Combine with ice; shake. Strain and add ice.

LOVER'S BALM

1 quart hard cider
3 oz. cognac
2 oz. curacao
1½ oz. sugar
3 tsp. lemon juice
Grated lemon rind
Club soda

Dissolve the sugar with the lemon juice in a large pot; add the rinds, brandy, curacao, and cider. Stir until foamy and well-blended. Store in the refrigerator until ready to use. Serve with ice and soda.

LOVER'S DELIGHT

¾ oz. Cointreau
¾ oz. cognac
¾ oz. Forbidden Fruit

Combine with ice; shake well. Strain and add ice.

LUCHOW'S GRAND PRIZE

1 oz. bourbon
1 oz. cherry liqueur
1 oz. lime juice

Combine with ice; shake. Strain and add ice.

LUGGER

1 oz. brandy
1 oz. calvados
A few drops apricot brandy

Combine with ice; shake well. Strain; add ice and a twist of orange.

YOUR OWN RECIPE

YOUR OWN RECIPE

Use a bartender's mixing glass whenever the instructions state "combine" ingredients. Strain the drink from the mixing glass into the drinking glass suggested by the illustration alongside the ingredients.

The glass pictured for each drink is our suggestion; other drinking cups may be used as well.

MABI PUNCH

1 oz. mabi bark, crushed
1 oz. whole ginger
A cinnamon stick
5 cups brown sugar

Clean the bark, slice the ginger and boil with the cinnamon stick in 1½ cups of water for 5 minutes; strain, cool and chill. Boil the brown sugar in 3 qts. of water; add mabi brew and stir to blend. Strain into a large pot; strain and ladle until foamy. Loosely top the pot or cap lightly in a bottle. Allow to ferment for several days. Store uncovered in the refrigerator until ready to use.

MACARONI

1½ oz. Pernod
2 tsp. sweet vermouth

Combine with ice; shake well. Strain and add ice.

MACKINNON

1½ oz. Drambuie
1½ tsp. white rum
1½ tsp. lime juice
Several drops lemon juice
Club soda

Combine everything except the soda with ice; shake well. Strain; add ice and fill the glass with club soda.

MADEIRA MINT FLIP

1½ oz. Madeira
1 tbs. chocolate mint liqueur
1½ tsp. sugar syrup
1 egg

Combine with ice; shake extremely well. Strain and add ice with nutmeg.

MADEIRA PUNCH

1 bottle Madeira
1 quart club soda
4 oz. brandy
Powdered sugar
Sliced peaches, strawberries, lemons and oranges

Combine the Madeira and the brandy and sugar to taste. Decorate with fruit. Add the club soda plus chunks of ice.

MADISON AVENUE

2 oz. vodka
2 oz. clam juice
2 oz. tomato juice
A few drops of lemon juice
1-2 dashes Worchestershire sauce
A pinch of salt

Combine with ice; shake. Strain straight up.

MAHUKONA

1 oz. white rum
2 tsp. Triple Sec
2 tsp. lemon juice
A few drops of rock candy syrup
A few dashes of Angostura bitters
A pineapple slice
Mint sprigs

Combine everything except the pineapple slice with ice; shake. Strain over crushed ice. Garnish with the pineapple slice and mint.

MAI KAI NO

1 oz. white rum
1 oz. 151-proof rum
2 tsp. Jamaican rum
2 tsp. passion fruit juice
2 tsps. honey
1 shot lime juice
A few dashes of Angostura bitters
Club soda
Mint sprigs
1 pineapple stick

Combine (except soda and garnishes) over crushed ice. Touch up with a spritz of soda and top with pineapple stick and a few mint sprigs.

MAIDEN'S BLUSH

1½ oz. dry gin
1 tsp. curacao
Several drops grenadine
A few drops lemon juice

Combine with ice; shake well. Strain and add ice.

MAIDEN'S KISS

Combine equal parts curacao, maraschino, Benedictine, yellow chartreuse and Creme de Roses in a pony glass and stir gently.

MAIDEN'S PRAYER

¾ oz. gin
¾ oz. Cointreau
1 tsp. lemon juice
1 tsp. orange juice

Combine with ice; shake well. Strain and add ice. Lillet can be used in instead of the Cointreau, with 2 teaspoons each of calvados and apricot brandy instead of the juices.

MAINBRACE

¾ oz. gin
¾ oz. Triple Sec
1 tbs. grape juice

Combine with ice; shake well. Strain and add ice.

MAI-TAI

3 oz. white rum
2 tsp. lime juice
1 tsp. Triple Sec
1 tsp. almond extract
1 tsp. sugar syrup
1 mint sprig
1 pineapple stick

Combine (except the mint and the pineapple stick) with ice; shake. Strain and add lots of ice. Top with the mint, pineapple stick and a lime slice.

MAI-TAI NO. 2

2 oz. Jamaican rum
1½ tbs. lime juice
2 tsp. curacao
2 tsp. apricot brandy
1 pineapple stick

Combine (except the pineapple stick) with ice; shake well. Strain and add ice. Top with pineapple stick.

MAJOR BAILEY

2 oz. gin
1 tsp. powdered sugar
Several drops of lime juice
Several mint leaves

Muddle the sugar, juice and leaves on the bottom of a julep glass. Fill with crushed ice; pour in the gin and stir briskly until the glass begins to frost.

MAMIE TAYLOR

3 oz. Scotch
1 tbs. lime juice
Ginger ale

Combine the Scotch and the lime juice; add ice and fill with ginger ale. Stir gently and decorate with a lemon slice.

MANANA

1½ oz. white rum
2 tsp. apricot brandy
1 tsp. lemon juice
1 tsp. grenadine

Combine with ice; shake. Strain and add ice.

MANDARIN FIZZ

1½ oz. gin
1½ oz. mandarin juice
2 tsp. sugar syrup
Club soda

Combine everything except the soda with ice; shake. Strain. Add ice and fill with soda. Decorate with a mandarin slice.

MANDEVILLE

1½ oz. white rum
1 oz. Jamaican rum
1 tbs. lemon juice
2 tsp. cola
1 tsp. Pernod

Combine with ice; shake. Strain and add ice. Top with an orange slice.

MANGO COOLER

1½ oz. vodka
3 oz. mango nectar
2 tbs. orange juice
2 tsp. lemon juice
2 tsp. Cointreau
Mango slices

Combine (except the fruit slices) with ice; shake. Strain; add lots of ice. Top with mango or orange slices.

MANGO DAIQUIRI

2 oz. white rum
1½ oz. lime juice
1 oz. curacao
1 tbs. powdered sugar
4 oz. pureed mango
8 oz. crushed ice

Combine in a blender at a low speed for 15 seconds. Strain straight up. Serve with straws. Serves two.

MANGO MINT

1 oz. rum
1½ oz. mango nectar
2 tsp. white creme de menthe
3 oz. crushed ice

Combine in a blender at low speed for 15 seconds. Strain and add ice.

MANHASSET

1½ oz. whiskey
2 tsp. lemon juice
1 tsp. dry vermouth
1 tsp. sweet vermouth

Combine with ice; shake. Strain. Add ice and a twist of lemon with its peel.

MANHATTAN

2½ oz. rye
1 oz. sweet vermouth

Combine and stir. Top with a cherry. There are many variations to the MANHATTAN. Some people prefer less vermouth and a dash of bitters. Others use a different kind of whiskey rather than rye, still others like a dash of Benedictine tossed in for effect. For a DRY MANHATTAN use dry vermouth instead of sweet, with a twist of lemon peel or an olive in place of the cherry; A SPANISH MANHATTAN is made with dry sherry instead of vermouth.

MANHATTAN COOLER

4 oz. claret
2½ oz. lemon juice
A few drops gold rum
2 tsp. sugar syrup

Combine; add ice and stir well. Top with fruit slices

MANHATTAN MANEATER

1½ oz. whiskey
2 tbs. Southern Comfort
1-2 dashes orange bitters

Combine with ice; shake. Strain and add ice; garnish with a cherry.

MANHATTAN VIEUX CARRE

2 oz. bourbon
1 oz. sweet vermouth
a few drops of sugar syrup

Combine without ice; stir to blend and refrigerate in a small sealed jar for a day or two. Serve straight up with a cherry.

MARASCHINO PUNCH

1 bottle sweet wine
2 pints brandy
1½ oz. maraschino
Red and green cherries

Combine the wine, brandy and maraschino stir. Add chunks of ice. Decorate with cherries.

MARCIA DELANO

2 oz. Puerto Rican rum
1 oz. brandy
1 egg
1 tbs. sugar

Beat the egg with the sugar until foamy; combine it with the brandy and the rum; add boiling water and stir. Top with nutmeg.

MARCONI WIRELESS

1½ oz. apple brandy
1 tbs. sweet vermouth
1-2 dashes orange bitters

Combine with ice; shake. Strain and add ice.

MARGARET DUFFY

1½ oz. Swedish Punch
2 tsp. brandy
A few dashes of Angostura bitters

Combine with ice; shake. Strain and add ice.

MARGUERITA

2 oz. tequila
2 tsp. Cointreau
1 tbs. lime juice
½ lime

Combine (except the lime) with ice, shake well. Rub the lime around the rim of glass and press it in salt. Strain straight up.

MARIA THERESA

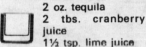

2 oz. tequila
2 tbs. cranberry juice
1½ tsp. lime juice

Combine with ice; shake. Strain and add ice.

MARQUISE PUNCH

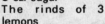

1 quart sauterne
1 pint cognac
8 oz. sugar
The rinds of 3 lemons
A few whole cloves
Cinnamon sticks

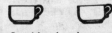

Combine in a large saucepan; heat and stir but do not boil. Serve hot and spicy.

223

MARSALA MARTINI

¾ oz. dry Marsala
¾ oz. gin
1 tbs. dry vermouth

Combine with ice; shake. Strain straight up; add a twist of lemon plus the peel.

MARTINEZ COCKTAIL

2 oz. Old Tom gin
3 oz. dry vermouth
A few drops maraschino
A few dashes of Angostura bitters

Combine with ice; shake. Strain and add ice.

MARTINI

2 oz. gin
1 tsp. dry vermouth

Combine straight up and stir with an olive. **MARTINIS** *can be made stronger and dryer (less vermouth) or weaker and dryer (more vermouth) or sweeter (half sweet, half dry vermouth). They can also be made with vodka instead of gin. Can be served on the rocks too. A twist of lemon or orange can be used instead of the olive. For a* **MARTINI, HOLLAND STYLE,** *use Dutch genever gin. For a* **MARTINI MAJADOR,** *use tequila instead of gin.*

MARTINIQUE MILK PUNCH

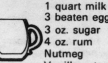

1 quart milk
3 beaten egg yolks
3 oz. sugar
4 oz. rum
Nutmeg
Vanilla extract

Bring the milk almost to a boil. Remove from heat; add the yolks and sugar, plus nutmeg and vanilla to taste. Stir until the sugar is dissolved. Pour in the rum; stir and serve piping hot. Touch up with a twist of lemon plus the peel.

MARY GARDEN

1½ oz. Dubonnet
1 tbs. dry vermouth

Combine with ice; shake. Strain and add ice. Equal parts Dubonnet and vermouth can be used if you like.

MARY PICKFORD

1½ oz. white rum
1½ oz. pineapple juice
Several drops grenadine
Several drops maraschino

Combine with ice; shake. Strain and add ice.

MATADOR

1 oz. tequila
2 oz. pineapple juice
1 tbs. lime juice

Combine with ice; shake. Strain and add ice.

MATINEE

1 oz. gin
2 tsp. sambuca
2 tsp. lime juice
½ egg white
1 tsp. heavy cream

Combine with ice; shake extremely well. Strain and add ice.

MAUI COCKTAIL

1 oz. vodka
½ oz. banana liqueur
2 tsp. pineapple juice concentrate
1 tsp. lemon juice

Combine with ice; shake well. Strain over crushed ice.

MAURICE

1½ oz. dry gin
1 tbs. sweet vermouth
1 tbs. dry vermouth
A few dashes of Angostura bitters

Combine with ice; shake. Strain and add ice.

MAXIM

1½ oz. dry gin
1 tbs. dry vermouth
A few drops white creme de cacao

Combine with ice; shake. Strain and add ice.

MAY BLOSSOM FIZZ

1½ oz. Swedish Punch
1½ oz. lemon juice
1 tsp. grenadine
Club soda

Combine (except the soda) with ice; shake. Strain, add ice and fill with soda.

MAY COCKTAIL

1½ oz. whiskey
1 tsp. kirschwasser
1 tsp. strawberry liqueur
May wine

Combine (except the wine) with ice; shake well. Strain, add ice and wine. Top with a lemon slice.

MAY WINE BOWL

2 bottles white wine
4 oz. sugar
8 oz. clean, whole small strawberries
Fresh woodruff

Cover the woodruff with the sugar in a small glass and allow to stand for several hours. Add 2 cups of wine to the sugar and woodruff and allow to stand again, overnight. Turn out the sweetened wine into a large punch bowl; add the remaining wine plus chunks of ice immediately before serving. Decorate with the strawberries.

McBRANDY

1½ oz. brandy
1 tbs. apple juice
1 tsp. lemon juice

Combine with ice; shake well. Strain and add ice. Top with a lemon slice.

McCLELLAND

1½ oz. sloe gin
1 tbs. curacao
1-2 dashes orange bitters

Combine with ice; shake. Strain and add ice.

McCRORY

1 oz. whiskey
A few dashes of Angostura bitters
Powdered sugar
Club soda

Combine the whiskey and the bitters; add sugar to taste and stir until it is dissolved. Add soda and ice.

McKINLEY'S DELIGHT

1½ oz. whiskey
1 tbs. sweet vermouth
A few drops Pernod
Several drops cherry brandy

Combine with ice; shake well. Strain and add ice.

MEAD

4 cups honey
8 oz. brown sugar
4 egg whites
A package of dry, active yeast
1½ oz. lemon juice
Grated lemon rind
Several pinches of mace
Ground cloves, nutmeg, ginger, cinnamon, pepper and rosemary

Combine everything except the yeast in a large pot and simmer for at least one hour in 2 gals. of water. Remove from heat and strain; add the yeast when lukewarm. Turn out the brew into a crock pot; seal tightly and allow to ferment for several months. Strain and bottle for future use. Serve ice cold.

MEDIEVAL PUNCH

5 cups port
6 oz. sugar
2 tsp. orange liqueur
Grated nutmeg, whole cloves, cinnamon
2 oz. brandy
2 large oranges, sliced

Combine the wine with the fruit slices and spices in a saucepan; add the sugar, stir and simmer until the sugar has dissolved. Add 2 cups of boiling water, the orange liqueur, and the brandy; heat thoroughly but do not allow to boil. Serve warm and unstrained.

226

MEETINGHOUSE PUNCH

Serves hundreds. You'd better have a good reason to use it, or you risk arrest.

4 kegs of beer
24 gallons Jamaican rum
35 gallons white rum
7 gallons sugar syrup
25 lbs. brown sugar
Enough lemons to fill a wheelbarrow

Combine in a large punch bowl a little at a time, i.e. a tenth of everything, and keep replenishing it — or prepare a dozen or so punch bowls at the same time. Make sure you have plenty of volunteers and a mixing system well beforehand.

MELON COCKTAIL

2 oz. dry gin
A few drops lemon juice
A few drops maraschino

Combine with ice; shake. Strain and add ice. Top with a cherry.

MELON PRESERVE

1 large melon cantalope, cranshaw or honeydew
3 cups sugar
1½ oz. brandy
1½ tsp. lemon juice

Slice and dice the melon meat; cook in enough water to cover until soft. Combine in a bowl with the lemon juice and brandy; allow to stand several hours. Boil the sugar in enough water to make a syrup; add the melon meat and cook a few more mins. Allow to stand overnight, then cook again until clear. Allow to cool before bottling for future use.

MERRY WIDOW

1½ oz. sherry
2 tbs. sweet vermouth

Combine with ice; shake. Strain. Add ice and a twist of lemon; plus the peel.

MERRY WIDOW No. 2

1½ oz. cherry brandy
1½ oz. maraschino

Combine with ice; shake well. Strain and add ice. Top with a cherry.

MERRY WIDOWER

1 oz. dry gin
1 oz. dry vermouth
Several drops Pernod
A few drops Benedictine
1-2 dashes Peychaud's bitters

Combine with ice; shake well. Strain add ice and a twist of lemon.

METROPOLITAN

1½ oz. brandy
1½ oz. sweet vermouth
½ tsp. sugar syrup
A few dashes of Angostura bitters

Combine with ice; shake well. Strain. Add ice.

MEURICE COCKTAIL

1 oz. vodka
1 oz. creme de banana
1 oz. heavy cream

Combine with ice; shake. Strain straight up.

MEXICAN FLAG

2 oz. tequila
1 tbs. sugar syrup
2 tsp. lime juice
1 green grape
1 small scoop vanilla ice cream

Combine the tequila, sugar and juice with ice; shake. Strain and add plenty of ice. Top with the grape, vanilla ice cream and a cherry.

MEXICANO

2 oz. white rum
2 tsp. kummel
2 tsp. orange juice
A few dashes of Angostura bitters

Combine with ice; shake. Strain and add ice.

MEXICO MARTINI

1½ oz. tequila
1 tbs. dry vermouth
A few drops vanilla extract

Combine with ice; shake well. Strain and add ice.

MEXICO PACIFICO

1½ oz. tequila
1 oz. passion fruit juice
2 tsp. lime juice
3 oz. crushed ice

Combine in blender at a low speed for 15 seconds. Strain straight up and top with a lime slice.

MEXITINI

1½ oz. dry vermouth
1 tbs. tequila
1 chili bean

Combine the vermouth and the tequila and stir. Top with the bean.

MIAMI BEACH

¾ oz. Scotch
¾ oz. dry vermouth
1 tbs. grapefruit juice

Combine with ice; shake. Strain and add ice.

MIAMI SUNSET

2 oz. bourbon
1 oz. Triple Sec
1 tsp. grenadine
Orange juice

Combine the bourbon and the Triple Sec with ice; shake. Strain; add ice and the orange juice. Stir and float the grenadine.

MIDNIGHT COCKTAIL

1 oz. apricot brandy
2 tsp. curacao
2 tsp. lemon juice

Combine with ice; shake. Strain and add ice.

MIDNIGHT SUN

1½ oz. aquavit
2 tsp. unsweetened grapefruit juice
1½ tsp. sugar syrup
A few drops grenadine

Combine with ice; shake well. Strain straight up and with an orange slice.

MIKADO

1¼ oz. brandy
A few drops curacao
A few drops almond extract
1-2 dashes creme de noyaux
A few dashes of Angostura bitters

Combine with ice; shake well. Strain and add ice.

MILITARY CUP

1 bottle claret
3 oz. Benedictine
3 oz. cherry bounce
2 oz. lemon juice
Mint sprigs
A few drops of cognac
4 oz. sugar
Grated lemon rind
Whole strawberries
1 bottle club soda

Dilute the claret with 2 quarts of water in a large punch bowl; add the sugar, juice and rind. Stir well until the sugar has dissolved. Add the Benedictine, cherry bounce, and cognac. Add the soda plus chunks. Garnish with strawberries and mint.

MILK LEMONADE

12 oz. milk
6 oz. sugar
4 oz. lemon juice
4 oz. sherry

Dissolve the sugar with a pint of boiling water; remove from heat and add the lemon juice and sherry. Allow to cool. Add the milk and strain through cloth until clear.

MILK PUNCH

2½ oz. rum
1 tsp. sugar
Milk

Combine the rum and the sugar with ice; shake well. Strain; add ice and fill with milk. Brandy or whiskey can be used instead of rum.

MILLIONAIRE

1½ oz. gin
1 tbs. Pernod
1 egg white
A few drops anisette

Combine with ice; shake. Strain and add ice.

MILLIONAIRE NO. 2

1½ oz. bourbon
2 tsp. curacao
1 egg white
A few grenadine

Combine with ice; shake. Strain and add ice.

MILLIONS COCKTAIL

1½ oz. gin
1 tbs. sweet vermouth
2 tsp. pineapple juice
1 egg white
Several drops grenadine

Combine with ice; shake. Strain and add ice.

MINT CORDIAL

2 bottles brandy
2 large bunches fresh mint
Sugar

Combine half the mint (whole) and half the brandy in a crock pot and allow to stand for several days. Add the remaining mint and brandy, plus at least a pint of water and sugar to taste. Strain and bottle to use as a cordial.

MINT DELIGHT

4 oz. white creme de menthe
6 oz. vanilla ice cream
4 oz. light cream

Combine in a blender at high speed until smooth. Serve straight up.

MINT JULEP PUNCH

8 oz. rum
8 oz. cold water
4 oz. powdered sugar
4 doz. mint sprigs
2 bottles bourbon

Muddle the mint leaves with the water, rum and sugar; strain carefully into a punch bowl filled with ice. Pour in the bourbon and stir.

MINT TEQUILA

1½ oz. tequila
2 tsp. lemon juice
1½ tsp. sugar syrup
½ doz. mint leaves, torn
4 oz. crushed ice

Combine in a blender at a low speed for 15 seconds. Strain into an old-fashioned glass and add ice.

MISSISSIPPI MULE

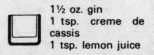

1½ oz. gin
1 tsp. creme de cassis
1 tsp. lemon juice

Combine with ice; shake. Strain and add ice.

MISSISSIPPI PUNCH

1½ oz. rum
1 oz. whiskey
1 oz. brandy
1½ tsp. sugar syrup
Several drops lemon
juice
A few dashes of
Angostura bitters

*Combine with ice; shake.
Strain and add plenty of ice.
Top with fruit.*

MISTS

MISTS *are frappes served up
in old-fashioned glasses.
Straight* **MISTS** *are the most
simple — 2 oz. of Scotch,
bourbon or brandy over 4 oz.
of well-packed crushed ice;
add a twist of lemon plus the
peel.*

MISTY MANHATTAN

2 ozs. Canadian Mist
whiskey
1 tbs. sweet ver-
mouth
A few dashes of
Angostura bitters

*Combine with ice; shake.
Strain and decorate with a
cherry.*

MIXED BLESSING

4 oz. pineapple juice
2 tbs. gold rum
2 tbs. crushed
pineapple
2 tsp. 151-proof rum
1 tbs. Falernum
A few drops lime
juice
2 oz. crushed ice

*Combine in a blender at high
speed until smooth.*

MIXED MOCHA FRAPPE

¾ oz. Kahlua
1 tsp. white creme
de menthe
1 tsp. white creme
de cacao
1 tsp. Triple Sec

*Combine without ice and stir.
"Sugarfrost" the rim with
water. Pour over crushed ice.*

MOBILE MULE

2 oz. white rum
1½ tsp. lime juice
Ginger beer

*Combine the rum and the
lime juice with ginger beer,
and stir. Add ice; touch up
with a twist of lime plus the
peel.*

MOCHA MINT

¾ oz. Kahlua
¾ oz. white creme
de menthe
¾ oz. white creme
de cacao

*Combine with ice; shake.
Strain and add ice.*

MOCKINGBIRD

1½ oz. tequila
1 oz. lime juice
1 tbs. white creme
de menthe

*Combine with ice; shake.
Strain straight up. Top with a
lime slice.*

231

MODERN

1½ oz. sloe gin
1 tbs. Scotch
A few drops Pernod
A few drops grenadine
1-2 dashes orange bitters

Combine with ice; shake well. Strain into an old-fashioned glass and add ice.

MODERN NO. 2

3 oz. Scotch
A few drops Jamaican rum, Pernod and lemon juice
1-2 dashes orange bitters

Combine with ice; shake. Strain and add ice. Top with a cherry.

MODERN LEMONADE

1½ oz. sloe gin
1½ oz. sherry
3 oz. lemonade
3 tbs. sugar syrup
Club soda

Combine (except the soda) with ice; shake well. Strain; add ice and soda. Touch up with a twist of lemon plus the peel.

MOJITO

2 oz. white rum
1½ tsp. lime juice
1½ tsp. sugar syrup
Club soda
Mint leaves

Combine the rum, lime juice and sugar with equal parts crushed ice and club soda; stir. Top with mint leaves.

MOLDAU

1½ oz. gin
2 tsp. plum brandy
1 tsp. orange juice
1 tsp. lemon juice
1 brandied cherry

Combined with ice; shake. Strain and add ice. Top with the cherry.

MONAHAN

1½ oz. whiskey
1 tbs. sweet vermouth
1-2 dashes Amer Picon

Combine; add ice and stir.

MONKEY GLAND

1½ oz. gin
1 tbs. orange juice
A few drops Benedictine
A few drops grenadine

Combine with ice; shake. Strain and add ice.

MONTANA

2 oz. cognac
2 tsp. dry vermouth
2 tsp. port

Combine; add ice and stir.

MONTE CARLO

1¼ oz. rye
½ tbs. Benedictine
A few dashes of Angostura bitters

Combine with ice; shake. Strain and add ice.

MONTMARTRE

1½ oz. gin
2 tsp. Triple Sec
2 tsp. sweet vermouth

Combine with ice; shake. Strain and add ice. Top with a cherry.

MONTREAL CLUB BOUNCER

1½ oz. gin
1½ oz. Pernod

Combine, add ice and stir.

MONTREAL GIN SOUR

2 oz. gin
2 tsp. lemon juice
1 tsp. sugar syrup
1 egg white

Combine with ice; shake. Strain and add ice.

MOOD INDIGO

3 ozs. peppermint schnapps
3 ozs. milk
1 tbs. unflavored gelatin
3 ozs. crushed ice

Heat the milk and combine it with the gelatin in a blender at a high speed for 30 seconds. Add the schnapps, chips, and ice, and blend another 30 seconds. Refrigerate until set.

MOONGLOW

1½ oz. brandy
1½ oz. white creme de menthe

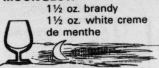

Combine without ice; stir until blended. Keep chilled. Serve straight up.

MOONLIGHT

3 oz. calvados
3 tsp. lemon juice
2 tsp. sugar syrup
Club soda

Combine (except the soda) with ice; shake. Strain; add ice and soda. Top with fruit slices.

MORNING

1 oz. brandy
1 oz. dry vermouth
A few drops Pernod, maraschino and curacao
1-2 dashes orange bitters

Combine with ice; shake. Strain and add ice. Top with a cherry.

MORNING AFTER

3 oz. Pernod
1 tsp. anisette
1 egg white
Club soda

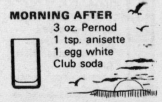

Combine (except the soda) with ice; shake. Strain and add ice. Touch it up with a spritz of soda.

233

MORNING GLORY

1 oz. Scotch
1 oz. brandy
A few drops curacao
1 dash Pernod
1-2 dashes Angostura bitters
½ tsp. sugar syrup
Club soda
Powdered sugar

Combine (except the soda and powdered sugar) with ice; shake well. Strain, add ice and soda. Stir with a wet spoon coated with powdered sugar.

MORNING GLORY FIZZ

2 oz. Scotch
2 tsp. lemon juice
1½ tsp. sugar syrup
1 tsp. Pernod
½ egg white
1-2 dashes Peychaud's bitters
Club soda

Combine (except the soda) with ice; shake. Strain; add ice and soda. Top with a lemon slice.

MORNING SUN

1½ oz. gin
2 tbs. grapefruit juice
2 tbs. orange juice
1-2 dashes Angostura bitters
A few drops cherry juice

Combine with ice; shake. Strain and add ice.

MOROCCAN COCKTAIL

1 oz. gin
1 oz. Cointreau
1 oz. mandarin liqueur

Combine with ice; shake well. Strain straight up.

MORRO

1 oz. gin
2 tsp. gold rum
2 tsp. lime juice
2 tsp. pineapple juice
1 tsp. sugar syrup
Falernum
Sugar

Combine everything except the Falernum and sugar in a mixing glass filled with ice; shake well. "Sugarfrost" the rim of a glass with Falernum. Strain in the drink; add ice if desired.

MOSCOW MULE

1½ oz. vodka
1½ tsp. lime juice
Ginger beer
1 cucumber peel

Combine the vodka and the lime juice with ice; shake. Strain add ice and top with the peel or lime slice. Ginger ale can be used instead of ginger beer. Decorate with the peel or a slice of lime.

MOSELLE PUNCH

1 bottle Moselle wine
½ gallon frozen lemon sherbet

Combine stir until smooth. Serve while ice cold.

MOSELLE SUPPER

1 bottle chilled Moselle
1 bottle chilled sparkling Moselle
3 ripe peaches, peeled, pitted and quartered
1½ oz. Benedictine
1 doz. cherries

Combine the plain Moselle and the Benedictine; add the fruit plus plenty of ice. Add the sparkling Moselle immediately before serving.

MOTHER SHERMAN

1½ oz. apricot brandy
1 tbs. orange juice
Several dashes orange bitters

Combine with ice; shake. Strain and add ice.

MOULIN ROUGE

1½ oz. sloe gin
1 tbs. sweet vermouth
A few dashes of Angostura bitters

Combine with ice; shake. Strain and add ice.

MOUNT FUJI

1½ oz. gin
3 tsp. lemon juice
2 tsp. heavy cream
1 tsp. pineapple juice
1 egg white
A few drops maraschino

Combine with ice; shake. Strain straight up; garnish with cherry.

MOUNTAIN

1½ oz. whiskey
A few drops lemon juice
A few drops of dry and sweet vermouths
1 egg white

Combine with ice; shake. Strain and add ice.

MS. MANHATTAN

2½ oz. dry gin
1 tsp. orange juice
1 tsp. sugar syrup
A few drops lemon juice
A few mint leaves, crushed

Combine with ice; shake. Strain and add ice.

MULBERRY WINE

3 quarts ripe mulberries
3 lbs. brown sugar
1½ lbs. raisins
2 tsp. gelatin dissolved in a few drops of hard cider

Crush the mulberries. Boil the sugar in 1½ gals. of water for 15 minutes, skimming constantly until clear. Add the crushed berries, allow to cool and strain. Combine the sweetened juice with the raisins and dissolved gelatin in a large cask or jar. Store until fermentation has stopped; strain and bottle for future use.

MULE'S HIND LEG

½ oz. gin
½ oz. apple brandy
2 tsp. Benedictine
2 tsp. apricot brandy
2 tsp. maple syrup

Combine with ice; shake. Strain and add ice.

MULLED CIDER

3 pints hard cider
4 oz. rum
3 oz. sugar
Cinnamon sticks
Allspice

Combine in a large pot; heat but do not allow to boil; stir constantly. Strain clean and serve hot.

MULLED CLARET

5 oz. claret
1½ tsp. lemon juice
1 cube sugar
1-2 dashes orange bitters
Ground cinnamon

Dissolve the sugar with 2 oz. of boiling water. Stir in the remaining ingredients and mull with a red-hot poker before serving.

MULLED WINE WITH EGGS

12 eggs, separated
2 bottles dry red wine
1 bottle spring water

Heat the wine with the water in a large saucepan. Scramble the yolks and beat the egg whites until dry but not stiff; combine them and slowly stir into the wine just before the wine reaches the boiling point. Serve piping hot. Top with nutmeg.

MURPHY'S DREAM (for three)

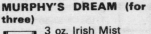

3 oz. Irish Mist
3 oz. gin
3 oz. lemon juice
Several dashes orange bitters
1 egg white

Combine with ice; shake. Strain; add ice.

MULLED VERMONT CIDER

2 quarts sweet cider
8 oz. apple brandy
Cinnamon sticks, ground cloves, allspice
1 tbs. brown sugar

Dissolve the sugar with the cider in a large saucepan; bring to a boil. Wrap spices in a cloth bag and infuse in the boiling cider for 15 minutes, stirring constantly. In a separate pot, warm the brandy. When the spices have saturated, remove them; add the warm brandy and stir. Serve piping hot in mugs.

MUSCADINE WINE

2 quarts muscadine juice
3 cups sugar
4 oz. hop yeast

Combine the juice with the sugar in a large pot; add 2 pints of water. Heat and stir until the sugar has dissolved. Remove from heat. Add the yeast when lukewarm; cover tightly and allow to ferment for a week and a half. Recook until smooth; strain and re-bottle. Store for several months; re-strain and bottle for use.

MUSCATEL FLIP

2 oz. brandy
2 oz. muscatel
1 tbs. heavy cream
1½ tsp. sugar syrup
1 egg
4 oz. crushed ice

Combine in blender at a high speed for a half minute. Strain; top with nutmeg.

MUSKMELON

1½ oz. white rum
2 oz. sliced ripe cantalope
2 tsp. lime juice
2 tsp. orange juice
1 tsp. sugar syrup
3 oz. crushed ice
1 small cantalope ball

Combine (except the cantalope ball) in blender at a low speed for 15 seconds. Strain straight up and top with the cantalope ball, speared and bridged across the glass.

MYRTLE BANK PUNCH

1½ oz. 151-proof rum
1½ tbs. lime juice
1½ tsp. sugar syrup
1 tsp. maraschino

Combine (except the maraschino) with ice; shake. Strain over crushed ice and float the maraschino on top.

YOUR OWN RECIPE

YOUR OWN RECIPE

Use a bartender's mixing glass whenever the instructions state "combine" ingredients. Strain the drink from the mixing glass into the drinking glass suggested by the illustration alongside the ingredients.

The glass pictured for each drink is our suggestion; other drinking cups may be used as well.

NAPOLEON

3 oz. gin
A few drops Dubonnet, curacao and Fernet Branca

Combine with ice, shake and strain. Serve over ice.

NARRAGANSETT

1½ oz. whiskey
1 tbs. sweet vermouth
A few drops anisette

Combine; add ice and stir.

NAVY GROG

1 oz. Jamaican rum
2 tsp. white rum, lime juice, orange juice, pineapple juice and guava nectar
1 tsp. Falernum
A few large mint leaves
4 oz. crushed ice

Combine (except the mint leaves) in a blender at a low speed for 15 seconds. Strain; add ice and top with the mint leaves, partially torn.

NAVY PUNCH

1 pint dark rum
1 pint cognac
1 pint Southern Comfort
4 bottles champagne
2 cups pineapple chunks
3 oz. lemon juice
Sugar

Combine everything except the champagne stir. Add the champagne plus chunks of ice before serving.

NECTARINE COOLER

2 oz. vodka
3 oz. orange juice
2 oz. sliced ripe nectarines
1 tsp. sugar
3 oz. crushed ice
Club soda

Combine everything (except the soda and a slice of nectarine) in an electric blender at a low speed for 20 seconds. Strain; add ice and a spritz of soda. Top with the nectarine and a slice of lemon.

NEGRONI

¾ oz. Campari
¾ oz. sweet vermouth
1 tbs. gin

Combine with ice; shake. Strain and add ice. Top with a twist of lemon plus the peel.

NEGRONI COOLER

1½ oz. Campari
1½ oz. sweet vermouth
2 tbs. gin
Club soda

Combine (except the soda and orange slice) with ice; shake. Strain; add ice and club soda. Top with the orange slice.

NEGUS

1 pint port
10 cubes sugar
3 tsp. lemon juice
1 lemon twist

Rub the cubes of sugar with the lemon twist and add them with the lemon juice to the port. Pour in a quart of boiling water and stir. Top with nutmeg and serve piping hot.

NEVINS

1½ oz. bourbon
2 tsp. grapefruit juice
1 tsp. lemon juice
1 tsp. apricot liqueur
A few dashes of Angostura bitters

Combine with ice; shake. Strain and add ice.

NEW ORLEANS

1½ oz. white rum
2 tsp. lime juice
2 tsp. orange juice
1-2 dashes Peychaud's bitters
Ginger ale

Combine (except the ginger ale) with ice; shake. Strain; add ice and ginger ale. Stir and top with a lime slice.

NEW ORLEANS GIN FIZZ

2½ oz. gin
1 oz. lemon juice
2½ tsp. sugar syrup
1 tsp. heavy cream
A few drops of orange-flower water
½ egg white
Club soda

Combine (except the soda) with ice; shake. Strain; add ice and soda. Top with a lemon slice.

NEW WORLD

1¾ oz. whiskey
2 tsp. lime juice
1 tsp. grenadine

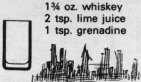

Combine with ice; shake. Strain. Add ice and a twist of lime plus the peel.

NEW YORK

2 oz. rye
1½ tbs. lime juice
1 tsp. sugar syrup
A few drops of grenadine

Combine with ice; shake. Strain. Add ice and a twist of orange plus the peel.

NEW YORK SOUR

2 oz. whiskey
1½ oz. lemon juice
1 tbs. claret
1½ tsp. sugar syrup

Combine (except the claret) with ice; shake. Strain straight up. Top with a slice of lemon or a cherry and float the claret on top.

NEWBURY

1½ oz. gin
1½ oz. sweet vermouth
A few dashes curacao

Combine with ice; shake. Strain and add ice. Top with an orange or lemon slice.

NEWTON'S APPLE COCKTAIL

1½ oz. apple brandy
2 tsp. curacao
A few dashes of Angostura bitters

Combine with ice; shake. Strain and add ice.

NICOLOSCAR

1 square slice of lemon peel
Coarse-ground coffee
Sugar
1½ oz. brandy

Place the coffee and the sugar on the lemon peel waferlike and chew it. Wash it down with the brandy.

NIGHTCAP

1 oz. brandy
1 oz. orange curacao
1 oz. anisette
1 egg yolk

Combine without ice; stir. Pour; add hot water and allow to stand a few minutes before drinking.

NIGHTMARE

¾ oz. gin
¾ oz. Dubonnet
2 tsp. cherry brandy
2 tsp. orange juice

Combine with ice; shake. Strain and add ice.

NIGHTSHADE

1½ oz. bourbon
2 tsp. sweet vermouth
2 tsp. orange juice
A few drops yellow chartreuse

Combine with ice; shake. Strain and add ice. Top with a slice of orange and lemon.

NINE-PICK

1 oz. Pernod
1 oz. brandy
1 tbs. curacao
1 egg yolk

Combine with ice; shake and strain. Serve over ice.

NINETEEN

3 oz. dry vermouth
2 tsp. gin
2 tsp. kirsch
A few drops sugar syrup
A few drops Pernod

Combine with ice; shake. Strain and add ice.

NINETEEN PICK-ME-UP

1½ oz. Pernod
1 tbs. gin
A few drops sugar syrup
1-2 dashes Angostura and orange bitters
Club soda

Combine (except the club soda) with ice; shake. Strain; add ice and a spritz of soda.

NINOTCHKA

1½ oz. vodka
2 tsp. white creme de cacao
2 tsp. lemon juice

Combine with ice; shake. Strain and add ice.

NONE BUT THE BRAVE

1½ oz. brandy
1 tbs. Pimento Dram
1½ tsp. sugar syrup
A few drops lemon juice
1 pinch ginger

Combine with ice; shake. Strain and add ice.

NORTH EXPRESS

1 oz. Canadian whiskey
1 oz. dry vermouth
1 oz. Cordial Medoc

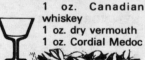

Combine without ice; stir until well-blended. Pour out over ice. Decorate with a cherry.

NUPCIAL

1 oz. tequila
1 tbs. white creme de cacao
1 tbs. white syrup
1¼ oz. evaporated milk
4 oz. crushed ice

Combine in a blender at a low speed for a minute and a half. Strain straight up and top with a cherry.

YOUR OWN RECIPE

Use a bartender's mixing glass whenever the instructions state "combine" ingredients. Strain the drink from the mixing glass into the drinking glass suggested by the illustration alongside the ingredients.

NOTE: The number of glasses or cups shown alongside a recipe do not necessarily indicate the quantity of drinks the recipe will produce.

OCHO RIOS

1½ oz. Jamaican rum
1 oz. guava nectar
2 tsp. lime juice
2 tsp. heavy cream
1 tsp. sugar syrup
3 oz. crushed ice

Combine in a blender at a low speed for 15 seconds. Strain straight up.

OGGE

1 quart beer
4 egg yolks
1½ oz. sugar

Add sugar to yolks; beat until sugar is dissolved. Heat beer in a saucepan until ready to boil. Slowly add the yolk mixture, stirring constantly. Serve immediately. Top it with nutmeg.

O'HEARN SPECIAL

2½ oz. brandy
A few mint sprigs, broken
Ginger ale

Pour the brandy; add ice, mint and ginger ale. Touch it up with a twist of lemon.

OLD BOURBON COOLER

3 oz. bourbon
2 tsp. grenadine
1 tsp. powdered sugar
A few drops white creme de menthe
A few dashes orange bitters
Club soda
1 pineapple stick

Combine (except the soda and the pineapple stick) with ice; shake. Strain; add ice and soda. Top with a slice of orange, a cherry and the pineapple stick.

OLD CASTLE PUNCH

2 bottles Rhine wine
1 pint rum
2 cups sugar

Dissolve the sugar in a quart of boiling water; reduce heat and slowly add the wine and the rum, stirring constantly. Do not boil. Serve piping hot.

OLD-FASHIONED

2½ oz. bourbon
Several drops of sugar syrup
A few dashes of Angostura bitters

Combine and stir. Top with orange slice, a cherry or a twist of lemon. Any whiskey can be used.

OLD-FASHIONED PUNCH

1 quart bourbon
1 doz. sugar cubes dipped in Angostura bitters
1½ oz. Maraschino cherry juice
A whole orange rind

Combine in a large jar; seal tightly and allow to stand for at least 36 hours. Remove the orange peel; re-cover and store in a cool place for at least three weeks. Serve over fruit slices and ice.

OLD MAN'S MILK

2 oz. Scotch
2 tsp. Drambuie
2 tsp. sugar syrup
1 egg beaten
8 oz. milk

Combine in a saucepan; heat but do not allow to boil, stirring constantly to prevent the milk from scalding.

OLD PAL

1¼ oz. whiskey
2 tsp. sweet vermouth
2 tsp. grenadine

Combine with ice; shake. Strain and add ice.

OLE

1½ oz tequila
1 oz. Kahlua
1 tbs. sugar syrup
Heavy cream

Combine everything except the cream without ice; stir until well blended. Pour over crushed ice; float a little cream.

OLYMPIC

¾ oz. brandy
¾ oz. curacao
1 tbs. orange juice

Combine with ice; shake. Strain and add ice.

ONE IRELAND

1 oz. Irish whiskey
1 tbs. green creme de menthe
2 oz. vanilla ice cream

Combine in a blender at a high speed until smooth. Serve straight up.

OOM PAUL

1 oz. calvados
1 oz. Dubonnet
A few dashes of Angostura bitters

Combine with ice; shake. Strain and add ice.

OPAL

1 oz. gin
2 tsp. orange juice
2 tsp. Triple Sec
½ tsp. sugar syrup
A few drops orange flower water

Combine with ice; shake. Strain and add ice.

OPEN HOUSE PUNCH

1 fifth Southern Comfort
3 quarts 7-UP
6 oz. lemon juice
6 oz. frozen lemonade concentrate
6 oz. frozen orange juice concentrate

Combine (except the 7-UP); stir until blended. Top with slices of fruit. Add 7-UP and chunks of ice before serving.

OPENING

1 oz. rye
2 tsp. sweet vermouth
2 tsp. grenadine

Combine with ice; shake. Strain and add ice.

OPERA

1½ oz. gin
1 tsp. Dubonnet
1 tsp. maraschino

Combine with ice; shake. Strain. Add ice and a twist of orange, plus the peel.

ORANGE BLOOM

1 oz. gin
2 tsp. Cointreau
2 tsp. sweet vermouth

Combine with ice; shake. Strain and add ice. Top with a cherry.

ORANGE BLOSSOM

1 oz. orange juice
2 tbs. gin

Combine with ice; shake. Strain and add ice. Top with orange slice.

ORANGE BLOSSOM BLENDER

2 oz. orange juice
2 tbs. gin
2 tsp. lemon juice
2 tsp. curacao
A few drops orange flower water
2 oz. crushed ice

Combine in a blender at a low speed for 10 seconds. Strain straight up and top with an orange slice.

ORANGE BUCK

1 oz. orange juice
2 tbs. gin
2 tsp. lemon juice
Ginger ale

Combine (except the ginger ale) with ice; shake. Strain; add ice and ginger ale. Top with orange slice.

ORANGE COMFORT

½ oz. Southern Comfort
½ oz. anisette
1 tbs. orange juice
2 tsp. lemon juice

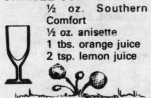

Combine, with ice; shake. Strain and add ice. Top with orange slice.

249

ORANGE COOLER IN A SHELL

1 oz. 151-proof rum
2 tsp. curacao
2 tsp. lime juice
1½ tsp. sugar syrup
1 large California orange

Slice off the top eighth of the orange and carefully cut out the fruit, leaving the skin intact; save 1½ oz. of the juice. Combine everything with the orange juice and with ice and shake. Strain into the orange shell. Serve with a straw in a bed of crushed ice.

ORANGE FIZZ

2 oz. gin
2 tbs. orange juice
2 tsp. lemon juice
2 tsp. Triple Sec
1½ tsp. sugar syrup
1-2 dashes orange bitters
Club soda

Combine all but the soda with ice; shake. Strain; add ice and the soda. Top with orange slice.

ORANGE FLOWER

1 oz. curacao
2 tsp. orange juice
2 tsp. cherry liqueur
1 tsp. lemon juice
A few drops orange flower water
3 oz. crushed ice.

Combine in a blender at a low speed for 15 seconds. Strain straight up.

ORANGE FLOWER RATAFIA

8 oz. orange blossoms
5 cups brandy
2 cups sugar

Pound the orange blossoms into a loose powder and soak them with the brandy in a pot for at least two weeks. Combine the sugar with 6 oz. of water; stir until syrupy. Add to the orange blossoms when ready. Strain and bottle for future use.

ORANGE MILK CORDIAL

1 doz. small oranges
8 oz. sugar
2 quarts milk
1 pint brandy
Grated lemon rind

Peel and separate the oranges; combine them with the milk in a large saucepan. Add lemon rind to taste; bring to a boil, stirring constantly. Boil for several minutes. Allow to cool; add the sugar and the brandy and stir until well-blended. Strain clean and bottle for future use.

ORANGE OASIS

1½ oz. gin
4 oz. orange juice
2 tsp. cherry liqueur
Ginger ale

Combine (except the ginger ale) ice; shake. Strain add ice and ginger ale. Top with orange slice.

ORANGE POSSET

1 pint white wine
8 oz. sugar
1 tsp. grated lemon rind
1 tsp. white bread, grated
2 tsp. almond paste
4 oz. brandy

Simmer the grated bread and rinds with a cup of water in a saucepan; add the sugar and allow to cool. Add the almond paste, wine and brandy. Beat until foamy and serve over ice.

ORANGE SANGAREE

4 oz. claret or Bordeaux
2 oz. orange juice
1½ oz. sugar
Club soda
2 tbs. lemon juice
A whole clove
Allspice

Combine everything except the soda with ice; shake. Chill for one hour. Strain and add ice. Fill with club soda

ORANGE VODKA

4 cups cooking alcohol
1 lb. sugar
The rinds of 2 large oranges, in pieces

Combine the fruit rinds with the alcohol in a jar or bottle; seal and allow to stand for several days in a warm place. Boil the sugar in enough water to make a syrup; combine with the rinds and alcohol when ready. Strain and bottle for future use.

ORANGE WARMER

8 oz. Grand Marnier
6 cups orange juice
6 tsp. tea leaves steeped in 6 cups of boiling water
4 oz. sugar
Whole orange slices stuck with cloves

Strain the brewed tea into a large chafing dish. Dissolve sugar in hot orange juice and combine with tea. Add the Grand Marnier and top with orange slices and cloves. Serve warm.

ORANGE WATER

½ doz. large oranges
3 oz. orange blossoms
7 pints brandy
4 pints sugar

Peel the oranges and squeeze out the juice; combine the peels and the juice with the brandy in a jar; seal and allow to stand for at least one week. Boil the sugar in enough water to make a syrup; add to the brandy when ready. Strain and bottle for future use.

ORANGE WINE
1 peck oranges
3 lbs. sugar

Squeeze the juice from the oranges and mince enough rinds to make approx. 3 ozs. of rinds. Combine the juice, minced rinds and sugar in a large kettle and bring to a boil. Allow to cool; strain clear and add another cup of fresh juice. Pour into a crock pot; seal and allow to ferment, skimming often. Bottle and store for future use.

ORCHID

2 oz. gin
1 egg white
A few drops Creme Yvette

Combine with ice; shake. Strain and add ice.

ORDINARY HIGHBALL
½ oz. rye
Club soda

Pour rye over ice; add club soda.

ORIENTAL COCKTAIL

1 oz. whiskey
2 tsp. curacao
2 tsp. sweet vermouth
1½ tsp. lime juice

Combine with ice; shake well. Strain and add ice.

OSTEND FIZZ

1½ oz. kirschwasser
2 tsp. lemon juice
2 tsp. creme de cassis
1½ tsp. sugar syrup
Club soda

Combine everything except the club soda with ice; shake well. Strain; add ice and fill the glass with soda. Decorate with a slice of lemon.

OVER HILL 'N' DALE

1½ oz. apple brandy
2 tbs. white creme de menthe
Several drops Pernod

Combine with ice; shake. Strain and add ice.

YOUR OWN RECIPE

YOUR OWN RECIPE

Use a bartender's mixing glass whenever the instructions state "combine" ingredients. Strain the drink from the mixing glass into the drinking glass suggested by the illustration alongside the ingredients.

NOTE: The number of glasses or cups shown alongside a recipe do not necessarily indicate the quantity of drinks the recipe will produce.

The glass pictured for each drink is our suggestion; other drinking cups may be used as well.

PACIFIC PACIFIER

1 oz. Cointreau
1 tbs. banana liqueur
1 tbs. light cream

Combine with ice; shake. Strain over crushed ice.

PADDY COCKTAIL

1½ oz. Irish whiskey
1½ oz. sweet vermmuth
1-2 dashes Angostura bitters

Combine with ice; shake. Strain and add ice.

PAGO PAGO

1½ oz. gold rum
2 tsp. lime juice
2 tsp. pineapple juice
A few drops green chartreuse
A few drops white creme de cacao

Combine with ice; shake. Strain and add ice.

PAISLEY MARTINI

2½ oz. gin
2 tsp. dry vermouth
1 tsp. Scotch

Combine shake well. Strain and add ice.

PALACE MARTINI

3 oz. dry gin
1 tbs. dry vermouth
1 tbs. Cordial Medoc

Combine with ice; shake. Strain straight up.

PALM BEACH

1½ oz. gin
1 tsp. sweet vermouth
½ tbs. grapefruit juice

Combine with ice; shake. Strain and add ice.

PALMETTO

1½ oz. white rum
2 tbs. sweet vermouth
1-2 dashes orange bitters

Combine with ice; shake. Strain into glass. Add ice and a twist of lemon; drop in the peel.

PANAMA

1½ oz. Jamaican rum
1 tbs. dark creme de cacao
1 tbs. heavy cream

Combine with ice; shake well. Strain into glass and add ice.

PANAMA COOLER

2 oz. Rhine wine
2 oz. dry sherry
1 oz. orange juice
1-2 dashes Angostura bitters
Club soda
2 tsp. maraschino
1 tsp. lime juice

Combine all but the soda with ice; shake. Strain into glass; add ice and soda. Top with a lemon slice.

PAN-AMERICAN

1¼ oz. rye
½ lemon
A few drops sugar syrup

Muddle the lemon with the sugar in a serving glass; add ice and the rye, and stir.

PANCHO VILLA

1 oz. white rum
1 oz. gin
1 tbs. apricot brandy
1 tsp. cherry brandy
1 tsp. pineapple juice

Combine with ice; shake. Strain into glass straight up.

PANDEMONIUM PUNCH

3 quarts pineapple juice
1½ quarts orange juice
4½ oz. lemon juice
6 oz. citric acid
8 lb. sugar
8 bottles ginger ale
Mint sprigs, crushed
Grated orange rind

Dilute the citric acid in a gallon and a half of boiling water; allow to cool. Combine in a large punch bowl with the fruit juices and sugar; stir until the sugar has dissolved. Garnish with the grated rind and mint. Add the ginger ale and ice before serving.

PANTOMIME

1½ oz. dry vermouth
A few drops almond extract
A few drops grenadine
1 egg white

Combine with ice; shake well. Strain and add ice.

PANZERWAGEN

1 oz. vodka
1 oz. gin
1 oz. Cointreau

Combine with ice; shake. Strain and add ice.

PAPAYA SLING

1½ oz. gin
3 tsp. lime juice
1 tbs. papaya syrup
Several dashes Angostura bitters
Club soda

Combine everything except the soda with ice; shake well. Strain add ice and fill the glass with soda.

PARADISE

1 oz. gin
1 oz. apricot brandy
1½ oz. orange juice

Combine with ice; shake well. Strain and add ice.

PARADISE COOLER

1 oz. white rum
1 oz. orange juice
2 tsp. Falernum
1 tsp. cherry brandy
1½ tsp. lime juice
Mint sprigs dipped in powdered sugar

Combine everything except the sprigs with ice; shake. Strain; add ice. Garnish with the powdered mint and a cherry. Serve with a straw.

PARFAIT D'ARMOUR

3 oz. lime rinds
1½ oz. lemon rinds
Rosemary sprigs
Ground cloves
Orange blossoms
2½ gallons cooking alcohol
20 cups sugar
caramel

Grate the fruit rinds, pound the rosemary sprigs, and combine them with the alcohol in a pot. Seal the pot tightly and store for at least two weeks. Soak the sugar in 5 quarts of water, add to the fruit and rosemary when ready. Add a little caramel for coloring; bottle and store for future use.

PARISIAN

1 tbs. dry gin
1 tbs. dry vermouth
1 tbs. creme de cassis

Combine with ice; shake well. Strain and add ice.

PARISIAN BLONDE

1 tbs. Jamaican rum
1 tbs. curacao
1 tbs. heavy cream

Combine with ice; shake very well. Strain and add ice.

PARK AVENUE

2 oz. gin
1 oz. pineapple juice
2 tsp. sweet vermouth
A few drops curacao

Combine with ice; shake well. Strain and add ice.

PARK AVENUE ORANGE BLOSSOM

3 bottles champagne, iced
2 quarts orange juice, as freshly squeezed as possible
A small bottle maraschino cherries

Combine the orange juice and the cherries in a large punch bowl; add the champagne immediately before use.

PARLOR PUNCH

8 oz. Jamaican rum
8 oz. raspberry syrup
2 tbs. tea steeped in 1 pint boiling water
2 lb. sugar
Club soda

Peel and grate the rinds of three of the lemons; combine with the sugar and 1 quart of boiling water in a large saucepan. Stir and continue to boil for 10-15 minutes. Cool and add the juice of all the lemons; strain in the tea. Stir well and refrigerate. Strain in the rum and the raspberry syrup immediately before using. Serve over ice. Touch up each glass with a spritz of soda.

PARSNIP WINE

3 lb. parsnips
3 lb. sugar
1 package dry, activated yeast

Slice the parsnips and boil them in a gallon of water until soft; carefully strain out all the juice. Add enough water to balance out at a gallon again and dissolve the sugar in it. Cool to lukewarm and add the yeast; turn out into a crock pot and ferment several weeks, stirring daily the first week. Strain, allow to stand a few days, then seal and store for half a year. Store in wooden casks, not glass.

PARTY JULEP

2 bottles bourbon
Sugar
Mint sprigs

Reserve two large punch bowls of different sizes; fill the larger of the two with ice, then comfortably hammer home the smaller one inside it. In this bowl, muddle plenty of mint with plenty of sugar. Fill this bowl with crushed ice and pour in the bourbon. Garnish with more mint. Serve in tall glasses, catching up a bit of mint, sugar, ice, and bourbon in each.

PARTY PUNCH

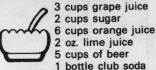

3 cups grape juice
2 cups sugar
6 cups orange juice
2 oz. lime juice
5 cups of beer
1 bottle club soda

Combine everything except the beer and the soda; stir to blend. Add the beer and the soda plus chunks of ice before serving.

PASSION DAIQUIRI

1½ oz. white rum
2 tbs. lime juice
2 tsp. passion fruit juice
1½ tsp. sugar syrup

Combine with ice; shake well. Strain and add ice.

PASSION FRUIT COOLER

2½ oz. white rum
4 oz. passion fruit nectar
1 oz. gin
1 oz. orange juice
2 tsp. lemon juice
A few mint sprigs, broken

Combine in a mixing glass; fill with ice; shake well. Strain over plenty of ice. Decorate with mint.

PATIO COCKTAIL

1½ oz. gin
1 tbs. dry vermouth
1 tbs. sweet vermouth, clear
A few drops of Cointreau

Combine with ice; shake well. Strain and add ice.

PEACH BRANDY

10 large peaches
8 oz. sugar
1 pint brandy

Slice the fruit, remove the pit. Crush the kernels from the center of the pit and combine with the sliced fruit, brandy, and sugar in a large jar or bottles. Store at room temperature for a month, shaking daily. When ready, strain, bottle, and store for half a year before using.

PEACH BUCK

1¼ oz. vodka
2 tsp. lemon juice
2 tsp. peach brandy
Ginger ale
1 peach slice

Combine everything except the ginger ale and the peach slice with ice. Shake. Strain over ice.

PEACH DAIQUIRI

2 oz. white rum
½ ripe peach, peeled
1 tbs. lime juice
1½ tsp. sugar syrup
6 oz. crushed ice

Combine in a blender at a low speed for 15 seconds. Strain straight up.

PEACH EGGNOG

1 pint peach brandy
1 pint heavy cream
8 oz. milk
8 oz. powdered sugar
½ doz. egg yolks
Grated nutmeg

Combine the egg yolks and the sugar in a large bowl; beat together until creamy. Slowly add the brandy. Allow to stand; add the milk and refrigerate several hours. Before serving, whip the cream and fold it into the nog. Whole eggs, separated, can be used. Beat the whites until stiff and fold into the nog after the whipped cream.

PEACH FLIP

2 oz. vodka
1 oz. almond extract
3 tsp. lemon juice
2 ripe peaches
3 oz. crushed ice

Peel and dice the peaches. Combine with the remaining ingredients in a blender at high speed until smooth. Serve straight up.

PEACH SANGAREE

4 oz. claret
1½ oz. lemon juice
2 tbs. sugar
Cinnamon, allspice, and salt
4 oz. sliced peaches
Club soda

Combine everything except the soda and the sliced peaches with ice; shake well. Add the peaches to the mixing glass; stir well and chill for one hour. When ready, strain and add ice. Fill the glass with soda and decorate with a slice of peach.

PEACH VELVET

1½ oz. peach brandy
2 tbs. white creme de cacao
2 tbs. heavy cream
2 oz. crushed ice

Combine in a blender at a high speed for 10 seconds. Serve straight up.

PEACH WEST INDIES

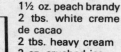

1½ oz. white rum
½ peach, peeled
A few drops of lime juice
A few drops of maraschino
3 oz. crushed ice

*Combine in a blender at a high speed for 15 seconds. Strain. To make a **BANANA WEST INDIES**, substitute 1½ oz. of banana liqueur for the peach.*

PEACHBLOW FIZZ

2 oz. gin
2 tsp. lemon juice
2 tsp. strawberry liqueur
1 tsp. sugar syrup
1 tsp. heavy cream
Club soda
1 strawberry

Combine everything except the soda and the strawberry with ice; shake extremely well. Strain. Add ice and fill the glass with soda. Decorate with the strawberry.

PEAR RICKEY

1½ oz. pear brandy
1 tsp. lime juice
Club soda
Pear slices

Pour the brandy into a highball glass. Add the lime juice plus ice; fill the glass with club soda and stir. Touch it up with a twist of lime. Decorate with pear slices.

PEACHED WINE

1 bottle Burgundy
1 cup peaches, peeled and sliced
3 oz. sugar
Lemon slices

Combine; dilute with a pint of water and stir until the sugar has dissolved. Allow to stand at room temperature for at least one hour. Add ice.

PEAR LIQUEUR

1 quart pears peeled
Whiskey
Sugar

Combine enough water and sugar to make enough syrup to cover the pears on the bottom of a crock pot. Seal the pot and allow to stand for a few days. Open the pot; strain and double with whiskey. Rebottle and use as a liqueur.

PEGGY COCKTAIL

1½ oz. dry gin
1 tbs. dry vermouth
A few drops Pernod
A few drops
Dubonnet

*Combine with ice; shake well.
Strain and add ice.*

PEGU CLUB

1½ oz. gin
1 tbs. orange
curacao
1 tsp. lime juice
1-2 dashes
Angostura and
orange bitters

*Combine with ice; shake.
Strain straight up.*

PENDENNIS COCKTAIL

1½ oz. gin
1 tbs. apricot brandy
3 tsp. lime juice
1-2 dashes
Peychaud's bitters

*Combine with ice; shake well.
Strain and add ice.*

PENSACOLA

1½ oz. white rum
2 tsp. guava nectar
2 tsp. lemon juice
2 tsp. orange juice
3 oz. crushed ice

*Combine in a blender at a
low speed for 15 seconds.
Strain straight up.*

PEPPER TREE PUNCH

1½ oz. white rum
1 tbs. dark rum
1 tbs. lime juice
2 tsp. sugar
1-2 dashes
Angostura bitters
A pinch cinnamon
A pinch cayenne
pepper

*Combine with ice; shake well.
Strain and add ice.*

PERFECT MARTINI

1½ oz. gin
2 tsp. dry vermouth
2 tsp. sweet verm-
muth

*Combine with ice; shake well.
Strain straight up. Decorate
with an olive.*

PENDENNIS EGGNOG

1 bottle bourbon
1 dozen eggs,
separated
2 quarts heavy
cream
1 lb. sugar

*Combine the sugar with the
bourbon in a punch bowl; stir
until the sugar is dissolved
and allow to stand at room*
*temperature a few hours.
Beat the egg yolks into the
bourbon mixture and let
stand for a few hours. Just
before serving, beat the egg
whites until stiff, whip the
cream, and fold both into the
bourbon mixture. Garnish
with nutmeg and serve in
punch glasses.*

PERNOD COCKTAIL

2 oz. Pernod
2 tsp. water
A few drops sugar syrup
A few dashes of Angostura bitters

Combine with ice; shake well. Strain and add ice.

PERNOD CURACAO FRAPPE

2 tsp. Pernod
2 tsp. curacao
2 tsp. orange juice
1 tsp. lemon juice

Combine without ice; stir well. Pour over crushed ice. Decorate with a slice of orange.

PERNOD DRIP

1½ oz. Pernod
1 cube sugar

Pour the Pernod into a small glass. Place the sugar cube in a tea strainer above the glass; pack the strainer with crushed ice and wait until the ice melts, dissolves the sugar, and drips into the Pernod before drinking. Stir gently; add ice if you like.

PERNOD FLIP

1 oz. Pernod
2 tsp. Cointreau
2 tsp. lemon juice
1½ tsp. sugar syrup
1 egg

Combine with ice; shake well. Strain straight up.

PERNOD FLIP II

1½ oz. Pernod
1 oz. heavy cream
1 egg white
2 tsp. almond extract
4 oz. crushed ice

Combine in a blender; at high speed for five seconds. Pour straight up.

PERNOD FRAPPE

1½ oz. Pernod
2 tsp. anisette
A few dashes of Angostura bitters

Combine with ice; shake well. Strain over crushed ice.

PERNOD MARTINI

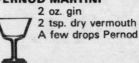

2 oz. gin
2 tsp. dry vermouth
A few drops Pernod

Combine with ice; shake well. Strain straight up. Decorate with an olive. The Pernod can be used as a garnish for a regular martini if you like.

PERPETUAL

1½ oz. sweet vermouth
1½ oz. dry vermouth
Several dashes Creme Yvette
A few drops white creme de cacao

Combine with ice; shake well. Strain and add ice.

263

PERSIMMON BEER

Several bunches of wild persimmon
1 quart slightly sugared water
8 oz. yeast

Mash the persimmon and simmer it in the boiling, sweet water at least a half hour. Allow to cool; add the yeast and allow to ferment for several weeks. Strain clean and bottle for future use.

PHILADELPHIA SCOTCHMAN

1 oz. apple brandy
1 oz. port
1 oz. orange juice
Club soda

Combine everything except the soda with ice; shake well. Strain; add ice and fill with soda.

PHILLY SPECIAL

1 oz. bourbon
1 oz. heavy cream
1 oz. dark creme de cacao

Combine with ice; shake. Strain straight up.

PHILOMEL

2 oz. sherry
1½ oz. Quinquina
2 tbs. orange juice
1 tbs. rum
1 pinch pepper

Combine with ice; shake well. Strain and add ice.

PHOEBE SNOW

1½ oz. brandy
1½ oz. Dubonnet
A few drops Pernod

Combine with ice; shake well. Strain and add ice.

PHILIP BROWN'S PUNCH

4 bottles dry white wine
1 quart brandy
1 quart gold rum

3 ounces frozen lemonade concentrate
2 quarts club soda

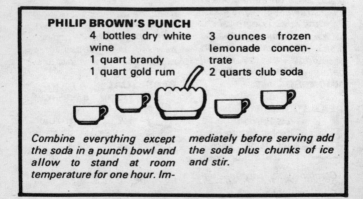

Combine everything except the soda in a punch bowl and allow to stand at room temperature for one hour. Immediately before serving add the soda plus chunks of ice and stir.

PICADILLY PUNCH

1 bottle cognac
1½ tbs. sugar
2 large lemons
Whole cloves
Cinnamon sticks
Ground nutmeg

Cut the peel off the lemons; stud the peels with cloves and combine in a pot with cinnamon sticks, sugar, nutmeg, and 1 pint of warm water. Squeeze in the juice of the lemons; simmer and stir until the sugar has dissolved. Pour an oz. or so of the cognac into a ladle; ignite and infuse the punch. Add the remaining cognac; stir well and serve hot in mugs, unstrained.

PICADOR

1½ oz. tequila
1 tbs. Kahlua

Combine with ice; shake well. Strain. Add ice and a twist of lemon.

PICASSO

1½ oz. cognac
2 tsp. lime juice
2 tsp. Dubonnet
1½ tsp. sugar syrup

Combine with ice; shake well. Strain; add ice and a twist of orange.

PICK-ME-UP

1 oz. cognac
1 oz. Dubonnet
1 tbs. anisette
1 egg white

Combine with ice; shake well. Strain; add ice and a twist of lemon.

PICKENS' PUNCH

1 oz. peach brandy
1 oz. white creme de menthe
1 oz. cherry liqueur

Combine with ice; shake well and allow to stand for a few minutes. Strain straight up.

PICON

2 tbs. Amer Picon
2 tbs. dry vermouth

Combine with ice; shake well. Strain and add ice.

PICON GRENADINE

1½ oz. Amer Picon
1 tbs. grenadine
Club soda

Combine the Amer Picon and the grenadine; stir well and add ice. Fill the glass with club soda.

PICON ON THE ROCKS

1½ oz. Amer Picon
2 tsp. lemon juice
Club soda

Combine the Amer Picon and the lemon juice; add ice and stir. Touch it up with a spritz of soda and decorate with lemon.

PICON PICON

1½ oz. Amer Picon
2 tbs. orange juice
Club soda.

Combine the Amer Picon and the orange juice; stir well and touch it up with a spritz of soda. Serve straight up.

PICON PUNCH

1½ oz. Amer Picon
1 tbs. cognac
A few drops grenadine
Club soda

Combine the Amer Picon and the grenadine; touch it up with a dash of soda and stir gently. Add ice and float the cognac.

PIED PIPER PUNCH

2 bottles Piper-Heidsieck champagne
1 pint cognac
1 pint cream sherry
3 oz. Contreau
3 oz. cherry liqueur

Combine everything except the champagne; stir well. Add a large block of ice. Pour in the champagne before serving.

PIMENTO DRAM

1½ quarts pimento berries
1 quart white rum
4 lb. sugar
1 pint lime juice
Cinnamon sticks

Soak the berries with the rum and the lime juice in a crock pot for several days. Break the cinnamon sticks and boil them in ½ gal. of water. Strain and re-boil the water with the sugar until the sugar has dissolved. Squeeze the liquid out of the pimento mixture; add to the sugar water when cool. Strain and bottle for future use.

PIMM'S CUP COCKTAIL

1½ oz. Pimm's Cup (gin sling)
7-UP
1 cucumber peel

Pour the Pimm's Cup into a tall glass; add ice, fill the glass with 7-UP, and stir. Decorate with the cucumber peel and a slice of lemon.

PINA BORRACHA

1 bottle tequila
3 cups crushed pineapple

Combine in a large jar; seal tightly and refrigerate at least 24 hours. Strain into a bottle which can be capped. Savor as a liqueur.

PINA COLADA

2 oz. gold rum
2 oz. cream of coconut
4 oz. pineapple juice
1 pineapple stick

Combine everything except the pineapple with ice; shake well. Strain. Decorate with the pineapple and a cherry. A PINA COLADA can also be mixed with a little crushed ice in a blender.

PINA FRIA

1 oz. white rum
2 oz. pineapple juice
1 oz. lemon juice
2 pineapple rings, torn in pieces
3 oz. crushed ice
Sprigs of mint

Combine everything except the mint in a blender at high speed for 15 seconds. Strain; garnish with mint and serve with a straw.

PINATA

1 oz. tequila
1 tbs. banana liqueur
1 oz. lime juice

Combine with ice; shake well. Strain straight up.

PINEAPPLE BEER

1 large pineapple
Sugar to taste

Slice the pineapple into small chunks, skin and all. Place the chunks in a deep saucepan and cover with boiling water; add sugar to taste and stir. Store in a warm place for 12 to 18 hours; strain and bottle the juice. Allow to stand for several days before using. Serve ice cold.

PINEAPPLE COCKTAIL PUNCH

3 oz. pineapple juice
6 oz. dry white wine
8 oz. crushed pineapple
9 oz. sherry
1 tbs. lemon juice
Pineapple wedges

Soak the crushed pineapple in the wine for 2-3 hours; combine both with the juices and the sherry and stir well. Strain and refrigerate. Serve over ice; decorate each glass with a pineapple wedge.

PINEAPPLE DAIQUIRI

1 oz. white rum
2 oz. pineapple juice
1 tsp. Cointreau
½ tsp. lime juice
4 oz. crushed ice

Combine in blender at a high speed for 15 seconds. Strain; serve straight up.

PINEAPPLE DELIGHT

1½ oz. Chablis
1½ oz. sherry
2 oz. crushed pineapple
1 tbs. white rum
2 tsp. lime juice
2 tsp. Cointreau

Combine without ice; refrigerate for several hours. Serve unstrained; add ice. Decorate with pineapple chunks.

PINEAPPLE LEMONADE

1½ oz. brandy
2 oz. crushed pineapple
2 tsp. sugar syrup
A few drops raspberry syrup
Club soda
1 pineapple stick

Muddle the crushed pineapple with the sugar syrup in a mixing glass. Add the brandy and raspberry syrup plus ice and shake well. Strain; add ice and fill with soda. Decorate with the pineapple stick and a twist of lemon.

PINEAPPLE MAUBY

1 large, ripe pineapple
2 tbs. ginger

Slice the pineapple into rings. Place the slices in a crock pot; add enough water to cover them and stir in the ginger. Seal and allow to stand for several days. When ready, crush the fruit, strain out the juice, and sweeten to taste. Serve over ice, garnished with ginger or mint.

PINEAPPLE MINT COOLER

2 oz. gin
2 tsp. white creme de menthe
1 oz. lemon juice
3 oz. pineapple juice
Club soda
1 pineapple stick and a green cherry

Combine everything except the soda and the garnishes in with ice; shake well. Strain; add plenty of ice and touch the drink up with a spritz of soda. Decorate with the pineapple stick and the cherry.

PINEAPPLE MIST

1½ oz. white rum
2 oz. crushed pineapple

Blend the pineapple with crushed ice. Pour in the rum and decorate with a cherry.

PINEAPPLE OKOLEHAO PUNCH

4 bottles okolehao
3 quarts pineapple juice
2 cups lemon juice
1 bottle club soda
Strawberries

Combine the okolehao and the juices. Add the club soda plus chunks of ice before serving. Garnish with strawberries.

PINEAPPLE PUNCH

1 quart pineapple juice
1 cup curacao
1 cup rum
1 quart lemonade

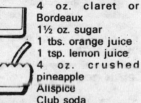

Combine; stir well. Serve over ice.

PINEAPPLE RUM PUNCH

5 cups white rum
4 oz. lime juice
6 cups pineapple juice
16 oz. sugar syrup

Combine; add ice and stir.

PINEAPPLE SANGAREE

4 oz. claret or Bordeaux
1½ oz. sugar
1 tbs. orange juice
1 tsp. lemon juice
4 oz. crushed pineapple
Allspice
Club soda

Combine everything except the allspice and the soda in with ice; shake. Chill for one hour. Strain and add ice. Fill glass with soda and garnish with allspice.

PINEAPPLE SUNRISE

1½ oz. tequila
1½ oz. pineapple juice
1 tbs. grenadine
1½ tbs. lime juice

Combine with ice; shake well. Strain straight up. Decorate with a cherry and a slice of pineapple.

PINEAPPLE WINE

5 lb. pineapple, sliced
4 lb. sugar
2 tsp. isinglass gelatin
Grated lemon rinds

Soak the pineapple slices in a gal. of water for several days; mixing well two times a day. Strain the liquid into a large pot; add the sugar and stir to dissolve. Add the rinds and gelatin; close tightly and allow to ferment for several days to a week. Strain clean, store for two weeks, then bottle and store for use.

PING-PONG

1¼ oz. sloe gin
1¼ oz. creme yvette
1 oz. lemon juice

Combine with ice; shake well. Strain and add ice.

PINK ALMOND

1 oz. whiskey
2 tsp. creme de noyaux, almond extract, kirsch, and lemon juice

Combine with ice; shake well. Strain and add ice. Decorate with slices of lemon.

PINK CALIFORNIA SUNSHINE

4 oz. pink champagne
4 oz. orange juice
1-2 dashes creme de cassis

Combine; pour straight up; stir gently.

PINK CREOLE

1½ oz. gold rum
2 tsp. lime juice
1 tsp. grenadine
1 tsp. heavy cream
1 rum-soaked black cherry

Combine everything except the cherry with ice; shake very well. Strain and add ice. Drop in the cherry.

PINK GIN

2 oz. gin
1-2 dashes Angostura bitters

Pour the bitters into an old-fashioned glass and tip the glass until its sides have been completely coated. Pour in the gin and add ice.

PINK LADY

2 oz. gin
1 oz. lemon juice
1 oz. sugar syrup
½ oz. heavy cream
Several drops grenadine

Combine with ice; shake very well. Strain and add ice.

PINK LEMONADE

5 oz. rose wine
2 oz. lemon juice
2 oz. orange juice
3 tsp. sugar syrup
2 tsp. kirschwasser

Combine; stir well and add ice. Decorate with a slice of lemon.

PINK PARADISE PUNCH

1 bottle bourbon
12 oz. apple brandy
8 oz. lemon juice
4 oz. white de cacao
2 tsp. grenadine
4 bottles 7-UP

Combine everything except the 7-UP; stir well. Add the 7-UP plus chunks of ice before serving.

PINK PEARL

4 oz. grapefruit juice
1 oz. cherry juice
3 tbs. vodka
2 tbs. lime juice

Combine with ice; shake well. Strain; add ice and decorate with cherry.

PINK ROSE

1 oz. gin
1 tsp. lemon juice
1 tsp. heavy cream
1 egg white
Several drops grenadine

Combine with ice; shake well. Strain; and add ice.

PINK RUM AND TONIC

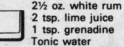

2½ oz. white rum
2 tsp. lime juice
1 tsp. grenadine
Tonic water

Combine everything except the tonic water with ice; shake well. Strain; add ice and fill with tonic. Decorate with lemon.

PINK VERANDA

1 oz. gold rum
1½ oz. cranberry juice
2 tsp. Jamaican rum
2 tsp. lime juice
1½ tsp. sugar syrup
½ egg white

Combine with ice; shake well. Strain and add ice.

PINK WHISKERS

1 tbs. apricot brandy
1 tbs. dry vermouth
2 tbs. orange juice
1 tsp. grenadine
A few drops white creme de menthe
1 oz. port

Combine everything except the port with ice; shake well. Strain; add ice and float the port.

PIONEER

2 oz. Jamaican rum
2 tsp. lime juice
A few drops orange curaçao
A few drops grenadine

Combine with ice; shake. Strain and add ice.

PIRATES' COCKTAIL

1½ oz. Jamaican rum
1 tbs. sweet vermouth
1-2 dashes Angostura bitters

Combine with ice; shake well. Strain and add ice.

PIROUETTER

1 oz. gin
1 oz. orange juice
2 tsp. Grand Marnier
1 tsp. lemon juice

Combine with ice; shake well. Strain. Add ice plus a twist of orange.

PISCO PUNCH

3 oz. Pisco brandy
1 tsp. lime juice
1 tsp. pineapple juice
A few pineapple cubes

Combine in a goblet. Add ice and fill with cold water; stir well.

PISCO SOUR

2 oz. Pisco brandy
1½ tsp. sugar syrup
1 tsp. lime juice
1 egg white
1-2 dashes Angostura bitters

Combine everything except the bitters with ice; shake well. Strain; pour straight up and add the bitters.

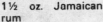

PLANTATION COFFEE

1 cup iced coffee
4 oz. brandy
1 small banana, sliced

Combine in blender at high speed until smooth. Serve straight up.

PLANTATION PUNCH

4 oz. dark rum
3 tsp. lemon juice
1 tsp. brown sugar
1 oz. sweet wine
Sprigs of mint
Slices of fruit

Dissolve the brown sugar with a few drops of water on the bottom of a large tumbler. Fill the tumbler with crushed ice; add the rum and the juice. Stir until the glass begins to frost. Float the wine. Garnish with mint and fruit slices.

PLANTER'S PUNCH

1½ oz. Myer's rum
1 oz. lemon juice
1 oz. sugar syrup
1 oz. orange juice
Several drops grenadine

Combine with ice; shake well. Strain onto crushed ice. Decorate with a cherry plus slices of fruit. Lime juice can be used instead of lemon juice; Angostura bitters instead of the grenadine. You can use two kinds of rum if you'd like. A bittered punch should be touched up with club soda.

PLANTER'S PUNCH II

2 oz. Puerto Rican rum
1 oz. Jamaican rum
2 tsp. sugar syrup
1 oz. lime juice
Several drops of Angostura bitters
Club soda

Combine everything except the soda with ice; shake well. Strain; add ice and fill with soda. Stir. Garnish with fruit.

PLAYBOY COOLER

1½ oz. gold rum
1½ oz. coffee liqueur
3 oz. pineapple juice
2 tsp. lemon juice
Cola
1 pineapple slice

Combine everything except the cola with ice; shake well. Strain; add plenty of ice and fill the glass with cola. Decorate with the pineapple slice.

PLAZA MARTINI

1 tbs. dry gin
1 tbs. dry vermouth
1 tbs. sweet vermouth
A few drops pineapple juice

Combine with ice; shake well. Strain; serve straight up.

272

PLUM APERITIF

1½ oz. dry vermouth
2 tsp. cognac
1 tsp. prunelle

Combine with ice; shake well. Strain and add ice. Decorate with a slice of lemon.

PLUM RICKEY

1½ oz. plum brandy
1 tbs. lime juice
Club soda
Plum slices

Combine the brandy and lime juice. Fill the glass with club soda; stir and add ice. Add a twist of lime. Decorate with plum slices.

PLUM WINE

6 lb. plums
3½ lb. sugar
1 oz. yeast, spread on a piece of toast

Slice the plums and place them in a pot with a gal. of boiling water. Stand several days, stirring occasionally. Strain out the juice into another pot; add the sugar and yeast on toast. Store several weeks, until bubbles begin to appear. Transfer to another jar and allow to ferment (the bubbles will stop rising). Strain out into another jar; seal and store in a cool place for at least half a year before bottling for serving.

POKER

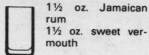

1½ oz. Jamaican rum
1½ oz. sweet vermouth

Combine with ice; shake well. Strain and add ice.

POLISH SIDECAR

¾ oz. gin
¾ oz. lemon juice
1 tbs. blackberry liqueur
Fresh blackberries

Combine everything except the blackberries with ice; shake well. Strain; and add ice. Float the blackberries.

POLLY'S SPECIAL

1 oz. Scotch
2 tsp. Cointreau
2 tsp. grapefruit juice

Combine with ice; shake well. Strain and add ice.

POLLYANNA

2 oz. gin
2 tsp. sweet vermouth
2 tsp. grenadine
Pineapple and orange slices

Combine everything except the fruit slices with ice; shake well. Strain and add ice. Decorate with the fruit slices.

POLO

1 oz. dry gin
2 tsp. lemon juice
2 tsp. orange juice

Combine with ice; shake well. Strain and add ice.

POLONAISE

1½ oz. brandy
2 tsp. dry sherry
2 tsp. blackberry liqueur
1 tsp. lemon juice
1-2 dashes orange bitters

Combine in a mixing glass filled with ice; shake well. Strain into an old-fashioned glass and add ice.

POLYNESIA

1½ oz. white rum
1 oz. passion fruit syrup
1 tsp. lime juice
½ egg white
3 oz. crushed ice

Combine in blender at a low speed for 15 seconds. Strain; serve straight up.

POLYNESIAN APPLE

1¼ oz. apple brandy
1 tbs. pineapple juice
2 tsp. Californian brandy
1 pineapple stick

Combine everything except the pineapple stick with ice; shake well. Strain and add ice. Decorate with the pineapple.

POLYNESIAN COCKTAIL

1½ oz. gin
1 tbs. cherry brandy
3 tsp. lime juice

Combine with ice; shake well. Line the rim of glass with lime juice and press it in sugar. Strain in the drink and add ice.

POLYNESIAN PARADISE

1½ oz. gold rum
1 tbs. lime juice
2 tsp. sweet vermouth
1 tsp. Triple Sec
1 tsp. brown sugar
3 oz. crushed ice

Combine in blender at a low speed for 15 seconds. Strain; serve straight up.

POLYNESIAN SOUR

2 oz. white rum
1 oz. orange juice
1½ tsp. lemon juice
A few drops almond extract
A few drops rock candy syrup
Sprigs of mint

Combine everything except the mint with ice; shake. Strain over crushed ice; garnish with mint.

POMPANO

1 oz. gin
1 oz. grapefruit juice
2 tsp. dry vermouth
Several dashes orange bitters

Combine with ice; shake well. Strain and add ice. Decorate with a slice of orange.

PONCE DE LEON

1½ oz. white rum
2 tsp. mango nectar
2 tsp. grapefruit juice
1 tsp. lemon juice

Combine with ice; shake well. Strain and add ice.

POOP DECK

1 oz. brandy
2 tsp. port
2 tsp. blackberry brandy

Combine with ice; shake well. Strain; and add ice.

POPO E IXTA

1 tbs. Kahlua
1 tsp. tequila

Combine. Serve straight up; stir well.

POPPY

1½ oz. gin
1 tbs. dark creme de cacao

Combine with ice; shake well. Strain and add ice.

POR MI AMANTE

Combine 4 cups of strawberries with a bottle of tequila in a large, tightly capped jar and refrigerate for a month. Strain into another bottle and keep capped. Savor as a liqueur.

PORT ANTONIO

1 oz. gold rum
2 tsp. Jamaican rum
2 tsp. lime juice
2 tsp. Tia Maria
1 tsp. Falernum

Combine with ice; shake well. Strain and add ice. Decorate with lime.

PORT COBBLER

1 tsp. curacao
1 tsp. orange juice
Port
1 pineapple stick

Fill a tumbler part-way with crushed ice; pour in the orange juice and the curacao and stir well. Fill the glass with port and decorate with the pineapple stick and a slice of orange.

PORT LIGHT

2 oz. bourbon
1 oz. lemon juice
2 tsp. passion fruit juice
2 tsp. honey
1 egg white
Mint sprigs
Grenadine

Combine everything except the mint and the grenadine with ice; shake. Coat the sides of a tumbler with grenadine; add ice and strain in the drink. Garnish with mint.

PORT MARIA

1½ oz. white rum
1 tbs. pineapple juice
2 tsp. lemon juice
1 tsp. Falernum

Combine with ice; shake well. Strain and add ice. Garnish with nutmeg.

PORT SANGAREE

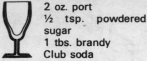

2 oz. port
½ tsp. powdered sugar
1 tbs. brandy
Club soda

Dissolve the sugar with a few drops of water; add the port plus ice and fill the glass with club soda. Garnish with nutmeg and float the brandy.

PORTALIA

1½ oz. vodka
1½ oz. dry white port
2 tsp. Campari
Several drops of grenadine

Combine without ice; stir. Strain straight up.

POTTED PARROT

2 oz. white rum
2 oz. orange juice
1 oz. lemon juice
2 tsp. orange curacao
1 tsp. almond extract
1 tsp. rock candy syrup
Mint sprigs

Combine everything except the mint with ice; shake. Strain; add ice. Garnish with mint.

POULET PUNCH

1 bottle orange wine
½ bottle sauterne
1 bottle gin
several dashes of Angostura bitters

Combine; add chunks of ice before serving.

POUSSE-CAFES

POUSSE-CAFES are usually liqueur drinks, served in many layers without ice in a pousse-cafe glass — tall and narrow. Here is one suggestion: Combine a few drops of maraschino, raspberry syrup, white creme de cacao, curacao, yellow Chartreuse, and brandy in a pousse-cafe glass; carefully and consecutively pouring each ingredient on top of the other so that they do not mix. If you haven't got the patience for so many layers, try simple twos, i.e.: coffee liqueur and sweet cream, dark creme de cacao and sweet cream. Pousse-cafe glasses are sometimes used interchangeably with their smaller cousins, pony glasses, for any liqueur straight up or over crushed ice like a frappe.

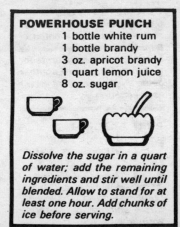

POWERHOUSE PUNCH

1 bottle white rum
1 bottle brandy
3 oz. apricot brandy
1 quart lemon juice
8 oz. sugar

Dissolve the sugar in a quart of water; add the remaining ingredients and stir well until blended. Allow to stand for at least one hour. Add chunks of ice before serving.

PRADO

1½ oz. tequila
1 tbs. lime juice
2 tsp. maraschino
1 tsp. grenadine
½ egg white

Combine with ice; shake well. Strain; serve straight up. Decorate with a slice of lemon.

PREAKNESS

1½ oz. whiskey
1 tbs. sweet vermouth
Several drops Benedictine
1-2 dashes Angostura bitters

Combine with ice; shake well. Strain. Add ice plus a twist of lemon.

PRESBYTERIAN

Pour 2½ ozs. of bourbon into a highball glass; add ice and fill the glass with equal parts ginger ale and club soda.

PRESIDENTE

1½ oz. white rum
1 tbs. dry vermouth
1-2 dashes grenadine
1-2 dashes orange curacao

Combine with ice; shake well. Strain and add ice.

PRESTO

1½ oz. brandy
1 tbs. sweet vermouth
A few drops orange juice
1-2 dashes Pernod

Combine with ice; shake well. Strain and add ice.

PRIMAVERA

4 oz. pineapple juice
2 tbs. white rum
½ doz. watercress sprigs

Slice off and save the leaves of the watercress sprigs; combine them with the juice in a blender at a high speed until the leaves are finely chopped. Pour unstrained; add the rum and fill the glass with ice. Stir well until the glass begins to frost.

PRINCE

1¼ oz. whiskey
1-2 dashes orange bitters
A few drops white creme de menthe

Combine the whiskey and bitters with ice; shake well. Strain and add ice. Float the white creme de menthe.

PRINCE EDWARD

1¾ oz. Scotch
2 tsp. Lillet
1 tsp. Drambuie

Combine with ice; shake well. Strain and add ice. Decorate with a slice of orange.

PRINCE GEORGE'S COCKTAIL

1½ oz. Bacardi rum
1 tbs. Grand Marnier
2 tsp. lime juice

Combine with ice; shake well. Strain and add ice; touch it up with a twist of lemon.

PRINCE OF WALES

1 oz. Madeira
1 oz. brandy
6 oz. champagne
Several drops curacao
1 - 2 dashes Angostura bitters

Combine everything except the champagne with ice; shake well. Strain; and add the champagne. Garnish with a slice of orange.

PRINCE REGENCE AU VICTOR'S PUNCH

4 gallons curacao
4 gallons maraschino
1 quart white wine
½ quart kirschwasser
½ quart brandy
Slices of pineapple, oranges, and lemons
Club soda

Combine all the beverages except the soda. Stir until well-blended. Add the fruit slices plus chunks of ice. Before serving, add an equal amount of club soda as there is existing punch.

PRINCE'S SMILE

2 oz. gin
1 oz. calvados
1 oz. apricot brandy
A few drops lemon juice

Combine with ice; shake well. Strain and add ice.

PRINCESS MARY

1 oz. gin
1 oz. white creme de cacao
1 oz. heavy cream

Combine with ice; shake very well. Strain straight up.

PRINCESS MARY'S PRIDE

1½ oz. calvados
1 tbs. Dubonnet
1 tbs. dry vermouth

Combine with ice; shake well. Strain and add ice.

PRINCETON

1½ oz. gin
2 tsp. port
1 - 2 dashes orange bitters

Combine with ice; shake well. Strain; add ice and a twist of lemon.

PUERTO APPLE

1¼ oz. apple brandy
1 tbs. Puerto Rican Rum
2 tsp. lime juice
1½ tsp. almond extract

Combine with ice; shake well. Strain and add ice. Decorate with a slice of lime.

PUERTO RICAN PINK LADY

1½ oz. gold rum
1 tbs. lemon juice
1 tsp. grenadine
½ egg white
3 oz. crushed ice

Combine in blender at a low speed for 15 seconds. Line the rim of a glass with lemon juice and press it in sugar. Strain in the drink straight up.

PUMPKIN COACH COCKTAIL

1 oz. Cesoriac
2 tsp. sweet vermouth
2 tsp. cherry juice

Combine without ice; stir well. Pour over crushed ice into a small glass. Add a twist of lime.

PUNCH ROMAINE

1 oz. rye
1 oz. Jamaican rum
3 tsp. lemon juice
2 tsp. sugar syrup

Combine with ice; shake well. Strain and add ice.

PUNT E MES NEGRONI

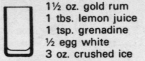

1 tbs. Punt e Mes
1 tbs. gin
1 tbs. sweet vermouth

Combine with ice; shake well. Strain; add ice and a twist of lemon.

PURPLE COW

1 oz. blackberry brandy
1 oz. light cream
1 tsp. Almond extract

Combine with ice; shake. Strain and add plenty of ice.

PURPLE PEOPLE EATER

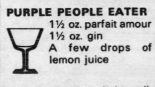

1½ oz. parfait amour
1½ oz. gin
A few drops of lemon juice

Combine with ice; shake well. Strain straight up.

YOUR OWN RECIPE

Use a bartender's mixing glass whenever the instructions state "combine" ingredients. Strain the drink from the mixing glass into the drinking glass suggested by the illustration alongside the ingredients.

NOTE: The number of glasses or cups shown alongside a recipe do not necessarily indicate the quantity of drinks the recipe will produce.

QUADRUPLE PINEAPPLE

6 oz. white rum
3 oz. orange juice
2 tbs. lime juice
2 tsp. maraschino
4 oz. pineapple sherbet
1 large pineapple

Slice off the top eighth or so of the pineapple with a sharp knife and carefully carve out the meat, leaving the shell intact. Save 4 oz. of the fruit and crush. Combine the crushed fruit with the remaining ingredients in a blender at a low speed for a few seconds.

QUARTER DECK

1½ oz. Jamaican rum
1 tbs. sherry
1 tsp. lime juice

Combine with ice; shake well. Strain and add ice.

QUEBEC

1½ oz. Canadian whiskey
2 tsp. dry vermouth
1 tsp. Amer Picon
1 tsp. maraschino

Combine with ice; shake well. Strain and add ice.

QUEEN ELIZABETH WINE

1 oz. dry vermouth
2 tbs. Benedictine
1 tbs. lemon juice

Combine with ice; shake well. Strain and add ice. Lime juice can be used instead of lemon juice.

Use a bartender's mixing glass whenever the instructions state "combine" ingredients. Strain the drink from the mixing glass into the drinking glass suggested by the illustration alongside the ingredients.

NOTE: The number of glasses or cups shown alongside a recipe do not necessarily indicate the quantity of drinks the recipe will produce.

The glass pictured for each drink is our suggestion; other drinking cups may be used as well.

RACQUET CLUB

1½ oz. gin
1 tbs. dry vermouth
1-2 dashes orange bitters

Combine with ice; shake well. Strain and add ice.

RAINBOW OLD-FASHIONED

2 oz. rye
1¼ oz. sugar syrup
1 tsp. cherry juice
A few dashes of Angostura bitters
1 strawberry

Combine everything except the strawberry; add ice and stir gently. Decorate with the strawberry, a slice of orange, and a cherry. Touch it up with a twist of lemon.

RAISIN WINE

2 lbs. raisins
4 oz. sugar
Cinnamon sticks
A whole ginger chunk

Combine in a large pot with a gal. of water; boil for several hours. Strain through cheesecloth and allow to stand until cold. Bottle unstrained. This wine can be drunk freshly made (when it will be mild) or stored to ferment longer (when it will be stronger and less sweet).

285

RAMOS GIN FIZZ

2 oz. gin
2 tsp. lemon juice
2 tsp. sugar
2 tsp. heavy cream
1 tsp. lime juice
1 egg white
A few drops orange flower water
6 oz. crushed ice
Club soda

Combine everything except the soda in a blender at a high speed for a few seconds. Strain, and fill the glass with soda.

RANGIRORA MADNESS

1½ oz. Jamaican rum
2 tbs. pineapple juice
2 tbs. orange juice
1 tsp. 151-proof rum
Lemon soda

Combine everything (except the 151-proof rum) with ice. Shake. Strain, add plenty of ice and fill with lemon soda. Float the 151-proof rum; decorate with a cherry.

RANGOON RUBY

2 oz. vodka
2 tbs. cranberry juice
½ lime
Club soda

Combine the vodka and the cranberry juice stir. Squeeze in the juice of the lime and drop in the peel. Add ice and fill with soda. Stir.

RASPBERRY CLARET CUP

4 oz. dry red wine
1 oz. brandy
1 oz. white raspberry brandy
1 oz. lemon juice
1 tbs. raspberry syrup
Club soda
Raspberries

Thoroughly chill the wine and the brandies before combining them with the raspberry syrup and lemon juice in a tall glass. Stir well and add ice. Fill the glass with soda and float a few raspberries.

RASPBERRY COCKTAIL

8 oz. raspberries, one raspberry left aside
4 oz. gin
4 oz. dry white wine
2 oz. kirsch

Mash the raspberries in a bowl; pour the gin over them and allow to stand for several hours. Strain the juice and gin with ice; add the wine and kirsch. Shake well. Garnish with a raspberry.

RASPBERRY RICKEY

1½ oz. white raspberry brandy
1 tsp. lime juice
Club soda
Raspberries

Pour the brandy into a glass; add the lime juice plus ice. Fill the glass with club soda and stir well. Touch it up with a twist of lime; float a few raspberries.

RATTLESNAKE

1½ oz. whiskey
1 tsp. lemon juice
1 tsp. sugar syrup
1 egg white
A few drops Pernod

Combine with ice; shake extremely well. Strain and add ice.

RAYMOND HITCHCOCKTAIL

3 oz. sweet vermouth
2 oz. orange juice
1-2 dashes orange bitters
1 pineapple slice

Combine everything except the pineapple slice with ice; shake well. Strain and add ice. Decorate with the pineapple slice.

RED APPLE

1 oz. 100-proof vodka
1 oz. apple juice
2 tsp. lemon juice
2 tsp. grenadine
1-2 dashes orange bitters

Combine with ice; shake well. Strain and add ice.

RED CLOUD

1½ oz. gin
2 tsp. apricot liqueur
2 tsp. lemon juice
1 tsp. grenadine
1-2 dashes Angostura bitters

Combine with ice; shake well. Strain into glass and add ice.

RED DEVIL

2 oz. Irish whiskey
1½ oz. clam juice
1½ oz. tomator juice
1 tsp. lime juice
A few drops Worchestershire sauce
A pinch pepper

Combine with ice; shake gently. Strain straight up.

RED GAVILAN

1 oz. Gavilan tequila
4 oz. tomato juice
A few dashes of Angostura bitters

Combine with ice; shake well. Strain add ice to fill. Decorate with a lime.

RED CIDER WINE

8 gallon cider
5 lb. honey
2 bottles dark rum
2 lb. sugar
2 lb. beet root
3 oz. red tartar
Sweet marjoran, sweet-briar

Combine the cider and honey with a gallon and a half of cold water; stir until blended. Seal in a crock pot and allow to ferment. When ready, add the remaining ingredients; stir very well. Strain and bottle for future use.

RED LION

1½ oz. Grand Marnier
1 tbs. gin
2 tsp. orange juice
2 tsp. lemon juice

Combine with ice; shake well. Strain. Add ice and a twist of lemon.

RED WINE COOLER

Chillled red wine
1 tbs. orange juice
1 tsp. sugar

Dissolve the sugar with a teaspoon of water; stir until the sugar is dissolved. Add the orange juice plus ice and fill the glass with wine. Decorate with a slice of lemon.

REGENT'S PUNCH

3 oz. Sauterne
2 tbs. Madeira
1 tbs. Jamaican rum
1 tsp. honey
Hot tea

Dissolve the honey with a few drops of the hot tea in a large mug; add the Sauterne, rum, and Madeira. Fill the mug with tea and stir very well.

REGENT'S PUNCH

8 oz. white wine
4 oz. Madeira
2 oz. rum
1 pint hot tea

Combine the wine, Madeira, and rum; and stir well. Pour in the tea and serve while hot.

REMSEN COOLER

2½ oz. Scotch
1 tsp. sugar syrup
Club soda

Combine the Scotch and sugar syrup in a tall glass. Add ice and fill the glass with club soda; stir well. Touch it up with a twist of lemon. Gin and ginger ale can be used instead of Scotch and club soda.

RENAISSANCE

1½ oz. gin
2 tsp. dry sherry
2 tsp. heavy cream

Combine with ice; shake very well. Strain and add ice. Garnish with nutmeg.

RENDEZVOUS

1½ oz. gin
2 tsp. kirschwasser
1 tsp. Campari

Combine with ice; shake well. Strain and add ice. Touch it up with a twist of lemon.

REPUBLIC CIDER PUNCH

1 quart hard cider
12 oz. sherry
8 oz. apple brandy
12 tbs. brown sugar
3 tsp. lemon juice
Lemon slices
Grated nutmeg
A slice of toast
1 bottle club soda

Dust the toast with nutmeg and place it on the bottom of a punch bowl; pile the sugar and lemon slices upon it. Fill the bottom of the bowl with ice, building it around the toast. Carefully add the remaining ingredients, soda last. Stir gently.

RESOLUTE

1½ oz. gin
1 tbs. apricot brandy
2 tsp. lemon juice

Combine with ice; shake well. Strain and add ice.

RHETT BUTLER

1½ oz. Southern Comfort
1 tbs. lemon juice
1 tsp. lime juice
1 tsp. curacao
1 tsp. sugar syrup

Combine with ice; shake well. Strain and add ice.

RHINE WINE CUP

1 bottle Rhine wine
2 tsp. Triple Sec
2 tsp. curacao
6 oz. club soda
Fruit slices
1 cucumber peel
A few mint sprigs

Combine the wine and the liquors; add the club soda plus ice and serve immediately, garnished with the fruit, peel, and mint.

RHINE WINE PUNCH

3 quarts Rhine wine
1 pint lemon juice
1 pint dry sherry
8 oz. brandy
8 oz. cold dark tea
8 oz. sugar syrup
1 quart club soda
Cucumber peels

Combine everything except the club soda and the peels; stir and add chunks of ice. Garnish with the peels and allow to stand at least 15 minutes before removing the peels and adding the soda.

RHUBARB WINE

2 gallon bottles white wine
3 oz. rhubarb, sliced
1 oz. ground cardamom seeds
2 tsp ground ginger
1½ pints cooking alcohol

Combine the rhubarb slices, cardamom, and ginger with the alcohol in a pot; close tightly and allow to stand for several days. Add the wine and bottle for future use.

RICHELIEU

2 oz. bourbon
1 oz. Dubonnet Blonde
1 tsp. Vieille Cure

Combine with ice; shake well. Strain and add ice. Touch it up: add a twist of orange and drop in the peel.

RICKEY

1½ oz. whiskey
1½ oz. lime juice
Club soda

Combine the whiskey and the lime juice. Add ice; fill the glass with soda and stir. Touch it up with a twist of lime.

RIVER PUNCH

1 bottle sweet wine
½ doz grapefruit
2 tbs. sugar
Powdered sugar

Line the rim of a large glass bowl or pitcher with water and press it in the powdered sugar. Squeeze in the juice of the grapefruit; add the tablespoon of sugar plus the wine and stir until the sugar is dissolved.

ROBBER COCKTAIL

1½ oz. Scotch
1 tbs. sweet vermouth
1-2 dashes Angostura bitters

*Combine with ice; shake well. Strain and add ice. Decorate with a cherry. For a **ROB ROY**, add an extra oz. of Scotch and a lemon peel.*

ROBSON

1 oz. Jamaican rum
2 tsp. grenadine
1 tsp. orange juice
1 tsp. lemon juice

Combine with ice; shake well. Strain and add ice.

ROCK AND RYE COOLER

1½ oz. vodka
1 oz. rock and rye
2 tsp. lime juice
Lemon soda

Combine everything except the soda in with ice; shake well. Strain; add ice and fill the glass with soda. Decorate with a slice of lime.

ROCK AND RYE TODDY

2 oz. rock and rye
3 oz. boiling water
1-2 dashes Angostura bitters
Lemon slice

Combine the rock and rye with the bitters add the lemon slice and pour in the boiling water. Garnish with the cinnamon stick and nutmeg.

ROCKY DANE

1 oz. gin
2 tsp. dry vermouth
2 tsp. Cherry Herring
1 tsp. kirsch

Combine with ice; shake well. Strain; add ice and a twist of lemon.

ROCKY GREEN DRAGON

1 oz. gin
1 tbs. green char-treuse
1 tbs. cognac

Combine with ice; shake well. Strain and add ice.

ROFFIGNAC

3 oz. whiskey
1 tbs. raspberry syrup
Club soda

Combine the whiskey and the raspberry syrup; stir well. Add ice and fill with soda.

ROLLS-ROYCE

1¼ oz. gin
2 tsp. dry vermouth
2 tsp. sweet ver-mouth
A few drops Benedictine

Combine with ice; shake well. Strain and add ice.

ROLLS ROYCE A PARIS

1 oz. Cointreau
1 oz. orange juice
1 tbs. cognac

Combine with ice; shake and strain. Serve over ice.

ROMA

2½ oz. dry gin
1 tbs. Strega
1 tbs. Amaro

Combine without ice; stir until well-blended. Pour straight up. Garnish with a slice of orange.

ROMAN COOLER

1½ oz. gin
2 tsp. Punt e Mes
2 tsp. lemon juice
1½ tsp. sugar syrup
Club soda

Combine everything except the soda in with ice; shake well. Strain; add ice and fill the glass with soda. Touch it up with a twist of lime.

ROMAN FRULLATI

3 oz. gin
2 oz. diced apples
2 oz. diced pears
2 oz. sliced peaches
1 oz. maraschino
1 oz. almond extract
4 oz. crushed ice

Combine in blender at a high speed for 20 seconds. Strain and add ice to the rim.

ROMAN PUNCH

1 quart lemon sherbert
8 oz. Jamican rum

Combine stir until smooth. Serve immediately.

ROMAN SNOWBALL

2 oz. Sambuca
A few coffee beans

Pour the Sambuca into a glass filled part-way with crushed ice; garnish with the beans. Chew the beans after they have absorbed the liqueur.

ROMPOPE

1 pint white rum
1 dozen egg yolks
1 quart milk
8 oz. sugar
1 vanilla bean

Combine the milk with the sugar and the bean in a saucepan; heat and stir until well-blended. Remove the bean and allow the sweetened milk to cool. Beat the yolks; add to the milk and re-heat until the eggs are cooked. Cool and add the rum. Strain into a bottle; seal well and refrigerate for a few days before serving.

ROOSEVELT

2 oz. Haitian rum
1 oz. dry vermouth
2 tsp. orange juice
A few drops sugar syrup

Combine with ice; shake well. Strain and add ice.

ROOT BEER

8 oz. Hires root beer extract
10 lb. sugar
1 pint dry, activated yeast

Dissolve the sugar in 10 gallons of warm water; add the root beer extract and the yeast. Stir until mixed; strain and seal in corked bottles. Store at room temperature for a few days before using. Ice before opening.

ROSE

1 oz. gin
2 tsp. lemon juice
2 tsp. apricot brandy
2 tsp. dry vermouth
1 tsp. grenadine

Combine with ice; shake well. Strain. Add ice and a twist of lemon.

ROSE HALL

1 oz. Jamaican rum
1 oz. orange juice
2 tsp. banana liqueur
1 tsp. lime juice

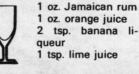

Combine with ice; shake well. Strain and add ice. Decorate with a slice of lime.

ROSE LEMONADE

2 bottles chilled rose wine
12 oz. frozen lemonade concentrate
1 quart club soda

Combine the wine and the lemonade concentrate in a large pitcher; stir until well-blended. Add the club soda plus ice before serving and stir.

ROSE OF PICARDY

1½ oz. gin
2 tsp. Cherry Kijafa
2 tsp. Dubonnet
1 tsp. dry vermouth

Combine with ice; shake well. Strain and add ice.

ROSEMARY

1½ oz. whiskey
1½ oz. dry vermouth

Combine with ice; shake well. Strain and add ice.

ROSY DEACON

2 oz. grapefruit juice
1 oz. sloe gin
1 oz. dry gin
1 pinch powdered sugar

Combine with ice; shake well. Line the rim of glass with water and press it in powdered sugar. Strain in the drink and add ice.

ROTATING PEACHES

1 large peach
Champagne

Rub the peach with a napkin or paper towel to remove the fuzz; pierce it several times with a fork. Place the peach in a glass goblet; fill the glass with champagne. The peach should float and spin in the glass.

ROY HOWARD LILLET

1½ oz. Lillet
1 tbs. orange juice
1 tbs. brandy
A few drops grenadine

Combine with ice; shake well. Strain and add ice.

ROYAL CLUB CLOVER

2½ oz. gin
1½ oz. lemon juice
1 tbs. grenadine
1 egg yolk

Combine with ice; shake extremely well. Strain and add ice.

ROYAL COCKTAIL

1½ oz. gin
1½ oz. lemon juice
1½ tsp. sugar syrup
1 egg

Combine with ice; shake extremely well. Strain and add ice.

ROYAL FIZZ

1¼ oz. gin
1½ tsp. sugar syrup
1½ tsp. lemon juice
1 egg
Club soda

Combine everything except the soda with ice; shake extremely well. Strain; add ice and fill the glass with soda.

ROYAL GIN FIZZ

2½ oz. gin
2 tbs. lemon juice
2½ tsp. sugar syrup
1 egg
Club soda

Combine everything except the soda with ice; shake extremely well. Strain; add ice and fill the glass with soda. Decorate with a slice of lemon.

ROYAL SMILE

1½ oz. gin
1½ oz. grenadine
A few drops lemon juice

Combine with ice; shake well. Strain and add ice.

RUBY FIZZ

2 oz. sloe gin
1½ tsp. lemon juice
1 tsp. powdered sugar
1 tsp. grenadine
1 egg white
Club soda

Combine everything except the soda with ice; shake extremely well. Strain; add ice and fill the glass with soda.

RUM AND BUTTER

1 quart Jamaican rum
5 quarts sweet cider
8 oz. brown sugar
8 oz. boiling water
Butter

Dissolve the brown sugar with the water in a large saucepan; stir until smooth. Add the cider; boil and add the rum. Serve piping hot in mugs. Garnish with cinnamon and top with butter.

RUM APERITIF

1 oz. white rum
1 oz. dry vermouth
2 tsp. lemon juice
1 tsp. Jamaican rum
1 tsp. raspberry syrup

Combine with ice; shake well. Strain. Add ice and a twist of lemon.

RUM BLOODY MARY

1½ oz. Puerto Rican rum
4 oz. tomato juice
1 tbs. lime juice
Several drops of Worchetershire sauce
Several drops of Tabasco sauce
A pinch of salt

Combine with ice; shake well. Strain straight up.

RUM BUCK

1½ oz. white rum
2 tsp. lime juice
Roasted almonds
Ginger ale

Combine the rum and the lime juice with ice; shake well. Strain. Add ice; fill the glass with ginger ale and stir well. Garnish with roasted almonds.

RUM CITRUS COOLER

2 oz. white rum
1 oz. orange juice
2 tsp. Cointreau
2 tsp. lime juice
1½ tsp. sugar syrup
7 UP

Combine everything except the 7-UP in with ice; shake well. Strain; add ice and fill the glass with 7-UP. Decorate with slices of lemon and lime.

RUM COCONUT COOLER

2½ oz. white rum
1 oz. cream of coconut
2 tsp. lemon juice
Club soda

Combine everything except the soda with ice; shake well. Strain and add ice; fill the glass with soda and stir. Decorate with a slice of lemon and a cherry.

RUM COCONUT FIZZ

2¼ oz. white rum
2 tsp. cream of coconut
2 tsp. lime juice
Club soda

Combine everything except the soda with ice; shake well. Strain and add ice; fill the glass with soda and stir. Decorate with a slice of lime.

RUM COLLINS

2 oz. white rum
1 tsp. sugar syrup
½ lime
club soda

*Combine the rum and the syrup stir. Squeeze in the juice of the lime, drop in the peel. Add ice and fill with soda; stir. A **RUM RICKEY** is a **RUM COLLINS** without the sugar.*

RUM CUIT

1½ oz. rum
3 tsp. lime juice
A few drops of dark
molasses

Combine with ice; shake very well. Strain into bamboo shoot cups, if you have them — or make them by cutting bamboo tubes just above the joint and fitting them around an appropriate glass.

RUM CURACAO COOLER

1 oz. Jamaican rum
1 oz. curacao
2 tsp. lime juice
Club soda

Combine all but the club soda with ice; shake well. Strain and add plenty of ice. Touch it up with club soda and decorate with orange and lime slices.

RUM CURE

1 oz. apiece Jamaican, white, and 151-proof rums
1 oz. apiece pineapple, lemon, and orange juice
2 tsp. brandy
2 tbs. grenadine
A few drops of curacao

Combine everything except the curacao with ice; shake well. Strain over crushed ice. Decorate with slices of fruit and float the curacao.

RUM DOUBLOON

1 oz. apiece Jamaican rum, white rum, and 151-proof rum
1 oz. grapefruit juice
1 oz. orange juice
A few drops of orange curacao
A few drops of Pernod

Combine with ice; shake. Strain with crushed ice. Decorate with an orange slice and a cherry.

RUM DUBONNET

1½ oz. white rum
1 tbs. Dubonnet
1 tsp. lime juice

Combine with ice; shake well. Strain. Add ice and a twist of lemon.

RUM FLIP

4 oz. rum
½ tbs. powdered sugar
1 egg

Combine in a saucepan; heat well and stir. Serve piping hot. Heavy brandies or port can be used instead of the rum.

RUM FRAPPE

2 oz. white rum
2 tbs. lemon sherbet

Combine and stir gently until smooth.

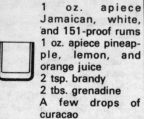

RUM FUSTIAN

1 quart ale
1 quart gin
1 pint dry sherry
6 egg yolks
1 cinnamon stick

Combine the yolks, ale, and gin in a large bowl and beat well. Set aside. Pour the sherry into a saucepan; add the cinnamon stick plus nutmeg and a twist of lemon and bring to a boil. Remove from heat; strain clean and combine with egg mixture. Serve piping hot in mugs.

RUM MARTINI

2 oz. white rum
A few drops dry vermouth

Pour the rum with vermouth and stir gently. Touch it up with a twist of lime. Decorate with an olive or a cocktail onion.

RUM MINT SQUASH

2 oz. gold rum
½ doz. mint sprigs
1-2 dashes Peyehaud's bitters
1-2 dashes rock candy syrup

Muddle the mint with the bitters and candy syrup in an oz. of cold water; turn out into an old-fashioned glass. Add ice and rum; stir briskly. Touch it up with a twist of lemon.

RUM MOCHA

2 oz. dark rum
4 oz. vanilla ice cream
Iced coffee

Combine the rum and the ice cream, stir until smooth. Add crushed ice and fill with iced coffee.

RUM PINEAPPLE FIZZ

2 oz. gold rum
3 oz. diced pineapple
2 tsp. 151-proof rum
2 tsp lemon juice and lime juice
1½ tsp. sugar syrup
½ egg white
4 oz. crushed ice
Club soda

Combine everything except the soda in a blender at a low speed for 15 seconds. Strain; fill the glass with ice and touch it up with a spritz of soda. Decorate with a slice of lime.

RUM PUNCH

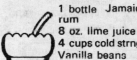

1 bottle Jamaican rum
8 oz. lime juice
4 cups cold strng tea
Vanilla beans

Steep a few vanilla beans in the bottle of rum for several hours, then combine the rum with the remaining ingredients in a large punch bowl and stir. Add ice before serving. (The ice should be made out of tea.)

RUM PUNCH FOR ONE

2 oz. dark rum
2 tsp. lime juice
2 tsp. sugar syrup
1 tsp. grenadine
A few drops of curacao

Combine with ice; shake well. Strain over crushed ice. Decorate with slices of fruit.

RUM ROYALE

1 oz. white rum
2 oz. sauterne
2 oz. pineapple juice
2 tbs. lemon juice
1½ tsp. sugar syrup
1-2 dashes Peychaud's bitters
1 pineapple chunk

Combine everything except the pineapple chunk with ice; shake well. Strain and add plenty of ice. Decorate with the pineapple chunk.

RUM SANGRIA PUNCH

1 bottle dry red wine
8 oz. Puerto Rican rum
8 oz. sugar
A large can of slices peaches
Slices of orange and lime

Combine the wine, rum, and sugar; in a large bowl stil until the sugar has completely dissolved. Add the fruit slices, squeezing out a little of the juice as you go along. Add the peach slices syrup; stir well. Add ice.

RUM SCREWDRIVER

1½ oz. white rum
3 oz. orange juice

Combine with ice; shake well. Strain and add ice. Decorate with a slice of orange.

RUM SHAKE

3 oz. Jamaican rum
1½ oz. Pernod
4 oz. pineapple juice

Combine with ice; shake well. Strain, add ice.

RUM SHRUB

4 quarts Jamaican rum
3 pints orange juice
1 lb. sugar cubes

Combine in a large pot; seal tightly and steep for several weeks. Strain and store well-capped.

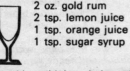

RUM SOUR

2 oz. gold rum
2 tsp. lemon juice
1 tsp. orange juice
1 tsp. sugar syrup

Combine with ice; shake well. Strain straight up. Decorate with a slice of lemon. A teaspoon of 151-proof rum may be used to top it off.

RUM SWIRL

1 oz. white rum
2 oz. banana liqueur
1 tsp. lime juice

*Combine with ice; shake well.
Strain and add ice.*

RUM SWIZZLE

3 oz. dark rum
2 tsp. water
1-2 dashes
Angostura bitters

*Combine with ice; shake well.
Strain with crushed ice; stir
until the glass begins to frost.
Drink in one gulp.*

RUM TEA

3-4 oz. Jamaican
rum
1 pot of hot tea
Whole cinnamon
sticks, whole cloves,
and nutmeg
Sprigs of mint

*Steep the spices in the tea for
several minutes; add the rum
when ready to serve.*

RUMRUNNER

1½ oz. white rum
1 tbs. orange juice
2 tsp. lime juice
1½ tsp. sugar syrup
1-2 dashes orange
bitters

*Combine with ice; shake well.
Strain. Add ice and a twist of
orange.*

RUSSIAN BEAR

1 oz. vodka
2 tsp. white creme
de cacao
2 tsp. heavy cream

*Combine with ice; shake very
well. Strain and add ice.*

RUSSIAN COCKTAIL

¾ oz. gin
¾ oz. vodka
1 tbs. white creme
de cacao

*Combine with ice; shake well.
Strain and add ice.*

RUSSIAN COFFEE

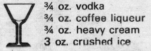

¾ oz. vodka
¾ oz. coffee liqueur
¾ oz. heavy cream
3 oz. crushed ice

*Combine in blender at a low
speed for 15 seconds. Strain
straight up.*

RUSSIAN ESPRESSO

1½ oz. vodka
2 tsp. espresso
coffee liqueur
Several drops lemon
juice

*Combine with ice; shake well.
Strain. Add ice and a twist of
lemon.*

RUSTY NAIL

1 oz. Scotch
1 oz. Drambuie

Combine; add ice and stir.

RYE AND DRY

1 oz. rye
2 oz. dry vermouth
1-2 dashes orange bitters

Combine with ice; shake well. Strain and add ice.

RYE COCKTAIL

2 oz. rye
1 tsp. sugar syrup
1-2 dashes Angostura bitters

Combine with ice; shake well. Strain and add ice.

RYE FLIP

1¼ oz. rye
1 egg
1 tsp. sugar syrup

Combine with ice; shake extremely well. Strain straight up. Garnish with nutmeg.

YOUR OWN RECIPE

Use a bartender's mixing glass whenever the instructions state "combine" ingredients. Strain the drink from the mixing glass into the drinking glass suggested by the illustration alongside the ingredients.

NOTE: The number of glasses or cups shown alongside a recipe do not necessarily indicate the quantity of drinks the recipe will produce.

The glass pictured for each drink is our suggestion; other drinking cups may be used as well.

SACK POSSET

½ pint sherry
½ pint ale
1 quart milk

Combine the ale and the sherry in a saucepan and bringing to a boil. Heat the milk in a separate saucepan and then combine it with the sherry and the ale. Sweeten to taste; add nutmeg and warm over low heat for a few hours. Serve while still warm in large mugs.

ST. AUGUSTINE

1½ oz. white rum
1 oz. grapefruit juice
1 tsp. Cointreau

Combine with ice; shake well. Line the rim of glass with water and press it in sugar. Strain in the drink. Add ice and a twist of lemon.

ST. CROIX MILK PUNCH

1 oz. Jamaican rum
1 oz. cognac
1 oz. gin
Sugar
Milk
Nutmeg
1-2 dashes Angostura bitters

Combine the rum, cognac, and gin. Warm enough milk to balance out the mug; combine with the liquors and sweeten to taste. Add the bitters and stir very well. Serve warm, garnished with nutmeg.

ST. LOU

1½ oz. gin
2 tsp. lemon juice
2 tsp. calvados
1½ tsp. sugar syrup

Combine with ice; shake well.

ST. RAPHAEL AND VODKA

3 oz. St. Raphael
2 tbs. vodka
Club soda

Combine the St. Raphael and vodka in a small goblet; add ice and stir gently. Touch it up with a spritz of soda and a twist of lemon.

SAKETINI

2 oz. gin
2 tsp. saki

Combine with ice; shake well. Strain straight up and decorate with an olive.

SALTY DOG

Line the rim of an old-fashioned glass with water and press it in salt. Pour in 2 oz. of vodka; add ice and fill the glass with grapefruit juice. Stir well. Serve with a salt shaker on the side.

SAMBUCA COFFEE FRAPPE

1 oz. sambuca
2 tsp. coffee liqueur
Roasted coffee beans

Combine the sambuca and the liqueur without ice; stir well. Pour over crushed ice. Serve with a few coffee beans on a saucer.

SAN FRANCISCO

¾ oz. sloe gin
1 tbs. dry vermouth
1 tbs. sweet vermouth
1-2 dashes Angostura bitters and orange bitters

Combine with ice; shake well. Strain and add ice. Decorate with a cherry.

SAN JUAN

1½ oz. Puerto Rican rum
1 oz. grapefruit juice
2 tsp. lime juice
2 tsp. 151-proof rum
1 tsp. cream of coconut
3 oz. crushed ice

Combine everything except the high-proofed rum in a blender at a low speed for 15 seconds. Strain straight up; float the rum.

SAN MARTIN

1 tbs. dry gin
1 tbs. dry vermouth
1 tbs. sweet vermouth
1 tsp. anisette
1-2 dashes Angostura bitters

Combine with ice; shake well. Line the rim of glass with water and press it in sugar. Strain in the drink and add ice.

SAN SEBASTIAN

1 oz. gin
2 tsp. grapefruit juice
2 tsp. lemon juice
1 tsp. 151-proof rum
1 tsp. curacao

Combine with ice; shake well. Strain and add ice.

SANCTUARY

1½ oz. Dubonnet
1 tbs. Cointreau
1 tbs. Amer Picon

Combine with ice; shake well. Strain and add ice.

SANGAREE COMFORT

1 oz. Southern Comfort
1 oz. bourbon
1 tsp. peach brandy
1 tsp. lemon juice
1 tsp. sugar syrup
Club soda

Combine everything except the soda with ice; shake well. Strain, add ice and touch it up with a spritz of soda. Garnish with nutmeg.

SAN'GRIA CALIFORNIA STYLE

2 gallons zinfandel
2 cups lemon juice
8 oz. brandy
8 oz. sugar
4 oz. Strega
2 quarts orange juice
2 quarts club soda
Orange and lemon slices

Dissolve the sugar with the orange and lemon juices and stir until the sugar is dissolved. Add everything else except the soda and the fruit slices; stir well. Add the soda and fruit plus chunks of ice before serving.

SAN'GRIA PUNCH

1 bottle Spanish red wine
4 oz. sugar syrup, fresh and still hot
1 orange and 1 lime, thinly sliced

Place the sliced fruit in a punch bowl and pour the sugar syrup over it; allow to stand for several hours. Combine the steeped fruit and sugar with the wine in a pitcher; add ice and stir.

SANGUENAY

1 oz. white rum
1 oz. dry vermouth
2 tsp. creme de cassis
1 tsp. lemon juice

Combine with ice; shake well. Strain and add ice.

SANO GROG

1 tbs. whiskey
1 tbs. curacao
1 tbs. Jamaican rum
1 tsp. powdered sugar

Combine in a mug. Fill with boiling water.

SANTA FE

1½ oz. brandy
2 tsp. dry vermouth
2 tsp. grapefruit juice
1 tsp. lemon juice

Combine with ice; shake well. Strain and add ice.

SANTIAGO

3 oz. white rum
Several drops lime juice
1-2 dashes grenadine

Combine with ice; shake well. Strain and add ice.

SAP BUCKET SPECIAL

2 oz. dark rum
1 oz. lemon juice
2 tsp. maple syrup

Warm the maple syrup in a ladle over a low flame; combine it with the rum and juice in a warmed wine glass straight up. Stir gently until well-blended.

SARATOGA

2½ oz. brandy
1 tsp. crushed pineapple
1-2 dashes maraschino
1-2 dashes Angostura bitters

Combine with ice; shake well. Strain and add ice. A half-teaspoon of pineapple syrup can be used instead of the crushed pineapple.

SARA'S SPECIAL

1½ oz. Amontillado
2 tbs. sweet vermouth

Combine, stir gently. Touch it up with a twist of lemon and add ice.

SASSAFRAS MEAD

4 large bunches sassafras roots
3½ pints molasses
3 cups honey
1 tbs. cream of tartar
Baking soda

Boil the sassafras roots in 2 quarts of water; strain clean. Boil the tea in a separate pot; add the molasses, honey, and tartar. Stir well. Allow to cool and strain. Bottle and store for 24 hours before use. To serve: Combine 1 tbs. mead with a tall glass of cold water; add ½ tsp. soda and stir.

SAUCY SUE

2 oz. apple brandy
Several drops apricot brandy
Several drops Pernod

Combine with ice; shake well. Strain and add ice. A **SAUCY SUE** *can also be made with equal parts plain and apple brandies, with less apricot brandy and Pernod and a twist of orange.*

SAUTERNE CUP

2 bottles sauterne
2 tbs. brandy, curacao, and maraschino
½ pint club soda

Combine; stir gently and serve in a bed of crushed ice. Garnish with fruit slices.

SAUTERNE PUNCH

1 bottle Sauterne
1 quart orange juice
1 pint pineapple juice
8 oz. lemon juice
1 bottle club soda

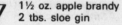

Combine everything except the soda; stir. Add the soda plus chunks of ice before serving.

SAUZALIKY

2 oz. tequila
4 oz. orange juice
1 tsp. lemon juice
1 very ripe banana
3 oz. crushed ice

Combine in blender at a high speed for 15 seconds. Strain straight up. Serves two.

SAVOY HOTEL

1 tbs. brandy
1 tbs. Benedictine
1 tbs. dark creme de cacao

Pour each ingredient into a pony or pousse cafe glass, carefully and one at a time, floating each upon the one beneath it.

SAVOY TANGO

1½ oz. apple brandy
2 tbs. sloe gin

Combine with a few ice cubes; stir to chill. Strain straight up.

SAZ

2 oz. bourbon
Several dashes Peychaud's bitters
A few drops Pernod

Combine the bourbon and the bitters with ice; shake well. Pour the Pernod into a freezing cold glass and tilt the glass around until the Pernod has coated its sides. Strain in the drink straight up and touch it up with a twist of lemon.

SAZERAC

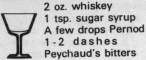

2 oz. whiskey
1 tsp. sugar syrup
A few drops Pernod
1-2 dashes
Peychaud's bitters

Combine the whiskey, sugar and bitters with ice; shake well. Pour the Pernod into a freezing-cold glass and tilt the glass until the Pernod has coated its sides. Strain in the drink. Add ice and a twist of lemon.

SCAFFAS ━━━━━━━

A SCAFFA is a combination of Benedictine and gin, rum, or whiskey — equal parts served straight up in a small glass with a dash or two of Angostura bitters. **BRANDY SCAFFAS** *are made with maraschino instead of Benedictine.*

SCANDIA

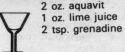

2 oz. aquavit
1 oz. lime juice
2 tsp. grenadine

Combine with ice; shake well. Strain straight up.

SCARLETT O'HARA

1½ oz. Southern Comfort
½ peach, soaked in brandy
3 tsp. lime juice
Several marashino cherries
3 oz. crushed ice

Combine in blender at a high speed for 15 seconds. Strain straight up.

SCANDANAVIAN GLOGG

1 bottle vodka
1 bottle red wine
1 cup sugar cubes
1 cup blanched almonds
1 cup raisins
Grated orange peels
Dried figs
Cardamon seeds
Cinnamon sticks
Whole cloves

Combine everything except the sugar cubes in a large saucepan; heat thoroughly but do not allow to boil. Lower heat and simmer for several minutes. Pile the sugar cubes on a large ladle; dip quickly in the glogg and ignite. Pour the burning sugar into the glog; stir well. Serve at once in mugs.

308

SCANDANAVIAN GLOGG II

2 quarts red wine
1 pint apiece port, vodka, rye, and cognac
4 oz. dry vermouth
1 cup blanched almonds
1 cup raisins
Cloves, anise, and fennel seeds
Sugar
Grated orange peels, cinnamon sticks, cardamom seeds

Tie the spices into a cloth sack; soak in a bowl with the wine, port, vermouth, raisins, and nuts overnight. When ready, heat, add sugar to taste, and stir until the sugar has dissolved. Simmer a few minutes, remove from heat; add the vodka, rye, and cognac. Re-heat but do not allow to boil. Remove spices and ignite. Serve hot.

SCARLETT O'HARA NO. 2

1½ oz. Southern Comfort.
1½ oz. cranberry juice
½ tsp. lime juice

Combine with ice; shake well. Strain and add ice.

SCHUSSBOOMER'S DELIGHT

1½ oz. cognac
1 tbs. lemon juice
Champagne

Combine the cognac and the lemon juice and add ice. Fill the glass with champagne and stir.

SCORPION

2 oz. white rum
2 oz. orange juice
1 oz. California brandy
2 tbs. lemon juice
2 tsp. almond extract
3 oz. crushed ice

Combine in blender at a low speed for 15 seconds. Strain and add ice. Decorate with a slice of orange.

SCOTCH AND VODKA

2½ oz. vodka
2 tsp. dry vermouth
A few drops of Scotch

Combine without ice; stir until well-blended. Pour straight up. Touch it up with a twist of lemon.

309

SCOTCH COBBLER

2 oz. Scotch
½ tsp. curacao
½ tsp. brandy

Combine over ice. Decorate with a slice of lemon and/or mint.

SCOTCH COOLER

3 oz. Scotch
Several dashes white creme de menthe
Club soda

Combine the Scotch and the creme de menthe and stir; add ice and fill the glass with soda.

SCOTCH EGGNOG

1 bottle Scotch
3 cups milk
1 doz. egg yolks
1 pint heavy cream
8 oz. powdered sugar
Grated nutmeg

Combine the egg yolks and the sugar in a bowl, beat together until creamy. Slowly add the Scotch, stirring constantly. Allow to stand several minutes; add the milk and refrigerate several hours. Just before serving, whip the cream and fold it into the nog. Garnish with nutmeg. Whole eggs, separated, can be used. Beat the whites until stiff and fold in after the whipped cream.

SCOTCH FLING

2 oz. Scotch
1 tsp. lime juice
Ginger ale

Combine the Scotch and the juice with ice; shake well. Strain, add ice and fill the glass with ginger ale.

SCOTCH FLIP

2 oz. Scotch
1 egg white
2 tsp. sugar syrup
Club soda

Combine the Scotch, egg white, and syrup with ice; shake well. Strain and add ice. Fill with soda.

SCOTCH HOLIDAY SOUR

2 oz. Scotch
1 oz. cherry liqueur
1 oz. lemon juice
2 tsp. sweet vermouth
½ egg white

Combine with ice; shake well. Strain, serve straight up. Decorate with a slice of lemon.

SCOTCH MILK PUNCH

Pour 2 oz. of Scotch into a highball glass; fill with milk. Add sugar to taste plus ice and stir very well. Garnish with nutmeg.

SCOTCH MIST

Pour 1½ oz. of Scotch into an old-fashioned glass packed with crushed ice. Touch it up with a twist of lemon. Other whiskeys can be used instead of Scotch.

SCOTCH ORANGE FIX

2 oz. Scotch
2 tsp. lemon juice
1 tsp. sugar
1 tsp. curacao
1 spiraled orange peel

Dissolve the sugar with 2 teaspoons of water. Drop in the peel; add the Scotch and the lemon juice and stir. Fill the glass with crushed ice and float the curacao on top.

SCOTCH SANGAREE

2 oz. Scotch
A few drops honey
Club soda

Combine the honey with the Scotch and stir until the honey is dissolved; add plenty of ice. Touch up with a spritz of soda and a twist of lemon. Garnish with nutmeg.

SCOTCH SAZ

1½ oz. Scotch
1 tsp. sweet vermouth
A few drops Pernod

Combine with ice; shake well. Strain, add ice.

SCOTCH SMASH

1½ oz. Scotch
1 tsp. sugar syrup
Club soda
A few mint sprigs

Muddle the mint with the sugar syrup; pour in the Scotch. Add ice; fill the glass with soda and stir. Decorate with slices of fruit.

SCOTCH SOUR

2 oz. Scotch
2 tsp. lime juice
1 tsp. powdered sugar
Club soda

Combine everything except the soda in with ice; shake well. Strain straight up; add a spritz of soda and decorate with a slice of orange and a cherry.

SCOTS GUARD

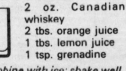

2 oz. Canadian whiskey
2 tbs. orange juice
1 tbs. lemon juice
1 tsp. grenadine

Combine with ice; shake well. Strain and add ice.

SCUPPERNONG WINE

Follow the recipe for **MUSCADINE WINE**, *substituting scuppernong juice for the muscadine juice.*

311

SEA CAPTAIN'S SPECIAL

1½ oz. rye
1 cube sugar
Several dashes Angostura bitters
A few drops Pernod
Champagne

Dissolve the sugar with the bitters. Add the rye plus ice and fill the glass with champagne; stir. Float the Pernod.

SEABOARD

1 oz. whiskey
1 oz. gin
2 tsp. lemon juice
1½ tsp. sugar syrup
A few mint leaves, partially torn

Combine everything except the mint with ice; shake well. Strain and add ice. Decorate with mint.

SECRET

1½ oz. Scotch
Several drops white creme de menthe
Club soda

Combine the Scotch and the creme de menthe with ice; shake well. Strain, add ice and fill the glass with soda.

SELF-STARTER

1 oz. gin
2 tsp. Lillet
1 tsp. apricot brandy
A few drops Pernod

Combine with ice; shake well. Strain and add ice.

SEPTEMBER MORN

1½ oz. white rum
2 tsp. lime juice
1 tsp. grenadine
½ egg white

Combine with ice; shake well. Line the rim of a glass with grenadine and press it in sugar. Strain in the drink and add ice.

SERPENT'S TOOTH

1½ oz. sweet vermouth
2 tbs. lemon juice
1 tbs. Irish whiskey
2 tsp. kummel
1-2 dashes Angostura bitters

Combine with ice; shake well. Strain and add ice.

SESAME

1½ oz. white rum
2 tsp. lime juice
2 tsp. sesame syrup

Combine with ice; shake well. Strain and add ice.

SEVILLA

1 oz. Jamaican rum
1 oz. sweet vermouth

Combine with ice; shake well. Strain and add ice.

SEVILLA FLIP

1 oz. white rum
1 oz. port
1 tsp. sugar syrup
1 egg

Combine with ice; shake well. Strain and add ice.

SEVILLE

1 oz. gin
2 tsp. dry sherry, orange juice, and lemon juice
1 tsp. sugar syrup

Combine with ice, shake well. Line the rim of a glass with water and press it in sugar. Strain in the drink and add ice.

SHAMROCK

1 oz. Irish whiskey
1 oz. dry vermouth
Several drops of green creme de menthe
Several dashes of green chartreuse

Combine with ice; shake well. Strain and decorate with an olive. The Irish whiskey can be augmented at the expense of the green Chartreuse.

SHANGHAI

1½ oz. Jamaican rum
1 tbs. lemon juice
2 tsp. anisette
A few drops grenadine

Combine with ice; shake well. Strain and add ice.

SHANGHAI PUNCH

1 bottle cognac
1 pint Jamaican rum
1 pint curacao
1 pint lemon juice
2 oz. almond extract
1½ oz. orange flower water
2 quarts fresh tea
Grated orange and lemon peels
Cinnamon sticks

Make sure the tea is boiling hot before combining it with the other ingredients in a large punch bowl. Stir serve while still hot.

SHARK'S TOOTH

2½ oz. gold rum
2 tsp. lemon juice
½ lime
1 - 2 dashes grenadine
A few drops rock candy syrup
Club soda
Mint sprigs

Combine everything except the lime and the mint with ice; shake well. Strain; add ice and fill with soda. Squeeze in the juice of the lime; stir gently. Garnish with mint.

SHARK'S TOOTH

1½ oz. gold rum
1 tsp. lemon juice, passion fruit syrup, sweet vermouth, and sloe gin
1 - 2 dashes Angostura bitters

Combine with ice; shake well. Line the rim of glass with water and press it in sugar; strain in the drink.

SHARKY PUNCH

1½ oz. calvados
2 tsp. rye
1 tsp. sugar syrup
Club soda

Combine everything except the soda with ice; shake well. Strain and add ice. Touch it up with a spritz of soda.

SHERMAN

1 oz. sweet vermouth
2 tsp. whiskey
Several drops Pernod
1-2 dashes Angostura and orange bitters

Combine and stir well; add ice.

SHERRIED COFFEE

1½ oz. cream sherry
1½ oz. coffee liqueur
2 tsp. light cream

Combine the sherry and the coffee liqueur with ice; shake well. Strain and add ice. Float the cream.

SHERRIED CORDIAL MEDOC FRAPPE

1 oz. Cordial Medoc
2 tsp. amontillado

Combine without ice; stir well. Pour over crushed ice.

SHERRY COBBLER

3 oz. sherry
1 tsp powdered sugar
1 tsp. orange juice
1 pineapple stick or mint sprigs

Stir the sherry, sugar, and juice together without ice; pour over crushed ice in a small goblet. Decorate with the pineapple stick or mint — and a slice of orange.

SHERRY COBBLER

16 oz. sherry
1 quart lemonade

Combine in a large pitcher; stir well. Pour over crushed ice. Garnish each with a twist of lemon.

SHERRIED SCOTCH

1½ oz. Scotch
1 oz. orange juice
2 tbs. cream sherry
1 tsp. honey
A few dashes of Angostura bitters
1 cinnamon stick

Combine everything except the cinnamon stick and the bitters into a saucepan; heat and stir until the honey is dissolved and the drink is ready to boil. Add the bitters and pour into a large mug. Garnish with the cinnamon and a slice of orange. Serve piping hot.

SHERRY SURPRISE

1 bottle cream sherry
¾ cup frozen orange juice concentrate

Dilute the orange juice concentrate in 6 oz. of water; combine with the sherry in a large pitcher and refrigerate; stir gently.

SHERRY TWIST

1½ oz. sherry
2 tsp. dry vermouth
2 tsp. brandy
Several drops Cointreau
A few drops lemon juice
1 cinnamon stick

Combine everything except the cinnamon stick with ice; shake well. Strain and add ice. Garnish with cinnamon.

SHERRY TWIST PUNCH

8 oz. sherry
6 oz. whiskey
4 oz. orange juice
2 tbs. Cointreau
1 tbs. lemon juice
2 cloves
1 pinch cayenne pepper

Combine; shake well. Strain over ice. Serves 4-6.

SIDECAR

2 oz. brandy
2 tsp. Cointreau
2 tsp. lemon juice

Combine with ice; shake well. Strain and add ice.

SILVER DOLLAR

1 oz. creme de banana
1 oz. white creme de menthe
1 oz. light cream

Combine with ice. Strain straight up.

SILVER KING

1½ oz. gin
1½ oz. lemon juice
1 egg white
A few drops sugar syrup
1-2 dashes orange bitters

Combine with ice; shake well. Strain and add ice.

SILVER KIRSCH

1 oz. kirsch
2 tbs. Positano
2 tsp. lemon juice
1½ tsp. sugar syrup
½ egg white
3 oz. crushed ice

Combine in a blender at a high speed for 10 seconds. Strain straight up.

SILVER STALLION

1 oz. gin
1 oz. vanilla ice cream
2 tbs. lemon juice
Club soda

Combine everything except the soda; stir until the ice cream has melted. Add ice and shake very well. Strain; add ice and fill the glass with soda.

SINGAPORE

1½ oz. Canadian whiskey
2 tsp. lemon juice
1 tsp. Rose's lime juice
1 tsp. sloe gin
1 cucumber peel

Combine everything except the peel with ice; shake well. Strain and add ice. Decorate with the peel.

SINGAPORE SLING

2 oz. gin
1 oz. Cherry Herring
½ lime
1-2 dashes Angostura bitters
A few drops of Benedictine
Ginger beer

Combine the gin, Cherry Herring, and bitters with ice; shake well. Strain; add ice. Squeeze on the juice of lime; drop in the peels; stir gently; add beer to fill the glass and float the Benedictine.

SINK OR SWIM

1½ oz. brandy
2 tsp. sweet vermouth
A few dashes of Angostura bitters

Combine with ice; shake well. Strain and add ice.

SIR WALTER

1½ oz. brandy
1 tbs. white rum
1 tsp. curacao, lime juice, and grenadine

Combine with ice; shake well. Strain and add ice.

61

3 oz. gin
1 oz. dry vermouth
1 oz. Strega

Combine with ice; shake well. Strain straight up.

SKEET SHOOTER'S SPECIAL

1½ oz. dark rum
2 tbs. apiece pineapple, grapefruit, and orange juices
1 oz. lemon soda
1 tbs. white rum
A pinch cinnamon

Combine with ice; shake. Strain, add ice and decorate with cherries.

SKI JUMPER'S PUNCH

1 bottle rum
4 oz. curacao
4 oz. orange juice
3 oz. lemon juice
8 oz. sugar
1 pint hot green tea

Dissolve the sugar with the juices in a large suacepan; add the tea. At the same time — in a separate pan — heat the curacao and the rum and then combine with the punch. Stir well and serve in a chafing dash piping hot.

SKIDMORE TIPPLE

2 oz. cognac
2 oz. kummel

Combine without ice; stir until blended. Serve straight up.

SKIPPER'S PARTICULAR

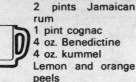

2 pints Jamaican rum
1 pint cognac
4 oz. Benedictine
4 oz. kummel
Lemon and orange peels

Combine in a punch bowl. Pour in 3 qts of boiling water; stir well and allow it to simmer a few minutes. Sugar to taste and serve hot.

SKY CLUB

1½ oz. whiskey
3 oz. orange juice
A few drops 151-proof rum

Combine, add ice and stir well.

SLEDGE HAMMER

1 tbs. brandy
1 tbs. rum
1 tbs. apple brandy
1-2 dashes Pernod

Combine with ice; shake well. Strain and add ice.

SLEEPER'S CIDER

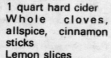

1 quart hard cider
Whole cloves, allspice, cinnamon sticks
Lemon slices

Combine the cider with spices in a large saucepan; cover and simmer for 20 minutes to a half hour. Strain and serve hot; garnish with a lemon slice.

SLEEPYHEAD

2½ oz. brandy
A few mint leaves, partially torn
Ginger ale

Pour the brandy into glass; add the mint leaves plus ice and a twist of orange. Fill the glass with ginger ale.

SLINGS

SLINGS are RICKEYS made with water: Combine 2 oz. of whiskey, brandy, gin, or vodka with 2 tablespoon of lemon juice in a highball glass. Add 1½ teaspoons sugar syrup plus ice and stir. Fill the glass with cold water.

SLOE BRANDY

2 oz. brandy
2 tsp. sloe gin
1 tsp. lemon juice

Combine with ice; shake well. Strain. Add ice and a twist of lemon.

SLOE GIN

1 pint sloes
2 oz. sugar
2 oz. rock candy
Gin

Place the sloes in a quart mason jar, poking each sloe through with a fork before hand. Add the sugar and candy, fill the jar with gin and seal. Shake the bottle every day for three weeks, then store in a cool dark place to ferment for at least one year.

SLOE GIN FIZZ

1 oz. sloe gin
1 oz. gin
1 tbs. lemon juice
Club soda

Combine everything except the soda with ice; shake well. Strain, add ice, and fill the glass with soda. Decorate with a slice of lemon.

SLOE LIME FRAPPE

1 tbs. sloe gin
1 tbs. white rum
1 tbs. lime liqueur

Combine without ice; stir well. Pour over crushed ice. Decorate with a slice of lime.

SLOE SCREW

1½ oz. sloe gin
Orange juice

Pour the sloe gin over ice. Fill the glass with orange juice and stir.

SLOE TEQUILA

1 oz. tequila
2 tsp. sloe gin
2 tsp. lime juice
4 oz. crushed ice
1 cucumber peel

Combine everything except the peel in blender at a low speed for 15 seconds. Strain; add ice to fill the glass. Decorate with the peel.

SLOE VERMOUTH

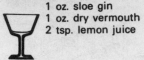

1 oz. sloe gin
1 oz. dry vermouth
2 tsp. lemon juice

Combine with ice; shake well. Strain and add ice.

SLOPPY JOE

1 tbs. white rum
1 tbs. dry vermouth
3 tbs. lime juice
A few drops curacao and grenadine

Combine with ice; shake well. Strain and add ice.

SNICKER

1½ oz. gin
1 tbs. dry vermouth
1 tsp. sugar syrup
1 egg white
A few drops maraschino
1-2 dashes orange bitters

Combine with ice; shake well. Strain and add ice.

SNOWBALL

1 oz. gin
1 tsp. white creme de menthe, heavy cream, anisette, and creme de violette

Combine with ice; shake well. Strain and add ice.

SOLDIER'S CAMPING PUNCH

2 bottles Jamaican rum
4 bottles brandy
4 lbs. sugar cubes
4 gallons strong hot coffee

Pour the rum and the brandy into a large saucepan. Add the sugar; heat and stir until the sugar is dissolved. Combine with the coffee in a large kettle; stir well and serve immediately.

SORGHUM BEER

3 lb. sorghum
4 lb. sugar
8 oz. hops
3 tbs. yeast

Boil the sorghum in 3 quarts of water until it becomes syrupy; strain back into the pot and boil the hops in the syrup for several minutes. Add 15 quarts of water and all but one lb. of the sugar; stir until the sugar has dissolved. Remove from heat. When lukewarm, add the yeast and stand at room temperature for 24 hours. Dilute the remaining sugar in a little hot water; add to the beer. Strain and bottle; store several days before serving.

SORREL BEER

2 large bunches wood sorrel
1 pint Jamaican rum
Crushed ginger

Combine the red sorrel blossom with the ginger in a crock pot; pour in 1 gallon of boiling water and allow to steep, sealed, for several days. When ready, add the rum and sugar to taste. Refrigerate until ready to use.

SOUL KISS

1 oz. Dubonnet
1 oz. orange juice
2 tbs. sweet vermouth
2 tbs. dry vermouth

Combine with ice; shake well. Strain and add ice.

SOUPED-UP GIBSON

2 oz. gin
2 tsp. dry vermouth
Pearl onions

Combine the gin and vermouth in a martini glass and stir well. Drop in several onions.

SOURS

Almost any liquor can be turned into a sour. Simply take 2½ oz. of any liquor of your choice and combine it with 2 tablespoons of lemon juice and 1 teaspoon of sugar syrup in a mixing glass filled with ice. Strain into a sour glass straight up. Decorate with fruit slices and a cherry.

SOUR APPLE WINE

1 gallon apple juice
2 lb. sugar
2 oz. isinglass gelatin
1 tbs. sourdough yeast
Wine vinegar

Combine the apple juice and the sugar in a large saucepan; boil until clear. Allow to cool. Add the yeast; stir well. Seal and store in a warm place several weeks. Strain and reseal in a wooden barrel. Store for at least one year. Re-strain; add the isinglass and an oz. of wine vinegar per gallon of cider. Bottle for use.

SOUR CITRUS WINE

1 doz. oranges
1 doz. lemons
1 lb. sugar
1½ oz. dry active yeast

Peel the fruit; boil the rinds in a gallon of water and then simmer for several hours. Squeeze in the fruit juices; add the sugar plus the yeast and stir until mixed. Turn out into a crock pot and seal tightly. Allow to ferment. After fermentation, allow the wine to stand until clear. Strain clean and bottle for future use.

SOUTH CAMP SPECIAL

1 tbs. Jamaican rum
1 tbs. dry gin
1 tbs. Scotch
A few drops lime juice, sweet vermouth, and cherry brandy

Combine with ice; shake well. Strain and add ice. Decorate with a cherry.

SOUTH PACIFIC

1½ oz. brandy
2 tsp. lemon juice
1½ oz. dry gin
1 tbs. grapefruit juice
A few drops maraschino

Combine with ice; shake well. Strain and add ice.

SOUTHERN BELLE

1 oz. bourbon
1 oz. heavy cream
1 tbs. green creme de menthe
1 tbs. white creme de cacao

Combine with ice; shake. Strain, serve straight up.

SOUTHERN COMFORT STRAWBERRY FRAPPE

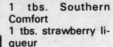

1 tbs. Southern Comfort
1 tbs. strawberry liqueur

Combine without ice; stir well. Pour over crushed ice. Touch it up with a twist of orange. Decorate with a slice of lemon.

SOUTHERN CROSS

1 bottle port
4 oz. grapefruit juice
2 oz. sugar syrup
3 tsp. lemon juice
½ tsp. all spice
2 oz. raisins

Combine everything except the raisins in a saucepan and heat thoroughly. Boil the raisins in a cup of water and add the raisins and the water to the wine mixture. Serve hot.

SOUTHERN GIN

2½ oz. gin
1-2 dashes orange bitters
A few drops curacao

Combine with ice; shake well. Strain; add ice and a twist of lemon.

SOUTHERN GINGER

1½ oz. 100-proof bourbon
1 oz. ginger ale
1 tsp. lemon juice
A few drops ginger brandy

Combine with ice; shake well. Strain. Add ice and a twist of lemon

SOUTHERN PUNCH

1½ oz. bourbon
1 oz. lemon juice
1 tbs. rum
2 tsp. brandy
2 tsp. sugar syrup
Club soda

Combine everything except the rum and the soda with ice; shake. Strain into glass filled partly with crushed ice. Almost fill glass with soda and float the rum on top.

SOUTHGATE

1¼ oz. whiskey
½ tsp. sugar syrup
A few dashes of Angostura bitters

Combine with ice; shake well. Strain and add ice. Touch it up with a twist of lemon.

SOVIET COCKTAIL

1½ oz. vodka
2 tsp. dry vermouth
2 tsp. amontillado

Combine with ice; shake well. Strain and add ice. Touch it up with a twist of lemon.

SOYER AU CHAMPAGNE

1 oz. vanilla ice cream
A few drops of brandy, maraschino, and curacao
4 oz. champagne

Combine the ice cream with the brandy, maraschino, and curacao; stir until blended and add the champagne. Decorate with a slice of orange and a cherry.

SPANISH MOSS

1½ oz. tequila
2 tbs. Kahlua
Several drops of green creme de menthe

Combine with ice; shake well. Strain over one cube of ice.

SPANISH TOWN

1½ oz. white rum
A few drops curacao

Combine with ice; shake well. Strain and add ice. Garnish with nutmeg.

SPANISH VODKA MARTINI

2½ oz. vodka
1 tbs. dry sherry

Combine with ice; shake well. Strain straight up; add a twist of lemon.

SPECIAL ROUGH

1½ oz. apple brandy
1½ oz. brandy
A few drops Pernod

Combine with ice; shake well. Strain and add ice.

SPENCER

1½ oz. gin
1 tbs. apricot brandy
A few dashes of Angostura bitters
A few drops orange juice

Combine with ice; shake well. Strain and add ice.

SPICED COFFEE

1 oz. brandy, rum, or bourbon
1 cup of hot coffee
Cinnamon, ground cloves, and nutmeg

Wrap the spices in cheesecloth or any other material for infusing; soak them in the coffee for several minutes. Add the brandy, rum, or bourbon when ready to drink.

SPICED ORANGE BLOSSOM

4 oz. orange juice
2 oz. gin
A few drops lemon juice
A few maraschino cherries
A few dashes of Angostura bitters
Several pinches cinnamon
A few drops cherry juice

Combine in a blender at a high speed until foamy. Serve unstrained.

SPIKED ALE

1 quart ale
4 oz. brandy
1 tbs. sugar
Cloves, nutmeg, and ginger

Combine in a large saucepan; heat but do not bring to a boil, stirring constantly. Strain clean and serve piping hot.

SPIKED PINEAPPLE PUNCH

2 quarts unsweetened pineapple juice
1 pint vodka
8 oz. Grand Marnier
8 oz. Maraschino
6 oz. Orange juice
1½ lemon juice
1 bottle club soda

Combine everything except the soda; stir well. Add the soda plus chunks of ice before serving.

SPINSTER'S NIGHT CAP

9 gallons hard cider
8 lb honey
2 oz. baking soda
2 bottles Jamaican rum
Ground cinnamon, cloves, and mace

Combine the cider, rum, and 2 quarts of cold water in a large crock pot; add the honey, baking soda, and spices to taste. Stir well until blended. Seal and allow to ferment. Stir, strain, and bottle for future use.

SPRING PUNCH

1 quart gin
2 6-oz. cans frozen lemonade concentrate
1½ bottles club soda
Cucumber peels

Combine the gin and defrosted lemonade concentrate; stir well to blend. Garnish with cucumber peels. Add the soda plus chunks of ice.

SPINGTIME VERMOUTH

1 oz. dry vermouth
2 oz. cranberry juice
6 strawberries

Combine the vermouth and the juice with ice; shake well. Strain and add ice. Fill with strawberries.

SPRITZER

5 oz. Rhine wine
Club soda

Thoroughly chill the wine and soda. Pour the wine into a large goblet; add ice and fill with soda. Stir. Decorate with spiral lemon peel or slices of fruit.

SPRUCE BEER

A bundle of spruce sprigs
1 pint molasses
3 oz. yeast
1 oz. hops
1 tsp. ginger

Boil the sprigs in just enough water to produce a tablespoon of strong juice. Boil the hops and the ginger in a gallon of water; strain out the spices. Add the molasses and the spruce juices. Allow to cool; add the yeast. Turn out into a crock pot; seal tightly and allow to ferment for a few days. Bottle for future use.

STAR

1 oz. apple brandy
1 oz. sweet vermouth
1-2 dashes orange bitters

Combine. Shake. Strain.

STAR DAISY

1 oz. dry gin
1 oz. apple brandy
1½ tsp. lemon juice
1 tsp. sugar syrup
1 tsp. grenadine

Combine with ice; shake well. Strain and add ice.

STARBOARD

1½ oz. gin
2 tbs. green creme de menthe

Combine with crushed ice; shake. Strain and add ice.

STARS AND STRIPES

1 tbs. green chartreuse
1 tbs. maraschino
1 tbs. creme de cassis

Slightly tip a pony glass and carefully pour in each ingredient. Do not mix.

STARS FELL ON ALABAMA

1¼ oz. corn whiskey
1 tsp. sugar syrup
Several drops Pernod
A few drops orange flower water
A few dashes of

Peychaud's and Angostura bitters

Combine with ice; shake well. Strain and add ice.

STINGERS

are simple, minted drinks which can be made with many kinds of liquors: Take 1½ oz. of your favorite brandy, Jamaican rum, gin, tequila, or vodka and combine it with 1 oz. of white creme de menthe. Shake them in a mixing glass filled with ice and strain into an old-fashioned glass.

STIRRUP CUP

1½ oz. Southern Comfort
1½ oz. cranberry juice
1 tbs. lemon juice
Grapefruit juice
Club soda
Mint sprigs

Combine the Southern Comfort plus the cranberry and lemon juices with ice; shake well. Strain; add ice and fill the glass with equal parts grapefruit juice and soda. Stir gently; decorate with mint.

STONE FENCE

2½ oz. apple brandy
1-2 dashes Angostura bitters
Sweet cider

Pour the brandy into a glass; add the bitters plus ice and fill with cider. Stir well.

STONE SOUR

1½ oz. bourbon
1 tbs. lemon juice
1 tsp. white creme de menthe
Club soda
Mint sprigs a few

Pour the bourbon, juice, and creme de menthe over crushed ice; stir well and fill the glass with club soda. Sweeten to taste. Decorate with sprigs of mint and a cherry.

STONEHENGE COLLINS

3 oz. gin
3 tsp. lemon juice
2 tsp. sugar syrup
1 tsp. white creme de menthe

Combine with ice; shake well. Strain over crushed ice. Garnish with fruit slices or mint.

STONEWALL

2 oz. cider
1 oz. Jamaican rum

Combine with ice; shake well. Strain and add ice.

STONYBROOK

1½ oz. whiskey
2 tsp. Triple Sec
½ egg white
A few drops almond extract

Combine with ice; shake well. Strain and add ice. Touch it up with a twist of orange and a twist of lemon.

STRAIGHT LAW

2½ oz. dry sherry
1 tbs. dry gin

Combine with ice; shake well. Strain and add ice. Touch it up with a twist of lemon.

STRATOSPHERE

1 oz. rum
2 tsp. California brandy
2 tsp. lemon juice
1½ tsp. sugar syrup
1 tsp. cherry liqueur

Combine filled with ice; shake well. Strain and add ice.

STRAWBERRY BOWL

2 bottles champagne, chilled
1 pint claret
2 quarts strawberries, sliced
8 oz. sugar

Combine the strawberries with the claret and sugar in a punch bowl; stir gently to blend and cool for at least one hour. Add the champagne before serving.

STRAWBERRY CORDIAL

1 peck strawberries
1 gallon brandy
16 oz. sugar
Ground cardamon, cinnamon, and cloves

Slice and simmer half the strawberries in a saucepan with just enough water to cover them, plus a few pinches of assorted spices. Strain the liquids out; add the sugar plus the remaining berries and allow to stand for several hours. Mash the berries through cheesecloth, combine the juice with the brandy, stir and bottle for future use.

STRAWBERRY CREOLE PUNCH

1½ quarts claret
1 quart strawberry juice
1 pint pineapple juice
2 cups sugar
2 bottles club soda
Whole strawberries

Dissolve the sugar with the fruit juices; add the wine and soda plus ice, and stir well. Garnish with strawberries and store in a freezer until semi-frozen.

STRAWBERRY PUNCH

½ peck strawberries
1 bottle white rum
1 lb. sugar
1½ gallons freshly brewed tea

Combine the berries with the sugar in a large bowl and refrigerate for at least two days. Strain clean and combine with the rum. Add chunks of ice plus the tea before serving.

STRAWBERRY RITA

1 oz. tequila
2 oz. whole strawberries
3 tsp. sugar syrup
3 oz. crushed ice
Sliced strawberries
Whipped cream

Combine everything except the sliced strawberries and the whipped cream in blender at a high speed for 15 seconds. Line the rim of a glass with water and press it in sugar; strain in the drink. Garnish with the sliced strawberries and whipped cream plus a slice of lime.

━━ STRAWBERRY RUM FLIP ━━

1½ oz. white rum
1 oz. strawberry liqueur
1½ tsp. sugar syrup
1 tsp. lemon juice
1 egg

Combine with ice; shake well. Strain straight up; garnish with nutmeg.

STRAWBERRY SANGAREE

4 oz. claret or Bordeaux
1½ oz. sugar
1 tsp. lemon juice
4 oz. strawberries, cleaned and crushed
Club soda

Combine everything except the soda with ice; shake well. Leave in glass and chill for at least one hour. Strain and add ice. Fill the glass wth soda and decorate with slices of fruit.

STRAWBERRY SWIG

1½ oz. gin
2 tsp. strawberry liqueur
1 tsp. lime juice
1-2 dashes orange bitters

Combine with ice; shake well. Strain and add ice. Decorate with a slice of lime.

STREGA FLIP

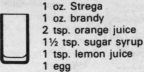

1 oz. Strega
1 oz. brandy
2 tsp. orange juice
1½ tsp. sugar syrup
1 tsp. lemon juice
1 egg

Combine with ice; shake extremely well. Strain straight up; garnish with nutmeg.

STREGA SOUR

1½ oz. gin
2 tsp. lemon juice
1 tsp. Strega

Combine with ice; shake well. Line the rim of glass with Strega and press it in sugar. Strain in the drink; add ice and decorate with a slice of lemon.

SUBURBAN

1 oz. whiskey
2 tsp. port
2 tsp. Jamaican rum
A few dashes of Angostura and orange bitters

Combine with ice; shake well. Strain and add ice.

STRAWBERRY WINE

2 quarts strawberries
1 quart sugar
1 quart potatoes, peeled and sliced

*Slice the strawberries and put them in a crock pot. Pour the sugar on top of them and add the potatoes. Seal the pot and allow to stand for several months **undisturbed**. Strain and bottle the wine when ready for use.*

SUGAR LOAF CORDIAL

8 oz. Puerto Rican rum
1 tbs. high-proof rum
8 oz. sugar
1 large orange

Carefully peel the orange, leaving the skin as intact as possible. Place the peel in the center of a wide, heat proof dish and fill it with sugar.

Pour the high-proof rum over the sugar; the Puerto Rican rum around it like a lagoon. Ignite the sugar loaf and serve while blazing. Place a spot of sugar in each cup of rum if you wish. Another alternative — lift the orange peel after igniting the sugar and let the flames and the sweetness disperse itself around the rum until dissolved, but not cool.

SUISSESSE

1½ oz. Pernod
Several drops anisette
1 egg white

Combine with ice; shake extremely well. Strain and add ice. A few drops of heavy cream can be added before mixing.

SUMMER BOURBON

1 oz. bourbon
2 oz. orange juice
1 pinch salt

Combine without ice; stir well. Pour over crushed ice.

SUMMER PUNCH

3 bottles dry white wine
12 oz. creme de cassis
1 pint strawberries
Orange slices

Combine the wine and the cassis and stir; float the strawberries and orange slices. Add chunks of ice before serving.

SUMMER WINE CUP

1 bottle white wine
4 oz. brandy
2 oz. sugar
Sliced strawberries, lemons, and oranges
Cucumber peels, sprigs of mint
1 pint club soda

Combine the brandy with the sugar; stir until the sugar has dissolved. Add the fruit slices and allow to stand for one hour. When ready add the wine, cucumber peels, and mint; stir. Pour in the soda plus chunks of ice.

SUN VALLEY

4 oz. Jamaican rum
1 quart heavy cream
4 egg yolks
2 tbs. powdered sugar
Milk

Pour the cream into a saucepan and almost bring to a boil; remove from heat. Beat the yolks with a little milk; add them plus the sugar to the cream. Pour in the rum and stir well. Serve piping hot in small mugs.

328

SUNDOWNER

2 oz. white rum
1 oz. lemon juice
2 tsp. grenadine
Tonic water

Combine the rum, juice, and grenadine with ice; shake. Strain, add ice and fill with tonic. Stir.

SUNSET

1½ oz. tequila
2 tsp. lime juice
2 tsp. grenadine
4 oz. crushed ice

Combine in a blender at a low speed for 15 seconds. Strain and add ice. Decorate with a slice of lime.

SUNSHINE PUNCH

1 bottle white wine
4 oz. brandy
2 oz. sugar
1 pint club soda
Sliced pears, apples, and oranges

Combine the wine, sugar, and fruit slices allow to stand for a few hours. Add the brandy and soda plus chunks of ice.

SUPERIOR COCKTAIL

2 oz. gin
1 oz. lemon juice
A few drops dry vermouth
1-2 dashes kirschwasser
1 tsp. sugar syrup
Button mushrooms

Combine everything except the mushrooms with ice; shake well. Strain straight up; drop in button mushrooms.

SUTTON PLACE SLING

1½ oz. Jamaican rum
2 tbs. orange juice
1 tsp. 151-proof rum
A few dashes of Angostura bitters
A few drops lime juice
A few drops cherry juice
Lemon soda

Combine everything except the soda and the 151-proof rum with ice; shake well. Strain; add ice and fill with lemon soda. Float the 151-proof rum.

SWEDISH SNOWBALL

1½ oz. Advockaat
lemon soda

Pour the Advockaat over ice. Fill the glass and stir. Decorate with lemon slice.

SWEET GRAPE WINE

10 lbs. grapes
2 lbs. sugar

Crush the grapes with the sugar in a large pot; seal and allow to ferment. When ready, strain into bottles and store for future use.

SWEET LILT

2 oz. Cognac
2 tbs. anisette
2 tbs. curacao
A chunk of fresh pineapple

Combine everything except the pineapple with ice; shake well. Strain straight up; garnish with pineapple.

SWISS COCKTAIL

2 oz. Dubonnet
1 tbs. kirschwasser

Combine with ice; shake well. Strain straight up; add a twist of lemon.

SW1

1 tbs. vodka
1 tbs. orange juice
1 tbs. Campari bitters

Combine with ice; shake well. Strain and add ice.

SWORE

1½ oz. 100-proof vodka
2 tsp. sweet vermouth
1 tsp. kirsch
1 tsp. orange juice

Combine with ice; shake well. Strain and add ice. Touch it up with a twist of orange.

SYLLABUB

16 oz. white wine
16 oz. light cream
3 cups milk
10 oz. sugar
4 egg whites
3 oz. lemon juice
Grated lemon rind
Nutmeg

Combine the wine, rinds (to taste), and juice. Add 1 cup of the sugar and stir until it dissolved. Combine the milk with the cream in a separate bowl; add it to the wine and beat until foamy. Beat the egg whites in another bowl, adding the remaining sugar slowly. When the whites hold peaks, add them in small puffs to the wine punch and garnish the tufts with nutmeg. Serve in punch glasses, a puff in each.

YOUR OWN RECIPE

Use a bartender's mixing glass whenever the instructions state "combine" ingredients. Strain the drink from the mixing glass into the drinking glass suggested by the illustration alongside the ingredients.

The glass pictured for each drink is our suggestion; other drinking cups may be used as well.

TABOO

1 oz. vodka
1 oz. white rum
2 tbs. pineapple juice
2 tsp. lemon juice
A few drops rock candy syrup
2 oz. crushed ice
Mint sprigs

Combine in a blender at a high speed for 15 seconds. Garnish with slices of fruit and sprigs of mint.

TAHITI CLUB

2 oz. gold rum
2 tsp. lime juice, lemon juice, pineapple juice, and maraschino

Combine with ice; shake well. Strain and add ice. Decorate with a slice of orange.

TAHITI TANTALIZER

1½ oz. vodka
1 tbs. pineapple juice concentrate
2 tsp. guava nectar
2 tsp. lemon juice

Combine with ice; shake well. Strain and add ice.

TAHITIAN WEDDING PUNCH

2 bottles white wine
1 bottle gold rum
2 cups crushed pineapple
8 oz. sugar
8 oz. lemon juice
Grated lemon rinds
Gardenia or other flower blossoms

Dissolve the sugar with the lemon juice in a large pot; stir until syrupy. Add the wine, rum, pineapple, and rinds; stir until blended. Seal, and allow to stand for several hours in a cool dark place. Add large chunks of ice plus the flower blossoms and rinds.

TAILSPIN

¾ oz. gin
¾ oz. sweet vermouth
1 tbs. green chartreuse
1-2 dashes orange bitters

Combine with ice; shake well. Strain and add ice. Touch it up with a twist of lemon and an olive.

TALL DUTCH EGG NOG

1½ oz. white rum
1 oz. orange juice
2 tbs. advocaat liqueur
2 tsp. 151-proof rum
1½ tsp. sugar syrup
6 oz. milk
4 oz. crushed ice

Combine in a blender at a high speed for 10 seconds. Strain and garnish with cinnamon.

TALL ISLANDER

2 oz. white rum
3 oz. pineapple juice
3 tsp. lime juice
1 tsp. Jamaican rum
1 tsp. sugar syrup
Club soda

Combine all but the soda with ice; shake well. Strain add plenty of ice and a spritz of soda. Stir well and decorate with a lime slice.

TANGO

1 oz. gin
2 tsp. sweet vermouth, dry vermouth, and orange juice
Several drops curacao

Combine with ice; shake well. Strain and add ice.

TANTALUS

¾ oz. brandy
¾ oz. lemon juice
1 tbs. Forbidden Fruit

Combine with ice; shake well. Strain and add ice.

TANGERINE MORNING PUNCH

1 quart brandy
1 doz. tangerines
1 lb. sugar
1 quart milk
1 quart light cream
Whipped cream

Slice the tangerines and place them in a deep saucepan. Add the milk and cream; stir gently while simmering for five to ten minutes. Strain into a large punch bowl; add the sugar while the punch is warm. Stir until the sugar is dissolved. Allow to cool and add the brandy. Top each cup with whipped cream.

TARPON

3 oz. orange juice
2 tbs. bourbon
2 tsp. Triple Sec
1 tsp. sugar
Club soda

Combine everything except the soda with ice; shake. Strain add ice and fill with soda. Decorate with pineapple.

TEA PUNCH

1 bottle vodka
1½ quarts strong hot tea
12 oz. frozen lemonade concentrate
8 oz. frozen orange juice concentrate
Fruit slices
Whole strawberries

Combine the frozen fruit juices with the tea and allow to cool. Add the vodka plus the fresh fruit slices and stir until well-blended. Add chunks of ice before serving.

TEMPERANCE PUNCH

1 quart sweet cider
3 oz. cognac
2 oz. sugar
Lemon slices
Club soda

Combine the cider, cognac, and sugar in a large pitcher; stir until the sugar has dissolved. Add ice. Serve in tall glasses over ice, 4 oz. of cider per glass. The rest is soda. Garnish each glass with lemon.

TEMPTATION COCKTAIL

1½ oz. whiskey
Several drops Pernod, Dubonnet, and curacao

Combine with ice; shake well. Strain and add ice. Touch it up with a twist of orange and of lemon.

TEMPTER

1½ oz. port
1½ oz. apricot brandy

Combine with ice; shake well. Strain and add ice.

TEN TON COCKTAIL

1½ oz. rye
1 tbs. dry vermouth
1 tbs. grapefruit juice

Combine with ice; shake well. Strain and add ice. Decorate with a cherry.

TENDER

1½ oz. gin
1 tbs. apple brandy
1 tbs. apricot brandy
A few drops lemon juice

Combine with ice; shake well. Strain and add ice.

TENNESSEE

3 oz. rye
2 tbs. maraschino
2 tsp. lemon juice

Combine with ice; shake well. Strain add ice.

TEQUILA A LA CANELA

1 oz. tequila liqueur
2 tbs. condensed milk
A few pinches cinnamon

Combine the liqueur and the milk; stir well. Add ice and cinnamon to taste.

TEQUILA COCKTAIL

1½ oz. tequila
1 tbs. dry vermouth
A few drops vanilla extract

Combine with ice; shake well. Strain and add ice.

TEQUILA COCKTAIL NO. 2

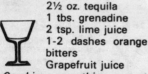

2½ oz. tequila
1 tbs. grenadine
2 tsp. lime juice
1-2 dashes orange bitters
Grapefruit juice

Combine everything except the grapefruit juice with ice; shake well. Strain; add ice and fill with grapefruit juice.

TEQUILA DAIQUIRI

1½ oz. tequila
1½ tsp. lime juice
1½ tsp. sugar syrup

Combine with ice; shake well. Strain.

TEQUILA DUBONNET

1½ oz. tequila
1½ oz. Dubonnet

Combine; stir well and add ice. Decorate with a slice of lemon.

TEQUILA FIZZ

1½ oz. tequila
1 tbs. grenadine
1 egg white
3 oz. ginger ale
3 oz. crushed ice

Combine in a blender at a low speed for a few seconds. Strain.

TEQUILA FRESA

1½ oz. tequila
1 tbs. strawberry liqueur
2 tsp. lime juice
A few drops orange bitters
1 slice of lime and a strawberry

Combine everything except the fruit with ice; shake well. Strain and add ice. Decorate with the fruit.

TEQUILA FROZEN SCREWDRIVER

1½ oz. tequila
3 oz. orange juice
3 oz. crushed ice

Combine in a blender at a low speed for 15 seconds. Strain and add ice. Decorate with a slice of orange.

TEQUILA GHOST

2 oz. tequila
1 oz. Pernod
2 tsp. lemon juice

Combine with ice; shake well. Strain and add ice.

TEQUILA GUAYABA

1½ oz. tequila
2 tsp. guava syrup,
orange juice, and
lime juice

*Combine with ice; shake well.
Strain and add ice. Touch it
up with a twist of orange.*

TEQUILA MANHATTAN

1½ oz. gold tequila
1 tbs. sweet ver-
mouth

*Combine with ice; shake well.
Strain Add ice and a twist of
lime; stir. Decorate with a
slice of orange.*

TEQUILA OLD-FASHIONED

1½ oz. tequila
1 tbs. sugar syrup
1-2 dashes
Angostura bitters
Club soda
1 pineapple stick

*Combine everything except
the soda and the pineapple
stick; add ice and stir. Touch
it up with a spritz of soda and
a twist of lemon; decorate
with the pineapple.*

TEQUILA PUP

1½ oz. tequila
3 tsp. lime juice
1 tsp. honey
1-2 dashes
Angostura bitters

*Combine with ice; shake very
well. Strain and add ice.*

TEQUILA RICKEY

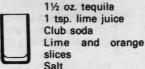

1½ oz. tequila
1 tsp. lime juice
Club soda
Lime and orange
slices
Salt

*Pour the tequila and the lime
juice into a highball glass;
add ice and stir well. Fill the
glass with soda. Twist in the
slice of lime. Sprinkle a little
salt over the drink. Decorate
with the orange slice.*

TEQUILA SOUR

1½ oz. tequila
2 tsp. lemon juice
1½ tsp. sugar syrup

*Combine with ice; shake well.
Strain straight up. Decorate
with a slice of lemon.*

TEQUILA SUNRISE

*Pour 2 oz. of tequila into a
highball glass. Add ice and 2
teaspoons of grenadine; fill
the glass with orange juice
and stir. A TIJUANA
SUNRISE is a TEQUILA
SUNRISE with a dash or two
of Angostura bitters instead
of the grenadine*

TEQUINI

2½ oz. tequila
1 tbs. dry vermouth

*Combine straight up and sitr
gently. Touch it up with a
twist of lemon.*

337

TEXAN

1½ oz. bourbon
2 tsp. apiece apricot
brandy, lime juice,
and grenadine

*Combine with ice; shake.
Strain over plenty of ice;
decorate with a slice of lime
and a green cherry.*

THANKSGIVING
COCKTAIL

1 oz. dry gin
1 oz. dry vermouth
1 oz. apricot brandy
Several drops lemon
juice

*Combine with ice; shake well.
Strain and add ice. Decorate
with a cherry.*

THIRD DEGREE

1½ oz. gin
1 tbs. dry vermouth
1 tsp. Pernod

*Combine with ice; shake well.
Strain and add ice.*

THIRD RAIL

2 oz. dry vermouth
A few drops of
curacao
Several drops white
creme de menthe

*Combine with ice; shake well.
Strain add ice and a twist of
lemon.*

THREE KINGS' PUNCH

8 oz. white rum
8 oz. anisette
4 egg yolks
A cinnamon stick
8 oz. sugar
8 oz. water
14 oz. undiluted
evaporated milk

*Combine the sugar, water,
and cinnamon stick in a
saucepan and heat until boiling. Remove from the heat
and take out the stick. Slowly
add the milk, rum, and
anisette. Fold in the yolks, stir
gently, and refrigerate. Turn
out into cups garnished with
cinnamon.*

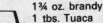

THREE MILLER

1½ oz. white rum
1 tbs. brandy
1 tsp. grenadine
A few drops lemon
juice

*Combine with ice; shake well.
Strain and add ice.*

THREE STRIPES
COCKTAIL

1 oz. dry gin
2 tsp. dry vermouth
2 tsp. orange juice

*Combine with ice; shake well.
Strain and add ice.*

THUMPER

1¾ oz. brandy
1 tbs. Tuaca

*Combine with ice; shake well.
Strain and add ice. Touch it
up with a touch of lemon.*

THUNDER

2½ oz. brandy
1 tsp. sugar syrup
1 egg yolk
1 pinch cayenne
pepper

Combine with ice; shake well. Strain and add ice.

THUNDERBIRD SPECIAL

1 oz. bourbon
1 oz. heavy cream
2 tsp. creme de banana
2 tsp. Cointreau

Combine with ice; shake. Strain with one ice cube.

TIDBIT

1½ oz. dry gin
1½ oz. vanilla ice cream
A few drops cream sherry

Combine without ice; stir until well-blended. Pour, and add ice to fill glass. Decorate with a cherry.

TIGER'S MILK

1 oz. Jamaican rum
1 oz. brandy
4 oz. heavy cream
3 tsp. sugar syrup

Combine with ice; shake very well. Strain and add ice.

TIGER'S TAIL

1½ oz. Pernod
6 oz. orange juice

Combine, stir well and add ice to fill the glass. Decorate with a slice of lime.

TIKI PUNCH

1 cup gin
1 cup Triple Sec
3 oz. lime juice
2 bottles champagne

Combine the gin, Triple Sec, and juice; add some ice and allow to stand until the ice melts. Add the champagne plus more ice.

TIPPERARY

¾ oz. Irish whiskey
¾ oz. sweet vermouth
1 tbs. green chartreuse

Combine with ice; shake well. Strain and add ice.

TNT 1½ oz. rye
1½ oz. Pernod
Combine with ice; shake well. Strain and add ice.

TOM AND JERRY

1½ oz. brandy
1½ oz. rum
Hot milk
2 tsp. sugar
2 eggs
A pinch of baking soda

Separate the eggs. Beat the whites until frothy; add the sugar and continue to beat the eggs until they form peaks. Beat the yolks in a separate bowl until creamy. Combine the yolks and the whites, and add the baking soda. Divide the egg mixture between two mugs; add half the brandy and rum to each and fill the mugs with hot milk.

TOM COLLINS

2 oz. gin
1½ oz. lemon juice
1½ tsp. sugar syrup
Club soda

Combine everything except the soda; stir well and add ice. Fill the glass with soda and decorate with a cherry. A **JOHN COLLINS** *is a* **TOM COLLINS** *using ginger ale instead of club soda.*

TOM MOORE

2 oz. Irish whiskey
1 oz. sweet vermouth
1-2 dashes Angostura bitters

Combine with ice; shake well. Strain and add ice.

TONGA PUNCH

1 quart white rum
1 quart orange juice
1 pint lemon juice
10 oz. orange curacao
6 oz. lime juice
4 oz. grenadine

Combine stir. Add chunks of ice plus slices of fruit.

TOREADOR

1½ oz. tequila
2 tsp. white creme de cacao
Whipped cream
Cocoa powder

Combine the tequila and the creme de cacao with ice; shake well. Strain and add ice. Top with whipped cream and sprinkle with cocoa.

TORPEDO

1½ oz. calvados
1 tbs. brandy
A few drops gin

Combine with ice; shake well. Strain and add ice.

TORRIDORA COCKTAIL

1½ oz. white rum
2 tsp. Tia Maria
1 tsp. heavy cream
1 tsp. 151-proof rum

Combine everything except the high-proof rum with ice; shake very well. Strain and add ice. Float the high-proof rum.

TRADE WINDS

2 oz. gold rum
2 tsp. lime juice
2 tsp. plum brandy
2 tsp. sugar syrup
3 oz. crushed ice

Combine in a blender at a low speed for 15 seconds. Strain straight up.

TRILBY

1½ oz. gin
2 tbs. sweet vermouth
2 tsp. Creme Yvette
1-2 dashes orange bitters

Combine everything except the Creme Yvette with ice; shake well. Strain and add ice. Float the Creme Yvette.

TRILBY NO. 2

¾ oz. Scotch
¾ oz. sweet vermouth
1 tbs. Parfait Amour
A few drops Pernod
A few dashes of Angostura bitters

Combine with ice; shake well. Strain and add ice.

TRINIDAD PUNCH

12 oz. white rum
4 oz. sugar
4 oz. lime juice
½ oz. Angostura bitters

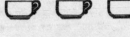

Boil the sugar in 4 oz. of water; after the sugar has dissolved, simmer another 5 minutes. Allow to cool. Combine the cool sugar syrup with the rum, juice, and bitters in a punch bowl; stir well. Refrigerate until ready to use. Add plenty of ice before serving.

TRIPLE C

1 oz. cognac
2 whole cardamom seeds
Hot coffee

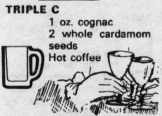

Drop the seeds into a coffee mug; break them open with a muddler. Add the cognac and the coffee; sugar to taste. Stir well.

TRIPLICE

1 oz. gin
1 oz. Benedictine
1 oz. dry vermouth

Combine with ice; shake well. Strain and add ice.

TRIPLE DESIRE (For Three)

1 oz. cognac, dry vermouth, coffee brandy, creme de noyaux, blackberry brandy, and lemon juice
2 tsp sugar syrup

Combine with ice; shake well. Strain and add ice.

TROIS RIVERES

1½ oz. Canadian whiskey
2 tsp. Dubonnet
1 tsp. Cointreau

Combine with ice; shake well. Strain and add ice. Touch it up with a twist of lemon.

TROLLEY

2 oz. bourbon
Pineapple juice
Cranberry juice

Pour the bourbon over ice. Fill the glass with equal parts pineapple and cranberry juices and stir gently. Decorate with a slice of orange.

TROPICAL COCKTAIL

2½ oz. gin
1 oz. frozen pineapple concentrate
1 oz. guava nectar

Combine with ice; shake well. Strain and add ice. Touch it up with a twist of orange.

TROPICAL SPECIAL

1½ oz. gin
1 oz. apiece orange and lime juice
2 tbs. grapefruit juice
2 tsp. sugar syrup

Combine with ice; shake. Strain into ice; decorate with fruit slices and a cherry.

TROPICAL EGGNOG PUNCH

16 oz. white rum
14 oz. undiluted condensed milk
4 egg yolks
2 coconuts, ripe
Nutmeg

Crack the coconuts into several large pieces, heat at 350 for approx. 5 minutes; remove and separate the meat from the shells. Grate the meat. Combine half the rum and a third of the coconut meat in an electric blender and blend thoroughly. Stir out all liquid. Add this liquid plus more meat to the blender and repeat the process until you have 2 cups of juice. Add the juice plus the yolks to the blender. Blend several seconds; add the milk and blend some more. Combine with the remaining rum. Refrigerate until ready to serve. Garnish with nutmeg.

TROPICALA

1½ oz. dry vermouth
2 tbs. white creme de cacao
2 tbs. maraschino
1-2 dashes Angostura and orange bitters

Combine with ice; shake well. Strain and add plenty of ice.

TRYST COCKTAIL

1 oz. Scotch
1 oz. sweet vermouth
1 oz. Parfait Amour
A few drops Pernod
1-2 dashes orange bitters

Combine with ice; shake well. Strain and add ice.

TULIP

1 tbs. apple brandy
1 tbs. sweet vermouth
1 tbs. lemon juice
2 tsp. apricot brandy

Combine with ice; shake well. Strain into an old-fashioned glass and add ice.

TURF

1 oz. gin
1 oz. dry vermouth
1 tsp. lemon juice
1 tsp. Pernod

Combine with ice; shake well. Strain and add ice. Decorate with a slice of lemon.

TURF COCKTAIL

1½ oz. gin
2 tbs. dry vermouth
A few drops maraschino and Pernod
1-2 dashes orange bitters

Combine with ice; shake well. Strain and add ice.

TURKISH COFFEE

1 cup coffee, hot and black
2 tsp. cognac
Sugar to taste

Combine; stir well and sip while still piping hot.

TUXEDO

3 oz. sherry
1 tbs. anisette
A few drops of maraschino
1-2 dashes Peychaud's bitters

Combine with ice; shake well. Strain and add ice.

TWELVE GAUGE GROG

1½ oz. Jamaican rum
1 tbs. 151-proof rum
2 oz. orange juice
1 oz. lemon juice
A few dashes of Angostura bitters
Sugar to taste
Grapefruit soda

Combine everything except the soda with ice; shake well. Strain; add ice and fill with grapefruit soda. Decorate with an orange slice and a cherry.

TWENTY-FOUR HOUR COCKTAIL

1 quart corn whiskey
1 doz lemons
1 doz. oranges
1 pint pineapple juice
8 oz. sugar
Cherries

Slice the lemons, saving the rinds. Squeeze the juice into a crock pot; add the sugar, corn whiskey, and a pint of boiling water. Drop in the rinds; close the crock and store overnight. The next afternoon, strain, squeeze in the juice of the oranges, and pour over chunks of ice. Garnish with cherries.

TWIN HILLS

2 oz. whiskey
2 tsp. Benedictine
1½ tsp. sugar syrup
1 tsp. lemon juice
1 tsp. lime juice

Combine with ice; shake well. Strain straight up. Decorate with slices of lemon and lime.

TWIN SIN COCKTAIL

1 oz. gin
2 tsp. sweet vermouth
2 tsp. orange juice
A few drops of grenadine
1 egg white

Combine with ice; shake well. Strain and add ice.

TWO-PART GLOGG

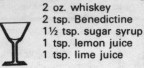

1 cup white rum
1 cup dry sherry
2 oz. sugar
Whole cloves, cinnamon sticks, raisins, whole shelled almonds.

Combine in a large saucepan; heat thoroughly but do not allow to boil. Immediately before serving, ignite. Stir with a long-handled spoon until the flame dies out. Serve in mugs; make sure each one gets a little bit of every spice.

YOUR OWN RECIPE

YOUR OWN RECIPE

Use a bartender's mixing glass whenever the instructions state "combine" ingredients. Strain the drink from the mixing glass into the drinking glass suggested by the illustration alongside the ingredients.

NOTE: The number of glasses or cups shown alongside a recipe do not necessarily indicate the quantity of drinks the recipe will produce.

ULANDA
1½ oz. gin
1 tbs. Cointreau
A few drops Pernod

Combine with ice; shake well. Strain and add ice.

ULYSSES
1 oz. brandy
1 oz. dry vermouth
1 oz. cherry brandy

Combine with ice; shake well. Strain and add ice. Touch it up with a twist of orange.

UNION JACK
1½ oz. gin
1 tbs. Creme Yvette

Combine with ice; shake well. Strain and add ice.

UNION LEAGUE
2 oz. Old Tom gin
1 oz. port
1-2 dashes orange bitters

Combine and stir gently. Add ice to fill the glass.

UNCLE HARRY'S PUNCH

2 bottles Rhine wine
2 bottles champagne
6 oz. curacao
6 oz. gold rum
4 oz. orange juice
4 oz. lemon juice
2 quarts club soda
Mint leaves
Fruit slices

Chill all the bottles well before using. Combine the wine, curacao, rum, and juices; add the mint and fruit slices and stir. Add the soda and champagne plus chunks of ice before serving.

UNISPHERE

1½ oz. gold rum
2 tsp. lime juice
1 tsp. grenadine
Several drops Benedictine and Pernod

Combine with ice; shake well. Strain and add ice.

UPSTAIRS

3 oz. Dubonnet
¾ oz. lemon juice
Club soda

Combine the Dubonnet and the lemon juice with ice; shake well. Strain and add ice. Fill the tumbler with club soda.

348

YOUR OWN RECIPE

Use a bartender's mixing glass whenever the instructions state "combine" ingredients. Strain the drink from the mixing glass into the drinking glass suggested by the illustration alongside the ingredients.

The glass pictured for each drink is our suggestion; other drinking cups may be used as well.

V

VALENCIA

2 oz. apricot brandy
1 oz. orange juice
1-2 dashes orange bitters

Combine with ice; shake well. Strain and add ice.

VAN DER HUM

5 bottles brandy
7½ oz. tangerine peel, clean and finely chopped
2½ oz. cinnamon
4 doz. cloves
Nutmeg, cardamon seeds, and orange blossoms
Rum

Combine the brandy with the peels and spices in an airtight cask; store at room temperature for at least a month, shaking once every day. When ready, strain out the spices and mix the brandy with rum — a few oz. of rum for every bottle of brandy. Store the finished **VAN DER HUM** *in air-tight bottles; shake at least once a day for a week before serving.*

VARIATION COCKTAILS
BRANDY VARIATION

1 oz. brandy
1 oz. gin
1 oz. dry vermouth
Club soda

Combine everything except the soda stir well and add ice. Fill the glass with soda.

FRENCH VARIATION

2½ oz. gin
Several drops Cointreau
Several drops dry vermouth
Ginger ale

Combine everything except the ginger ale stir well and add ice. Fill the glass with ginger ale.

GIN VARIATION

2 oz. dry gin
2 tsp. sugar syrup
Club soda

Combine everything except the soda stir well and add ice. Fill the glass with soda; touch it up with a twist of lemon.

VELVET HAMMER

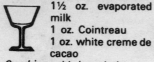

1½ oz. evaporated milk
1 oz. Cointreau
1 oz. white creme de cacao

Combine with ice; shake very well. Strain. Serve straight up.

VELVET ORCHID

1 oz. dry vermouth
1 oz. white creme de cacao
Several drops of black raspberry syrup

Combine with ice; shake. Strain. Serve straight up.

VERACRUZ COCKTAIL

1½ oz. Jamaican rum
2 oz. lime juice
1½ oz. dry vermouth
1-2 dashes pineapple juice

Combine with ice; shake well. Strain and add ice.

VERBOTEN

1 oz. gin
2 tsp. Forbidden Fruit, lemon juice and orange juice

Combine with ice; shake well. Strain and add ice. Decorate with a cherry.

VERMONT PUNCH

2 bottles whiskey
2 quarts lemon juice
1 quart maple syrup

Combine in a large saucepan; stir well. Heat but do not allow to boil; stirring occasionally to keep smooth. Serve hot in mugs.

VERMOUTH

1 pint dry white wine
1 tsp. wormwood extract

Combine in a bottle; seal, shake, and allow to stand until the wormwood ferments in the wine.

VERMOUTH CASSIS

1½ oz. dry vermouth
1 tbs. creme de cassis
Club soda

Combine the vermouth and the cassis stir well and add plenty of ice. Fill the glass with club soda; decorate with a slice of lemon.

VERMOUTH COOLER

1½ oz. sweet vermouth
1 tbs. vodka
1½ tsp. lemon juice
1½ tsp. sugar syrup
Club soda

Combine everything except the soda with ice; shake well. Strain add ice and fill the glass with soda. Stir gently.

VERMOUTH FLIP

3 oz. dry vermouth
1 egg white
1 oz. cognac
1½ tsp. lemon juice
1 tsp. powdered sugar
Club soda

Combine everything, except the soda with ice; shake well. Strain over ice. Fill with soda and stir gently.

VERMOUTH FRAPPE

2 tsp. dry vermouth
A few drops orange bitters
A few drops sugar syrup

Combine with a few cubes of ice; stir briskly. Strain. Serve straight up; add a twist of lemon.

VERMOUTH MARASCHINO

2 oz. dry vermouth
2 tsp. maraschino
2 tsp. lemon juice
1-2 dashes orange bitters

Combine with ice; shake well. Strain and add ice. Decorate with a cherry.

VERMOUTH TRIPLE SEC

1 oz. dry vermouth
1 oz. gin
2 tsp. Triple Sec
1-2 dashes orange bitters

Combine with ice; shake well. Strain; add ice and a twist of lemon.

VIA VENETO

1¾ oz. brandy
2 tsp. sambuca
2 tsp. lemon juice
1½ tsp. sugar syrup
½ egg white

Combine with ice; shake well. Strain and add ice.

VICTOR

1 oz. sweet vermouth
2 tsp. gin
2 tsp. brandy

Combine with ice; shake well. Strain and add ice.

VICTORY

1½ oz. Pernod
2 tbs. grenadine
Club soda

Combine everything except the soda with ice; shake well. Strain and add ice. Fill the glass with soda.

VIENNESE ICED TEA

Fill a tall glass part-way with crushed ice; pour in 1½ oz. of rum and fill the glass with dark, freshly brewed tea. Add sugar to taste and stir well.

VIKING

1½ oz. Swedish Punch
2 tbs. aquavit
2 tbs. lime juice

Combine with ice; shake. Strain and add ice.

VILLA IGIEA

1 oz. gin
1 oz. sweet vermouth
1 oz. Amaro

Combine with ice; shake and strain. Serve over ice.

VIN CHAUD

1 bottle red wine
4 oz. brandy
6-8 cubes sugar
Cinnamon sticks, whole cloves
Lemon slices and a spiral lemon peel

Place the sugar cubes in a large saucepan and dissolve them in a couple of tablespoons of hot water. Pour in the wine; heat but do not boil. Add the spices, the slices and the peel, and the brandy. Simmer a few minutes but do not allow to boil. Serve in a large chafing dish; keep warm.

VIN CRIOLLO

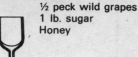

½ peck wild grapes
1 lb. sugar
Honey

Place the grapes in a large crock pot and add enough honey to cover them. Allow to stand for at least one week; then strain through cheesecloth. Put the sugar in the crock pot and pour the juice over it. Stir, then allow to ferment. Strain, bottle, and store in a cool place until ready to use.

VIRGIN

¾ oz. gin
¾ oz. white creme de menthe
1 tbs. Forbidden Fruit

Combine with ice; shake well. Strain and add ice.

VIRGINIA JULEP

2 oz. bourbon
1½ tsp. sugar syrup
Mint sprigs

Soak a few sprigs of mint in the bourbon for one hour. When ready, combine the minted bourbon with the sugar syrup and with ice and shake well. Strain over crushed ice. Stir and decorate with fresh mint.

VIRGINIA NIGHTCAP

2 doz. whole cloves
6 oz. cognac
1 oz. sugar
1 pint hard cider

Crush the cloves into a fine powder; combine with the sugar in a saucepan. Add the cognac and the cider; heat thoroughly but do not allow to boil. Serve hot in mugs.

VODKA CHAMPAGNE PUNCH

¾ oz. vodka
1 tbs. white rum
2 tsp. lime juice
2 tsp. strawberry liqueur
A few drops of grenadine
1 strawberry

Combine everything except the strawberry with ice; shake well. Line the rim of glass with water and press it in sugar; strain in the drink and decorate with the strawberry.

VODKA COCKTAIL

1½ oz. vodka
1 tbs. cherry brandy
1½ tsp. lemon juice

Combine with ice; shake well. Strain and add ice.

VODKA FRAISE

¾ oz. vodka
1 tbs. white rum
2 tsp. lime juice
2 tsp. strawberry liqueur
A few drops of grenadine
1 strawberry

Combine everything except the strawberry with ice; shake well. Line the rim of glass with water and press it in sugar; strain in the drink and decorate with the strawberry.

VODKA GIBSON

2½ oz. vodka
1 tbs. dry vermouth
1 pearl onion

Combine the vodka with the vermouth with ice; shake well. Strain straight up. Drop in the onion.

VODKA GIMLET

1½ oz. vodka
1 oz. lime juice
1½ tsp. sugar syrup

Combine with ice; shake well. Strain and add ice.

VODKA GRAND MARNIER

1½ oz. vodka
2 tsp. lime juice
2 tsp. Grand Marnier

Combine with ice; shake well. Strain and add ice. Decorate with a slice of orange.

VODKA GRASSHOPPER

¾ oz. white creme
de cacao
¾ oz. green creme
de menthe
1 tbs. vodka

*Combine with ice; shake very
well. Strain straight up.*

VODKA GYPSY

1½ oz. vodka
1 tbs. Benedictine
1-2 dashes orange
bitters

*Combine with ice; shake well.
Strain and add ice.*

VODKA ORANGE PUNCH

3 bottles vodka
18 oz. frozen orange
juice concentrate
8 oz. Cointreau

*Combine; stir until well-
blended and add ice. Touch it
up with several drops of
lemon juice and slices of
orange.*

VODKA SLING

2 oz. vodka
1½ tsp. Benedictine
1½ tsp. cherry bran-
dy
1 tsp. lemon juice
A few dashes of
Angostura and
orange bitters
Club soda

*Combine everything except
the soda with ice; shake well.
Strain; add ice and fill the
glass with soda.*

VODKA STINGER

1½ oz. vodka
2 tbs. white creme
de menthe

*Combine with ice; shake very
well. Strain and add ice.*

VOLGA BOATMAN

1½ oz. vodka
2 tbs. cherry brandy
2 tbs. orange juice

*Combine with ice; shake and
strain. Serve over ice.*

VOLSTEAD

1½ oz. Swedish
Punch
2 tbs. rye
1 tbs. orange juice
1 tbs. raspberry
syrup
A few drops anisette

*Combine with ice; shake well.
Strain and add ice.*

YOUR OWN RECIPE

YOUR OWN RECIPE

Use a bartender's mixing glass whenever the instructions state "combine" ingredients. Strain the drink from the mixing glass into the drinking glass suggested by the illustration alongside the ingredients.

The glass pictured for each drink is our suggestion; other drinking cups may be used as well.

WAGON WHEEL

2½ oz. Southern Comfort
2 tbs. cognac
1 tbs. lemon juice
Several drops grenadine

Combine with ice; shake well. Strain and add ice.

WALDORF

2 oz. Swedish Punch
2 tsp. dry gin
2 tsp. lemon juice

Combine with ice; shake. Strain and add ice.

WALTERS

2 oz. Scotch
1 oz. orange juice
1 oz. lemon juice

Combine with ice; shake well. Strain and add ice.

WARDAY'S COCKTAIL

1 oz. gin
1 oz. sweet vermouth
1 oz. apple brandy
1 tsp. yellow chartreuse

Combine with ice; shake well. Strain and add ice.

WARSAW

1½ oz. vodka
2 tsp. dry vermouth
2 tsp. blackberry brandy
1 tsp. lemon juice

Combine with ice; shake well. Strain and add ice. Touch it up with a twist of lemon.

WASHINGTON

1½ oz. dry vermouth
1 tbs. brandy
Several drops sugar syrup
1-2 dashes Angostura bitters

Combine with ice; shake well. Strain and add ice.

WASSAIL PUNCH

2 bottles dry sherry
16 oz. sugar
8 oz. brandy
6 eggs, separated
10 tiny, freshly baked apples, topped with brown sugar
Nutmeg, ground ginger, whole cloves, allspice berries, and a cinnamon stick

Combine the sherry and the spices with ½ cup of water in a large saucepan; heat but do not allow to boil. In separate bowls, beat the yolks until creamy and the whites until stiff; fold them together. Strain the spices out of the wine and gently fold in the egg mixture. Pour in the brandy and stir. Serve steaming hot in a large punch bowl; float the baked apples on top.

WATERBURY

2½ oz. brandy
1 tbs. lemon juice
1 tsp. sugar syrup
1 egg white
A few drops of grenadine

Combine with ice; shake extremely well. Strain and add ice.

WATERMELON CASSIS

2 oz. gin
1 tbs. lemon juice
2 tsp. creme de cassis
4 oz. diced seeded watermelon
4 oz. crushed ice
Club soda

Combine everything except the soda in a blender at a low speed for 15 seconds. Strain; add ice and touch it up with a spritz of soda. Decorate with a slice of lemon.

WATERMELON COOLER

2¼ oz. white rum
2 tsp. lime juice
1½ tsp. sugar syrup
4 oz. diced seeded watermelon
4 oz. crushed ice

Combine in a blender at a low speed for 15 seconds. Strain; add ice to fill the glass. Decorate with a slice of lime.

WEDDING BELLE

1 tbs. gin
1 tbs. Dubonnet
1 tsp. cherry brandy
1 tsp. orange juice

Combine with ice; shake well. Strain and add ice.

WEEP NO MORE

1½ oz. Dubonnet
1¼ oz. brandy
2 tbs. lime juice
A few drops of maraschino

Combine with ice; shake well. Strain and add ice.

WESTERN ROSE

1 oz. gin
2 tsp. dry vermouth
2 tsp. apricot brandy
A few drops lemon
juice

Combine with ice; shake well. Strain and add ice. To make an ENGLISH ROSE, add a few drops of grenadine before shaking. A FRENCH ROSE uses cherry brandy instead of the apricot brandy. For a WEBSTER, replace half the apricot brandy with lime juice and leave out the lemon juice.

WHALER'S TODDY

2 oz. Jamaican rum
4 oz. boiling water
1 tsp. sugar
Whole cloves
Pieces of cinnamon
Ground nutmeg

Pour the boiling water into a mug; add the sugar and stir until dissolved. Add the rum cloves, and cinnamon pieces and stir gently. Serve piping hot, garnished with nutmeg and decorated with a slice of lemon.

WHIP

1½ oz. brandy
1 tbs. sweet vermouth
1 tbs. dry vermouth
Several drops curacao
A few drops Pernod

Combine with ice; shake well. Strain and add ice.

WHISKEY COBBLER

2½ oz. whiskey
1 tbs. lemon juice
2 tsp. grapefruit juice
1½ tsp. almond extract
1 peach slice

Combine everything except the peach slice; stir well and add ice to fill the glass. Decorate with the slice of peach.

WHISKEY COCKTAIL

A WHISKEY COCKTAIL is an OLD-FASHIONED made with rye instead of bourbon.

WHISKEY CURACAO FIZZ

2 oz. whiskey
1 oz. lemon juice
2 tsp. curacao
1½ tsp. sugar syrup
Club soda

Combine everything except the soda with ice; shake well. Strain; add ice and fill the glass with soda. Decorate with a slice of orange.

WHISKEY DAISY

1½ oz. whiskey
1½ tsp. lemon juice
1½ tsp. sugar syrup
Several drops Cointreau
Club soda

Combine everything except the soda with ice; shake well. Strain; add ice and fill the glass with soda. Decorate with slices of fruit. A few drops of curacao or an oz. of raspberry syrup can be used instead of the Cointreau (in the latter case, half the sugar), or a teaspoon of yellow chartreause can be floated on top and the sugar eliminated altogether.

WHISKEY HOUND

1½ oz. 100-proof bourbon
2 tsp. 151-proof rum
2 tsp. grapefruit juice
2 tsp. orange juice
1 oz. lemon juice
1 tbs. sugar syrup
A few drops maraschino cherry juice

Combine with ice; shake. Strain and add ice.

WHISKEY KUMQUAT

3 oz. bourbon
A few drops of kumquat juice
A whole kumquat

Pour the bourbon into glass; add the juice plus the kumquat and stir gently. Add ice.

WHISKEY MAC

2 oz. Scotch
2 oz. ginger wine

Combine with ice; shake well. Strain and add ice.

WHISKEY OUZO FIX

2 oz. whiskey
2 tsp. lemon juice
1½ tsp. sugar syrup
1 tsp. ouzo

Combine everything except the ouzo; fill the glass with crushed ice and sir well. Touch it up with a twist of lemon; float the ouzo.

WHISKEY PUNCH

1½ bottles whiskey
4 cups orange juice
12 oz. lemon juice
3 oz. curacao
3 tbs. sugar syrup
2 quarts club soda

Combine the juices with the sugar syrup; pour in all the remaining ingredients except for the soda and stir. Decorate with slices of fruit. Add the soda plus chunks of ice before serving. Half the club soda can be replaced by iced tea.

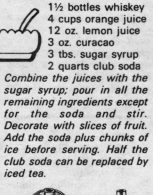

WHISKEY PUNCH

1 bottle bourbon
1 pint brandy
3 cups hot green tea
2 cups sugar
6 oz. orange juice
2½ lemon juice
Grated orange and lemon peels

Dissolve the sugar with the fruit juices peels, and tea. Allow to stand at room temperature for an hour. Add the brandy and the bourbon; strain out the rinds and store in the refrigerator until cold. Add ice.

WHISKEY SHAKE

2 oz. whiskey
2 tbs. lime juice
1 tsp. sugar syrup

Combine with ice; shake well. Strain and add ice.

WHISKEY SOUR IN THE ROUGH

2 oz. whiskey
1 tsp. sugar
Orange and lemon slices

Muddle the sugar with the fruit slices in a mixing glass; add the whiskey plus plenty of ice and shake well. Pour the entire contents of the mixing glass into an old-fashioned glass and allow to settle before drinking.

WHISKEY SOUR PUNCH

2 pints rye
2 pints bourbon
12 oz. sugar
6 oz. lemon juice
1-2 tsp. Angostura bitters
1 pint club soda

WHISKEY SOUR

2 oz. whiskey
1 oz. lemon juice
1 tbs. sugar syrup

Combine with ice; shake well. Strain straight up. Decorate with a slice of lemon. For a **WARD EIGHT,** *add a few drops of grenadine before mixing.*

Boil the sugar with enough water to make a syrup allow to cool. Combine with all the remaining ingrediens except the soda; Stir well. Add the soda plus chunks of ice.

363

WHITE COCKTAIL

3 oz. gin
1 tsp. anisette
A few drops orange bitters

Combine; stir gently.

WHITE DOVE

2 oz. white rum
2 oz. anisette

Combine with ice; shake. Strain over crushed ice. This drink can be touched up with a little club soda.

WHITE HORSE

1 oz. gin
1 oz. heavy cream
1 oz. Cointreau

Combine with ice; shake very well. Strain straight up.

WHITE LADY

2 oz. Cointreau
2 tsp. white creme de menthe
2 tsp. brandy

Combine with ice; shake well. Strain and add ice.

WHITE LILY

1 oz. gin
1 oz. white rum
1 oz. Cointreau
A few drops Pernod

Combine with ice; shake well. Strain and add ice.

WHITE LION

1½ oz. Jamaican rum
1½ oz. lemon juice
1½ tsp. sugar syrup
Several drops raspberry syrup
A few dashes Angostura bitters

Combine with ice; shake well. Strain and add ice.

WHITE ROSE

1¼ oz. gin
Orange juice
2 tsp lime juice
1½ tsp. sugar syrup
½ egg white

Combine with ice, shake extremely well. Strain and add ice.

WHITE WAY

1 oz. brandy
1 oz. Pernod
1 oz. anisette

Combine with ice; shake well. Strain and add ice.

WHITE WINE CUP

1 bottle white Burgundy
4 oz. sherry
2½ tbs. anisette
2½ tbs. brandy
1 bottle club soda
Lemon peels, pineapple slices, mint leaves
Sugar to taste

Combine everything except the soda. Add ice and the soda before serving.

WHITE WITCH

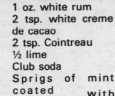

1 oz. white rum
2 tsp. white creme de cacao
2 tsp. Cointreau
½ lime
Club soda
Sprigs of mint coated with powdered sugar

Combine the rum, creme de cacao, and Cointreau with ice; shake well. Strain. Squeeze in the juice of the lime. Add ice and fill with soda; garnish with the mint.

WIDOW'S DREAM

3 oz. Benedictine
2 tbs. heavy cream
1 egg

Combine with ice; shake extremely well. Strain and add ice.

WIDOW'S KISS

1 oz. apple brandy
2 tsp. Benedictine
2 tsp. yellow chartreuse
1-2 dashes Angostura bitters
1 strawberry

Combine everything except the strawberry in a mixing glass filled with ice; shake well. Strain into an old-fashioned glass and add ice. Decorate with the strawberry.

WILD COW

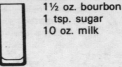

1½ oz. bourbon
1 tsp. sugar
10 oz. milk

Dissolve the sugar in the bourbon on the bottom of a glass; add the milk plus ice to fill the glass and gently stir. Garnish with nutmeg.

WINDJAMMER

2 oz. white rum
2 tbs. rock and rye
2 tbs. orange curacao
An orange peel, cut in a long strip
Brown sugar

Coat the orange peel with brown sugar; place it on the bottom of a mug. Heat the mug over a low flame until the sugar melts on the peel; add the remaining ingredients. Fill the mug with boiling water and stir well. Touch it up with a twist of lemon.

WINE BOWL

2 bottles champagne
Grenadine
Sliced strawberries

Pour the champagne over chunks of ice; add enough grenadine to color the wine a light pink. Garnish with strawberries.

WINE REFRESHER

1 gallon rose wine
3 cups unsweetened grapefruit juice

Chill well before combining. Serve over plenty of ice.

WITCH'S BREW

3 oz. Strega
2 tbs. orange juice
2 tbs. lemon juice
1 tbs. white creme de menthe
A few drops of Pernod

Combine everything except the Pernod with ice; shake very well. Strain over crushed ice; stir gently until the glass begins to frost. Float the Pernod. Decorate with slices of fruit.

WITCH'S STEW

1 quart cider
1 pint apiece orange and lemon sherbert
8 oz. curacao
1 large orange
2 doz. whole cloves
Nutmeg, cinnamon, allspice
1 bottle champagne

Stick the orange with the cloves; combine with the curacao in a saucepan and simmer several minutes, turning occasionally. Add the cider and spices and heat thoroughly. Allow to cool; turn out unstrained into a large punch bowl; add the sherbert in scoops. Before serving, add the champagne.

WIVES' NOG

1 quart hard cider
4 oz. sherry
2 oz. brandy
2 oz. curacao
½ oz. maple syrup
Grated nutmeg
Orange slices
Cucumber slices
Lemon peels

Combine the cider, sherry, brandy, curacao, and maple syrup; stir until the syrup has dissolved. Garnish with the nutmeg, fruit and vegetable slices, and peels.

WOODRUFF WINE BOWL

3 pints May wine
4 oz. sugar
2 bunches fresh woodruff, a few blossoms aside

Combine the woodruff, uncut, with the wine and sugar. Allow to stand, covered, at room temperature for half an hour. Strain; add ice and reserved woodruff blossoms just before serving. Stay light on the ice to keep the fragrance of the woodruff intact.

WOODSTOCK

1½ oz. gin
1 oz. lemon juice
1 tsp. maple syrup
1-2 dashes orange bitters

Combine with ice; shake very well. Line the rim of glass with water or maple syrup and press it in sugar. Strain in the drink and add ice.

WOODWARD

1 oz. Scotch
1 oz. grapefruit juice
1 oz. dry vermouth

Combine with ice; shake well. Strain and add ice.

WRIGHT SPECIAL

2½ oz. rye
2½ oz. port
3 tsp. lemon juice
2 tsp. sugar syrup
1½ egg whites

Combine with ice; shake extremely well. Strain into a tall glass and fill the glass with ice.

WORLD OF TOMORROW PUNCH

3 bottles champagne
2 bottles Tokay wine
1 bottle Madeira
2 pints brandy
1 oz. maraschino, curacao, Benedictine, and rum
2 bottles club soda
12 oz. sugar
Pineapple and orange slices
Whole strawberries

Pound the sugar with a few of the fruit rinds until the fruit color starts to bleed in. Add the fruit slices and pour the remaining ingredients over them; club soda last. Stir very well. This punch may be strained clean if you'd like.

YOUR OWN RECIPE

YOUR OWN RECIPE

YOUR OWN RECIPE

Use a bartender's mixing glass whenever the instructions state "combine" ingredients. Strain the drink from the mixing glass into the drinking glass suggested by the illustration alongside the ingredients.

xyz

XANTHIA

¾ oz. gin
¾ oz. cherry brandy
1 tbs. yellow chartreuse

Combine with ice; shake well. Strain and add ice.

XERES

3 oz. sherry
1-2 dashes orange bitters
1-2 dashes peach bitters

Combine with ice; shake well. Strain and add ice. To make a **SHERRY COCKTAIL,** *double the orange bitters and use and equal amount of dry vermouth instead of the peach bitters.*

XYZ

1 oz. Jamaican rum
1 tbs. Cointreau
1 tbs. lemon juice

Combine with ice; shake well. Strain and add ice.

YANKEE PUNCH

2 quarts rye
1 pint rum
Pineapple and lemon slices
4 quarts water
Sugar

Combine stir well. Add ice before serving.

YARD OF FLANNEL

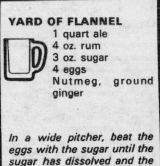

1 quart ale
4 oz. rum
3 oz. sugar
4 eggs
Nutmeg, ground ginger

In a wide pitcher, beat the eggs with the sugar until the sugar has dissolved and the eggs are creamy-colored. Add the rum and spices; stir. Heat the ale in a saucepan; do not boil. Remove from heat and slowly add to the egg mixture, stirring constantly. Serve hot in mugs.

YASHMAK

¾ oz. rye
¾ oz. dry vermouth
1 tbs. Pernod
1-2 dashes
Angostura bitters
A few drops sugar
syrup

Combine with ice; shake well. Strain and add ice. Campari can be used instead of the Pernod, omitting the bitters and the sugar.

YELLOW PARROT

¾ oz. apricot brandy
¾ oz. Pernod
1 tbs. yellow chartreuse

Combine with ice; shake well. Strain and add ice.

YELLOW PLUM

1½ oz. plum brandy
2 tsp. lemon juice
2 tsp. orange juice
1½ tsp. sugar syrup
1 tsp. maraschino

Combine with ice; shake well. Strain and add ice.

YODEL

1½ oz. Fernet Branca
1½ oz. orange juice
Club soda

Combine the Fernet Branca and the orange juice. Add ice and fill the glass with soda; stir gently.

YORK SPECIAL

2½ oz. dry vermouth
1 tbs. maraschino
Several dashes
orange bitters

Combine with ice; shake well. Strain and add ice. The bitters can be omitted.

ZENITH

2½ oz. gin
1 tbs. pineapple juice
Club soda
1 pineapple stick

Combine the gin and the juice stir well. Add ice and fill the glass with soda. Decorate with the pineapple stick.

ZOMBIE

1½ oz. gold rum
3 tsp. lime juice
1 tbs. Jamaican rum
1 tbs. white rum
1 tbs. pineapple and
papaya juice
1½ tsp. sugar syrup
1 tsp. 151-proof rum
1 pineapple stick
Granulated sugar

Combine everything except the high-proof rum, pineapple stick, and granulated sugar with ice; shake well. Strain and add ice. Decorate with the pineapple stick and a cherry; float the high-proof rum and sprinkle a little sugar over it. **ZOMBIES** *should be made with rums of various strengths, i.e. 90 and 86 proof. A little apricot brandy can be used as an addition to the fruit juices; sprigs of mint can be added to the garnishes.*

YOUR OWN RECIPE

NON-ALCOHOLIC DRINKS

AGUA LOJA

12 oz. molasses
1 oz. ground ginger
Cinnamon sticks

Boil the ginger and several cinnamon sticks in 5 cups of water for 15 minutes. Strain clean and allow to cool. Turn out into a bowl; add the molasses and stir until blended. Refrigerate until ready to serve.

ALMOND PUNCH

8 oz. almonds
4 oz. sugar

Boil the almonds in 2 cups of water for several minutes; remove from heat, cool, and peel the nuts. Pound the almonds into a pulp and combine with 1 quart of water in a pot. Strain clean into a separate bowl; add the sugar and stir until the sugar is dissolved. Refrigerate until ready to serve.

ANGEL PUNCH

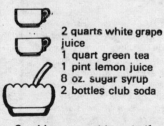

2 quarts white grape juice
1 quart green tea
1 pint lemon juice
8 oz. sugar syrup
2 bottles club soda

Combine everything except the soda; stir well and refrigerate several hours. Chill the soda. Serve on ice with soda.

APPLE COCKTAIL

8 oz. sliced, peeled apple
8 oz. orange juice
3 oz. lemon juice
Pineapple chunks
Sugar to taste
Maraschino cherries

Combine the fruit juices in a bowl; add sugar to taste and stir until the sugar is dissolved. Add the sliced apple and pineapple slices and refrigerate for at least an hour. Serve in large tumblers; garnish with a cherry.

APPLE JUICE

1 doz. baking apples
Sugar
Lemon juice

Slice the apples in their peels; boil in enough water to cover until soft. Strain the juice into a large bowl; add sugar to taste. Stir until the sugar has dissolved. Allow to cool. Add 2 teaspoons lemon juice for every pint of apple juice and stir. Dilute with ice-cold water before serving.

BANANA MILK SHAKE

1 large banana, sliced
8 oz. milk
1½ oz. orange juice
1 tbs. honey
A few drops almond extract
Whipped cream

Combine everything except the whipped cream; shake. Serve with whipped cream.

377

BARLEY PUNCH

2 oz. ground barley
2 oz. sugar
The peels of 1 large lime

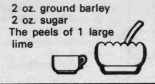

Combine in a large pot with 6 cups of water; bring to a boil and stir constantly until the barley is cooked. Strain out the punch and refrigerate until ready to serve.

BLACK AND WHITE MILK SHAKE

1 pint milk
2 oz. apiece vanilla and chocolate ice cream

Combine in a blender for a few seconds at a high speed.

BLACK COW

8 oz. sarsaparilla
2 oz. vanilla ice cream

Pour the sarsaparilla into a tall glass; add the ice cream and stir until well-blended.

BOSTON CREAM

2½ lb. sugar
2 oz. citric acid
1 tbs. concentrated lemon juice
Baking soda

Combine the sugar and citric acid in 3 pints of boiling water; stir well until the sugar has dissolved and allow to cool. Add the lemon juice and stir. Chill in the refrigerator; bottle and store. Serve as a tonic, with a pinch of baking soda and a teaspoon of **BOSTON CREAM** for each glass of water.

BOG PUNCH

1 pint cranberries
1 pint apple juice
8 oz. sugar
8 oz. cranberry juice
4 oz. lemon juice
8 oz. pineapple chunks, from the can and packed in their own sauce
1 bottle ginger ale

Boil the whole cranberries with the sugar in a pint of water; remove from heat and simmer until the berries are soft and the sugar has dissolved. Strain out the juice; allow to cool. Combine the fresh, warm juice with the *remaining ingredients*; refrigerate until ready to serve.

CARRY NATION PUNCH

1 quart orange juice
3 cups lemon juice
8 oz. pineapple juice
8 oz. sugar syrup
2 bottles ginger ale
Slices of fruit

Combine the juices and the sugar syrup, stir well and refrigerate several hours. Chill the ginger ale. Add the ginger ale and ice before serving. Decorate with fruit.

CHERRY BING

1 pint cherry juice
4 oz. orange juice

Dilute the cherry juice and orange juice with 10 oz. water; stir to blend. Add chunks of ice before serving.

CHERRY WATER

2 lb. cherries
8 oz. sugar
1 large lemon

Crush the cherries; strain the juice into a bowl. Squeeze in the juice of the lemon plus a few tsp. water; stir well and allow to stand for several hours. Strain into a pitcher when ready. Serve over crushed ice.

CHRISTMAS JUICE PUNCH

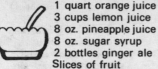

2 quarts apple juice
2 quarts cranberry juice
8 oz. lemon juice
8 oz. sugar
2 bottles ginger ale

Combine everything except the ginger ale. Stir well. Add the ginger ale plus chunks of ice before serving.

CIDER CUP

1 quart cider
3 oz. sugar
Whole cloves, cinnamon sticks

Combine in a large saucepan; heat until boiling, stirring constantly. Remove from heat and allow to cool. When cool enough, strain and refrigerate for several hours. Re-heat approx. one hour before serving.

CIDER EGGNOG FOR TWO

4 oz. light cream
1 egg
1 tsp. powdered sugar
Sweet cider
Ground nutmeg

Combine the cream, sugar, and egg with ice; shake well. Strain into two tall glasses; add ice and fill with cider. Dust with nutmeg.

CLAM JUICE COCKTAIL

5 oz. clam juice
1 tsp. catsup
1-2 dashes Tabasco sauce
A pinch of celery salt

Combine with ice; shake well. Strain into a tumbler and add ice. A **CLAMATO COCKTAIL** *uses half clam juice and half tomato juice, omitting the catsup.*

CONCORD GRAPE PUNCH

1 pint Concord grape juice
1 pint cold water
4 oz. sugar
4 oz. orange juice
3 oz. lemon juice

Combine; stir gently to blend and allow to stand until the sugar has dissolved. Add chunks of ice before serving.

CRANBERRY JUICE COCKTAIL

1 quart cranberries
4 oz. apiece lemon, orange, and pineapple juice
8 oz. sugar

Boil the cranberries in a quart of water until soft; allow to cool. Strain the juice; add the sugar and stir until it has dissolved. Add the fruit juices plus chunks of ice when ready to serve.

CRANBERRY PUNCH

1 quart pineapple juice
2 16 oz. cans cranberry juice
6 oz. brown sugar
Ground cloves cinnamon, allspice, nutmeg, salt, and cinnamon sticks
A spot of butter

Boil the brown sugar and spices (except for the cinnamon sticks) with a cup of water in a saucepan; add the pineapple juice and 3 more cups of water. Add the cranberry juice and bring to another boil; turn down the heat and simmer for several minutes. Stir and turn out into a deep chafing dish. Top with the butter. Serve in mugs, using the cinnamon sticks as swizzlers.

CRANBERRY TEA PUNCH

2 quarts cranberries
1 quart tea
2 cups sugar
Cinnamon sticks
Lemon slices
Ground nutmeg

Boil the cranberries in 2 quarts of water; when soft, strain. Pour the juice back into the pot; add the sugar and cinnamon sticks and simmer for several minutes. Allow to cool; add the tea and lemon slices. Re-heat. Serve hot in mugs garnished with nutmeg.

CRANBERRY WASSAIL

2 oz. ground orange pekoe tea
8 oz. orange juice
4 oz. lemon juice
2 small bottle cranberry juice
1 cup sugar
Ground nutmeg, cinnamon, and allspice

Combine the spices and ground tea in a cloth sack; infuse it in 2 quarts of boiling water. Immediately remove from heat; allow to steep for 15 minutes. Strain. Add sugar and juices; re-heat and stir until sugar has dissolved. Serve piping hot.

CREOLE COOLER

1 pint milk
8 oz. crushed pineapple, chilled
2 oz. orange juice
3 tsp. lime juice
Sugar

Combine the pineapple with the juices in a pitcher; add sugar to taste. Add the milk and mix well. Serve straight up.

EGG TISANA

2 egg whites
The grated peels of 1 lime
8 oz. sugar

Beat the egg whites until foamy; add the grated peel and continue beating until the whites hold peaks. Slowly add the sugar and continue beating the whites until stiff. Gradually combine the whites with 5 cups of water in a large bowl; beating carefully and constantly. Serve immediately.

EMERALD FROSTS

4 oz. mint jelly
3 tsp. lime juice
Lemon-lime soda
Lemon sherbert
Lime slices

Melt the jelly with 4 oz. water in a saucepan; cool and add the lime juice. Drop scoops of sherbert in several tall glasses; add 2 tsps. mint syrup to each glass. Fill the glasses with soda; stir very well. Add ice if you wish; garnish with lime slices.

ENRICHED COFFEE

12 oz. ground coffee
1 egg

Combine the coffee with the egg, well-beaten, and 4 oz. cold water. Stir to blend; tie up the soaked coffee in a cloth sack. Boil a gallon and a half of water; remove from heat and infuse with the coffee sack. Shake the sack in the water a few times, then drop it in, cover the pot, and allow it to brew for at least 12 minutes. When ready, remove sack, strain the coffee, add 4 oz. of cold water and serve immediately.

FLORIDA COCKTAIL

3½ oz. grapefruit juice
1½ oz. orange juice
1 tbs. lemon juice
2 oz. sugar syrup
Club soda
Mint sprigs
A pinch of salt

Combine everything except the soda and mint with ice; shake well. Strain over crushed ice. Add an oz. of soda to each glass and decorate with mint.

FLORIDA PUNCH

1½ quart orange juice
1½ quart grapefruit juice
16 oz. powdered sugar
12 oz. lime juice
3 cups water
1½ quart ginger ale

Combine the sugar and the water in a saucepan; heat and stir until the sugar is dissolved. Allow to cool. Combine the sugar syrup and the juices; stir well. Add the ginger ale plus chunks of ice before serving.

FRESH FRUIT PUNCH

8 oz. apiece of orange juice, pineapple juice, and grapefruit juice
1 bottle ginger ale
Sugar to taste

Combine the juices with the sugar. Stir until the sugar is dissolved and refrigerate. Add the ginger ale plus chunks of ice before serving.

FRESNO APRICOT COOLER

1 pint apricot nectar
6 oz. orange juice
3 tbs. lemon juice
1½ oz. sugar
1 pint ginger ale

Dissolve the sugar with the fruit juices. Add the nectar and stir to blend. Refrigerate until ready to serve. Add the ginger ale plus chunks of ice before serving.

FROSTED APRICOT SPECIAL

1 cup apricots
3 cups milk
8 oz. vanilla ice cream

Cook the apricots until soft; remove the skins and pits. Crush the pulp in a mixing bowl; add the milk and stir to blend. Place the ice cream on the bottom of a glass pitcher; pour the fruit and milk mixture over it and stir gently until smooth. Serve in punch glasses.

FROSTED CHOCOLATE SHAKE

3 pints hot chocolate, chilled
1½ pints vanilla ice cream

Combine in blender for a few seconds until smooth. Serve in a tall glass with a straw.

FROZEN CIDER

8 oz. sweet cider
4 oz. orange juice
1 tbs. applesauce
A few drops lemon juice
3 oz. crushed ice

Combine in blender at a high speed or until thick. Store in the freezer until thick enough to eat with a spoon. Serve in tall glasses.

FROZEN PINEAPPLE AND BANANA COOLER

8 oz. pineapple juice, frozen and chopped up
½ small banana, sliced
Several drops of lemon juice

Combine in a blender for several seconds, or until snowy.

FRUIT COCKTAIL PUNCH

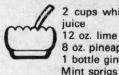

2 cups white grape juice
12 oz. lime juice
8 oz. pineapple juice
1 bottle ginger ale
Mint sprigs

Combine the fruit juices; chill in the refrigerator until ready to use. Before serving, add the soda plus chunks of ice. Garnish with mint.

FRUIT CUP

1 pineapple
½ doz. oranges
½ doz. grenadillas
Grated orange rind
Sugar syrup
Club soda

Peel and slice the fruit meats; combine and pound into a pulp. Add sugar syrup to taste and stir to blend. Dilute with club soda and ice before serving.

FRUIT JUICE PUNCH

1¼ quarts pineapple juice
3 quarts grape juice
Sugar
3 bottles ginger ale

Combine the fruit juices with a quart of water; add sugar to taste and stir until the sugar is dissolved. Add sugar, ginger ale, and ice chunks before serving; garnish with fruit slices.

FRUIT MILK SHAKE

1 pint apiece orange juice and grapefruit juice
1 pint milk
2 oz. sugar
A few drops vanilla extract, a few pinches of salt
8 oz. crushed ice

Combine the ingredients in a blender in four parts (i.e. 4 oz. milk, juices, ½ oz. sugar, etc.) Blend at a high speed until smooth. Serve with a straw.

GARDEN PARTY PUNCH

8 oz. orange juice
8 oz. pineapple juice
4 oz. lemon juice
8 oz. sugar
1 pint ginger ale
1 pint club soda
3 cups hot tea
Orange slices
Mint leaves

Combine the sugar with the hot tea; stir until the sugar has dissolved. Allow to cool. Combine the sweetened tea with the fruit juices; stir to blend. Add the ginger ale and soda plus chunks of ice before serving. Garnish with fruit slices and mint.

GENERAL HARRISON'S EGGNOG

sweet cider
1 egg
1 tsp. powdered sugar

Combine the egg and sugar and crushed ice; stir until well-blended. Strain; add ice and fill the glass with cider. Garnish with nutmeg.

GINGER ALE FLOAT

Ginger ale
Fruit sherbert
Sprigs of mint

Fill a tall glass half-way with ale; add ice and float a scoop of sherbet on top. Garnish with sprigs of mint.

GINGER GRAPE JUICE

1 quart grape juice
2 oz. sugar
3 tbs. lemon juice
1 pint ginger ale
Whole cloves, a cinnamon stick

Combine the grape juice, lemon juice, and sugar; tie cloves and cinnamon into a cloth sack. Heat the juices and infuse with the spices; stir until the sugar is completely dissolved and simmer for 15 minutes. Allow to cool; then refrigerate until ready to use. Add the ginger ale plus chunks of ice before serving.

GINGER MINT JULEP

Ginger ale
Sprigs of mint
Powdered sugar

Muddle the mint sprigs in plenty of sugar. Line the rims of several tall glasses with water and press them in fresh powdered sugar; divide out the minted sugar among them and fill each glass with crushed ice and ginger ale. Stir gently and serve garnished with mint.

GINGER PEACH COCKTAIL

8 oz. peach juice
8 oz. orange juice
4 oz. lemon juice
Whole ginger chunks
1 pint ginger ale

Combine the fruit juices; stir well. When ready to serve, add the ginger ale to the pitcher. Place a chunk of ginger in each serving.

GINGER PUNCH

8 oz. ginger, in chunks
8 oz. sugar
4 oz. orange juice
4 oz. lemon juice
1 bottle club soda

Boil the ginger and sugar in a cup of water for 15 minutes; allow to cool. Turn out into a large punch bowl; add the fruit juices and stir to blend. Add the soda plus chunks of ice before serving.

GOLDEN NECTAR

1½ pints grapefruit juice
8 oz. orange juice
2 oz. honey
4 eggs
A pinch of salt

Combine the egg yolks, well-beaten, with the fruit juices; stir briskly until well blended. Add the honey and salt; stir until the honey has dissolved. In a separate bowl, beat the egg whites until stiff; fold carefully into the nectar. Serve at once in pre-chilled wine glasses.

GOLDEN PUNCH

12 oz. orange juice
12 oz. lemon juice
4 oz. pineapple juice
2 cups sugar
1 bottle ginger ale

Boil the sugar in a cup of water for several minutes; allow to cool. In a large punch bowl, combine the fruit juices with the cool sugar syrup and another pint and a half of water; stir well. Add the ginger plus ice before serving.

GRANADILLA ADE

2 cups granadilla pulp
8 oz. orange juice
8 oz. sugar syrup
3 tsp. lemon juice

Combine with 2 cups of water; stir briskly until well blended. Add plenty of ice before serving.

GRAPE JUICE PUNCH

2 quarts grape juice
1 bottle ginger ale
Orange slices

Combine in a punch bowl. Add chunks of ice and oranges before serving. Garnish with mint.

GRAPE SODA

2 quarts white muscat grapes
1 bottle club soda

Squeeze the juice out of the grapes; combine with club soda and stir gently. Bottle well, if not for immediate use.

GRAPEFRUIT ADE

Several large grapefruit
Ginger ale
Mint leaves

Squeeze out the juice of the grapefruit; dilute with an equal amount of ginger ale and stir gently. Serve over ice garnished with mint.

HAWAIIAN PUNCH

8 oz. grated pineapple
4 oz. orange juice
2 oz. lemon juice
8 oz. strong iced tea
2 cups sugar
1½ bottles ginger ale

Boil the sugar in enough water to make a syrup; allow to cool. Combine with the grated pineapple and fruit juices in a large punch bowl; add the tea, stir well, and allow to stand for several hours. Add the ginger ale plus ice before serving.

HOLIDAY APPLE PUNCH

1½ quarts apple juice
2 bottles ginger ale
Lemon slices
Red and green cherries

Make this punch immediately before serving. Combine the apple juice and the ginger ale; stir gently to blend. Garnish with the fruit slices and cherries.

HONEY MILK SHAKE

8 oz. milk
1½ oz. vanilla ice cream
1 tbs. honey

Combine in a blender at a high speed until smooth. Serve with a straw.

HOT CHOCOLATE

½ lb. unsweetened chocolate
2 quarts milk
1½ cups sugar
Whipped cream

Cut the chocolate into small pieces; combine with the sugar over a double boiler and melt until the sugar has dissolved with the chocolate and they are well-blended. Add the milk and continue cooking until smooth. Serve immediately in mugs; top with whipped cream or a marshmallow.

HOT CRANBERRY-PINEAPPLE PUNCH

2 quarts cranberries
1 quart pineapple juice
8 oz. brown sugar
Cinnamon sticks, ground cloves, ground cinnamon, salt, and nutmeg
Butter

Boil the cranberries in a quart of water until soft; strain out the juice. Combine the warm juice with the sugar, ground spices, and another cup of water in a saucepan; add the pineapple juice and bring to a boil. Serve piping hot in mugs. Garnish with cinnamon sticks and a pat of butter.

HOT SPICED NOGGIN

2 quarts cider
6 oz. brown sugar
1 orange sliced
1 lemon, sliced
Cinnamon sticks
Whole cloves
Allspice
A pinch salt

Combine the sugar and spices in a saucepan; pound together into a fine powder. Add a quart of warm water; stir well and bring to a boil. In a separate saucepan, heat the cider with the fruit slices; do not allow to boil. Strain clean. Serve warm.

HOT SPICED PINEAPPLE JUICE

14 oz. pineapple juice
1 oz. lemon juice
A cinnamon stick
Sugar

Combine the juices with the cinnamon stick in a saucepan; heat but do not boil. Allow to simmer for 15 minutes. Strain; add sugar to taste. Stir well until the sugar is dissolved. Serve hot in mugs.

ICED CIDER PUNCH

Sweet cider
Mint leaves

Make a tray of ice cubes out of cider; use them in tall glasses filled with cider and garnished with mint.

ICED MINT TEA

1 doz. sprigs fresh mint
2 cups boiling water
1 quart cold water
Granulated sugar
Powdered sugar
Sprigs of mint ·
Spiral lemon peels

Combine the fresh mint with the boiling water in a saucepan and steep over hot water in a double boiler for at least ½ hour. Strain the minted water clean and allow to cool. Combine with the cold water in a large pitcher; add granulated sugar to taste and stir until the sugar is completely dissolved. Serve with ice. Garnish with spiral lemon peels and sprigs of mint dusted with

INDEPENDENCE DAY LEMONADE

1 doz. lemons
2 cups sugar

Boil the sugar in 2 cups of water. Allow to cool. Squeeze out the juice of the lemons into a large punch bowl; add the sugar syrup plus 3 quarts ice water. Stir well. Float the leftover rinds in the punch. Add chunks of ice before serving.

LEMONADE

2 cups lemon juice
Grated lemon peels
10 oz. sugar

Combine the sugar and lemon rinds with 1 cup of water in a saucepan; simmer for several minutes until syrupy. Allow to cool. Add the lemon juice and strain. Dilute the lemonade with water for each glass (for an average strength lemonade, use four times as much water as ade per serving).

LIME AND GINGER ALE

2 large limes
2 tbs. sugar
1 tbs. mint sprigs, cut finely
1 bottle ginger ale .

Peel the limes, slice them and combine with the sugar and chopped mint with 1½ cups boiling water. Allow to stand until cool, pressing the lime slices occasionally. Strain; add the ginger ale. Stir gently. Decorate with fresh lime slices.

LIME COOLER

4½ oz. lime juice
6 oz. orange juice
2 tbs. lemon juice
Mint sprigs, crushed
Sugar
16 oz. club soda

Combine the fruit juices with the crushed mint in a punch bowl; allow to stand at least one hour. Strain and add sugar to taste; stir well until the sugar is dissolved. Add the soda plus chunks of ice before serving.

LIMEADE

9 oz. lime juice
9 oz. sugar
3 cups of water

Boil the sugar with the water to make a syrup; combine the syrup with the lime juice in a large pitcher and stir until well-blended.

MAPLE NOG

1 pint milk
4 oz. whipped cream
3 oz. maple syrup
3 egg yolks, beaten
A pinch of salt
Ground ginger

Combine the maple syrup, beaten egg yolks, and milk; stir briskly until well-blended. In a separate bowl, dust the whipped cream with the ginger. Turn out the nog into several tall glasses; top each glass with a dab of the dusted cream.

MAPLE SHAKE

8 oz. milk
3 tbs. maple syrup
1 oz. vanilla ice cream
Slices of banana

Combine the maple syrup and the milk with ice; shake well. Strain into a tall glass; decorate with slices of banana and float the ice cream.

MINT AND FRUIT COCKTAIL

2 large bunches of mint leaves
9 oz. orange juice
6 oz. grapefruit juice
4 tbs. sugar

Boil one of the mint bunches in 3 oz. of water until the water is infused. Strain out the leaves. Combine the mint water with the juices, sugar, and 4-6 oz. of crushed ice in blender at a low speed for 15 seconds. Strain into several wine glasses straight up. Garnish with the remaining mint.

MINT COOLER

6 oz. orange juice
4½ oz. lemon juice
2 cups sugar
Mint sprigs, crushed
Grated orange and lemon rinds
Ginger ale

Boil the sugar in enough water to make a syrup; combine the hot sugar syrup with the mint and fruit juices in a punch bowl. Add the grated rinds and allow to cool. Strain clean, bottle, and store in the refrigerator until ready to use. Serve over crushed ice diluted with ginger ale.

MINT TEA PUNCH

3 cups orange juice
6 cups grape juice
2 cups lemon juice
8 oz. grapefruit juice
2 oz. lime juice
2 cups sugar syrup
Cucumber slices
Mint sprigs, in pieces
1½ bottles club soda
3 bottles ginger ale
1 quart hot tea

Infuse the mint in the tea; add the fruit juices and syrup (except grape) and stir well. Allow to cool; garnish with cucumber slices. Add the grape juice, ginger ale, and chunks of ice before serving.

MOCHA

2 oz. unsweetened chocolate
2 cups hot coffee
3 cups milk, scalded
6 oz. sugar
Ground cinnamon
A few drops of vanilla extract
A pinch of salt

Combine the chocolate with 1½ oz. hot water in a double boiler; heat and stir until the chocolate has melted. Add the sugar, salt, cinnamon, and coffee; stir to blend and simmer several minutes before adding the milk and vanilla extract. Simmer at least ½ hour; whip and serve hot.

MOCK CHAMPAGNE

4 oz. white grape juice
4 oz. grapefruit juice
1 pint club soda
A few drops concentrated lime juice
Angostura bitters

Chill all the ingredients extremely well. Combine the juices, stir well, and before serving add the soda; stir gently. Touch each serving up with a dash or two of bitters.

MOCK MANHATTAN

2 oz. orange juice
2 oz. cranberry juice
A few drops lemon juice
A few drops of maraschino cherry juice
1-2 dashes orange bitters

Combine with ice; shake well. Strain and add ice; decorate with a cherry.

MULTI-FRUIT PUNCH

1 quart orange juice
1 quart grapefruit juice
6 oz. lemon juice
1 pint apiece strawberry, pineapple, and raspberry syrup
1 bottle ginger ale
Banana slices

Combine everything except the ginger ale and banana slices; dilute with three quarts of water and stir well to blend. Add the sugar, ale plus chunks of ice before serving; garnish with banana slices.

NECTAR PUNCH

3 cups apricot nectar
6 oz. lime juice
4 oz. current jelly
6 oz. white corn syrup
4 oz. sugar
Ground cinnamon
Lemon slices

OATMEAL PUNCH

4 oz. oatmeal
The peels of one large lime

Soak the oatmeal in 1 qt. of water and the lime peels for ½ hour. Strain out the liquid; add the sugar and stir until the sugar is dissolved. Refrigerate until ready to serve.

ORANGE MILK SHAKE

4 oz. orange juice
2 oz. pineapple juice
1½ oz. honey
1 tbs. lemon juice
A pinch salt
2 cups milk

Combine with ice; shake very well. Strain straight up; serve with a straw.

ORANGE NOG

2 cups milk
4 eggs
10 oz. orange juice
2 oz. sugar
Ground nutmeg

Combine the eggs, sugar, and milk; stir until well-blended. Split among four glasses; add 4 oz. milk to each glass. Add ice and garnish each with nutmeg.

Boil the sugar, corn syrup, cinnamon, and fruit slices in a cup of water for several minutes; remove from heat. Take out the fruit slices and beat in the jelly; add the nectar and lime juice. Stir well. Refrigerate until ready to serve.

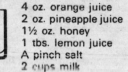

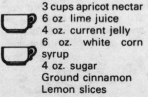

ORANGEADE

3 large oranges
3 tsp. lemon juice
4 oz. sugar

Peel and slice one of the oranges; combine it with the sugar in a cup and a half of water; stir gently until the sugar has dissolved. In a separate bowl; combine the juice of the remaining oranges with the lemon juice. Pour it over the sliced orange; allow to settle for a few minutes before using.

PARTY TEA

4 tbs. ground tea
2 cups orange juice
8 oz. lemon juice
4 cups sugar
Mint leaves

Combine the tea, sugar, and mint leaves with a quart of boiling water; allow to steep several minutes. Strain clean; add the juices plus 2 more quarts of water. Stir well. Add chunks of ice before serving.

PILGRIM'S PUNCH

12 oz. orange juice
3 oz. lemon juice
2 cups sugar
1 quart whole strawberries
1 bottle club soda
Mint leaves
1 cup iced tea, dark
2 cups pineapple juice
1 quart lemon sherbet

Boil the sugar with a cup of water for several minutes (longer than it takes to dissolve the sugar). Strain out the juice of the strawberries; add it to the sugar syrup with the tea, and all the fruit juices. Allow to cool.

PASSION FRUIT PUNCH

1 doz. large passion fruit
2 quarts grapefruit juice
1 quart orange juice
1 quart pineapple juice
4 oz. lemon juice
6 quarts lemonade
6 bottles ginger ale
Fruit slices

Squeeze the juice out of the passion fruit; combine with the remaining ingredients, except the ginger ale and fruit. Stir well. Add the ginger ale plus chunks of ice before serving; garnish with fruit.

PINEAPPLE ADE

1 large pineapple
1 cup orange juice
Grated orange rind
Sugar

Peel the pineapple and grate the meat; combine with the orange juice in a large bowl and set aside. Boil the pineapple skin and core with the orange rinds in 4 cups of water for 20 minutes. Strain and allow to cool. Combine with the grated pineapple; sweeten to taste and serve over ice.

PINEAPPLE EGG COCKTAIL

1 pint pineapple juice
5 oz. lemon juice
2 oz. sugar
2 egg whites
12 oz. crushed ice

Combine in a blender with 4 oz. cold water; blend at a high speed until foamy. Divide out among several glasses filled with ice; decorate each glass with a cherry.

PINEAPPLE MINT PUNCH

2 cups pineapple juice
3 cups milk
6 oz. light cream
2 oz. sugar
1 doz. mint leaves
2 teasps. lemon juice
A pinch of salt

Muddle the mint in a large punch bowl; remove the leaves, leaving the oils. Pour in all the ingredients and beat until frothy. Serve over ice in glasses garnished with fresh sprigs of mint.

PINEAPPLE PUNCH

1 large pineapple
1 cup sugar
1 bottle rose wine
3 bottles club soda

Peel the pineapple; dice the meat and combine with the sugar. Pour in the wine; stir to dissolve the sugar and allow to stand for a couple of hours. Add the club soda plus ice.

PINEAPPLE SHERBERT PUNCH

8 oz. apiece of orange juice, pineapple juice, and raspberry juice

8 oz. crushed pineapple

1 cup tea

1 quart pineapple sherbet

1 bottle club soda

A few drops of concentrated lime juice

Combine the fruit juices, crushed pineapple, and tea; stir well. Before serving, add the sherbet in small scoops, plus the soda.

PINEAPPLE TEA PUNCH

5 pints pineapple juice

1 pint lemon juice

4 cups powdered sugar

4 oz. tea, in leaf form

Infuse the tea in a gallon of boiling water several minutes; strain. Add the sugar and stir until the sugar has dissolved. Add the fruit juices and a quart of cold water; refrigerate until ready to serve. Turn out over chunks of ice.

PRAIRIE OYSTER

1 egg yolk

1 tsp. Worchestershire sauce

Several drops of vinegar

A few drops of Tabasco sauce

A pinch of salt and pepper

Slide the whole yolk into a wide champagne glass; add the remaining ingredients. Do not stir. A whole egg can be used if you'd like.

RASPBERRY DELIGHT

3 oz. raspberry sherbet

Ginger ale

Fresh raspberries

Scoop the sherbet into glass; add ice and fill the glass with ginger ale. Float a few raspberries and serve with a straw.

RASPBERRY REFRESHER

12 oz. of red raspberries

2 cups sugar

1 pint orange juice

Boil the sugar in enough water to make syrup. Add raspberries; macerate until smooth. Add the orange juice; stir and refrigerate for several hours. Strain before using. Serve wih ice.

RASPBERRY SHRUB

2 pints raspberries
Cider vinegar
Sugar

Combine the raspberries with the vinegar, allow to stand for 24 hours. When ready, strain out the berries; add sugar. Boil several minutes until the sugar has dissolved. Allow to cool. Bottle for future use. Serve diluted in water.

RECEPTION CHOCOLATE

8 oz. cocoa
8 oz. sugar
1 quart heavy cream
2 quarts milk
1 tsp. vanilla extract
A pinch of salt

Combine the sugar and the cocoa with a cup of boiling water; stir to blend. Heat in a saucepan; turn out into a double boiler; simmer at least ½ hour and allow to cool. Whip the heavy cream and fold it into the cocoa. Warm the milk with the vanilla and salt. Serve in tall glasses, a tablespoon of cocoa per glass of warm milk.

RHUBARB COCKTAIL

1 small rhubarb
4 oz. pineapple juice
1 tbs. orange juice and lemon juice

Break the rhubarb into pieces and boil it in just enough water to cover; strain out the juice and add sugar to taste. Stir until the sugar is dissolved; allow to cool. Combine the rhubarb juice with the remaining juices; shake very well. Serve over crushed ice.

RUSSIAN TEA

4 tsp. ground tea
6 oz. orange juice
3 tsp. lemon juice
A cinnamon stick
Whole cloves
Sugar

Boil the cinnamon sticks and cloves in 6 cups of water for a few minutes; add the tea, remove from heat and allow to simmer a few minutes more. Strain into a large bowl. Combine the juices; Serve hot in mugs.

SARATOGA

1½ oz. lemon juice
1 tsp. sugar syrup
A few dashes of Angostura bitters
Ginger ale

Combine everything except the ginger ale with ice; shake well. Strain into a tall glass; add ice and fill the glass with ginger ale. Club soda can be used instead of ginger ale.

SESAME SEED PUNCH

1 cup sesame seeds
4 ozs. sugar

Soak the seeds in 1 qt. of water for several hours; dry the seeds and crush them into a pulp. Combine the seed pulp with 2 cups of warm water; stir to blend and strain out the liquid into a separate bowl. Add the sugar to the sesame seed liquid; stir until the sugar has dissolved and refrigerate until ready to serve.

SHIRLEY TEMPLE

Fill a champagne glass with ginger ale and add several drops of grenadine; stir gently and decorate with a couple of cherries.

SODA FOUNTAIN CIDER

1 quart cider
1 pint orange juice
10 oz. sugar
4 oz. lemon juice

Boil the sugar in a pint of water stir until the sugar has dissolved. Combine the sugar syrup with the remaining ingredients in a large pot; allow to cool and strain clean. Freeze until thick before serving.

SOFT PUNCH

8 oz. pineapple juice
6 oz. orange juice
1½ oz. lemon juice
1 oz. sugar syrup
2 tbs. passion fruit juice

Combine; stir well. Add ice before serving.

SOUR ORANGE TEA

2 fresh, sour orange sprigs
1 tsp. sugar

Crush the sprigs and boil them in a cup of water. Strain out the infused water; add the sugar and stir until the sugar has dissolved. Serve hot in mugs.

SOURSOP PUNCH

2 lbs. ripe soursop fruit
6 oz. sugar

Slice the fruit; cut out the pulp and seeds with a paring knife. Combine the pulp and seeds with a cup of water; mash and strain out the liquid. Keep repeating this process with more water until the pulp is strained out. Add the sugar to the final straining; stir until the sugar has dissolved. Refrigerate until ready to serve.

SOUTHERN PUNCH

5 cups sweet cider
1 quart grape juice
Cinnamon sticks
Grated orange and lemon peels
4 oz. lemon juice
2 bottles ginger ale
Orange slices
Whole cloves

Simmer the cinnamon sticks and cloves with half the cider in a large saucepan for several minutes. Allow to cool; strain. Pour the remaining cider back into the empty pot; add the fruit juices and peels. Refrigerate. Combine the spiced and fruit cider; add the ginger ale, orange slices, and ice.

SPANISH HOT CHOCOLATE

8 oz. semi-sweet chocolate
8 oz. hot coffee
3 pints milk, warm
2 egg yolks
2 tsp. vanilla extract

Combine the chocolate with the coffee in a double boiler; heat unil the chocolate has dissolved and stir well to blend. Add the milk and warm over a low flame. When ready to serve; beat the yolks; add them to the chocolate. Add the vanilla and stir well. Serve in mugs. Add sugar to taste and top with whipped cream.

SPICE PUNCH

2 quarts ginger ale
3 8-oz. cans grape juice concentrate
4 oz. lime juice
Cinnamon sticks
Whole cloves

Combine the cinnamon sticks and cloves with a cup of water in a saucepan; bring to a boil. Let stand several minutes cooling, then strain. Combine this spiced water with the grape juice concentrate and the lime juice. Stir until well-blended. Add ice and ginger ale.

SPICED APPLE JUICE

½ doz. apples
8 oz. sugar
Cinnamon sticks, allspice berries, Whole cloves

Boil the apples in their peels with enough water to cover them; when soft, strain out all the juice. Tie up the spices in a cloth bag and infuse in boiling juice for several minutes; add the sugar and stir until the sugar is dissolved. Strain clean and serve piping hot.

SPICED LEMONADE

12 oz. lemon juice
8 oz. sugar syrup
1 doz. whole cloves
1 quart cold water
Cinnamon sticks

Simmer the sugar, cinnamon, and cloves in a saucepan for a few minutes; add the lemon juice and remove from heat. Allow to stand for at least one hour. Strain and combine with the water; stir well. Serve over crushed ice.

STRAWBERRY WATER

8 oz. strawberry juice
8 oz. sugar

Dilute the juice with a quart of water in a large bowl; add the sugar and stir well until the sugar is completely dissolved. Serve over ice. If you are using fresh strawberries, allow approx. twice as much volume for the fruit meat. RASPBERRY and PINEAPPLE WATER can be made with this recipe; merely change the fruits.

TAMARIND PUNCH

1 lb. whole tamarind seeds
1 cup sugar

Combine the seeds with a cup of water in a mixing bowl; mash to a pulp and strain out the juice with the water. Save the mashed seeds. Repeat this process until the seeds emit no more juice. Add the sugar to the punch; stir until the sugar is dissolved and refrigerate until ready to serve.

TEA PUNCH

3 cups strong, iced tea
16 oz. raspberry syrup
8 oz. lime juice
8 oz. crushed pineapple
1 quart orange juice
2 bottles club soda

Combine everything except the soda; add the soda plus chunks of ice.

TOMATO COCKTAILS

These are the most popular of non-alcoholic drinks. There are dozens of variations to a **TOMATO COCKTAIL;** all are made with 8 oz. of tomato juice and are mixed in an electric blender. Here a few suggestions.

TOMATO COCKTAIL WITH CARROTS

Combine the juice with 4 oz. of thinly sliced carrots, a pinch of salt, and a dash of Tabasco. Blend until smooth; serve over ice.

TOMATO COCKTAIL WITH HOT CHILI PEPPERS

Combine the juice with a can of peeled, green chili peppers and a few drops of lemon juice. Blend until smooth; serve over ice.

TOMATO COCKTAIL PROVENCALE

Combine the juice with a whole clove garlic (slightly chopped), several fresh basil leaves, a dash of salt, and a few drops of lemon juice. Blend until the garlic is finely distributed. Serve over ice.

TOMATO COCKTAIL CALIFORNIAN

Combine the juice with 4 oz. of thinly sliced raw carrots, ¾ oz. lemon juice, a few drops of Worchestershire sauce, a pinch of salt, and a few sprigs of parsley, finely chopped. Blend for at least 30 seconds or until the parsley is evenly distributed. Serve over ice; decorate with a scoop of sour cream and a dash of paprika.

TOMATO AND YOGURT COCKTAIL

Use only 4 oz. of tomato juice. Combine the juice with 4 oz. of plain yogurt, 1 oz. small, diced onion, and a few sprigs of chopped watercress. Blend until the watercress is evenly distributed. Serve over ice. Slices of cucumber can be used instead of the watercress.

YOGURT FRUIT COCKTAIL

8 oz. plain yogurt
2½ oz. frozen orange juice concentrate

Combine in blender at a high speed for a few seconds. Serve over ice. Pineapple juice (4 oz.) can be used instead of the orange juice concentrate.

TROPICAL AMBROSIA

2 small cans mandarin oranges, sliced
3 large apples
8 oz. grated coconut meat
A few drops lemon juice

Peel and slice the apples; arrange in a deep bowl with the orange slices. Dab with lemon juice and garnish with the grated coconut.

VISHNADA

1 lb. sour cherries
12 oz. sugar
2 tbs. lemon juice

Clean and stem the cherries; combine them with the sugar and lemon juice in a cup of water. Bring to a boil; lower the heat and simmer several minutes until the cherries soften, break, and blend with the rest. Cool, strain, and refrigerate. Use as a concentrate, one tablespoon per glass of water.

YULETIDE PUNCH

1 quart cider
2 cups cranberry juice
8 oz. orange juice
8 oz. cold tea
1 oz. lemon juice, grated lemon rinds, fruit slices

Combine the cider, juices, and tea; add grated rinds and fruit slices. Slide in chunks of ice before serving.

Low Calorie Drinks

This section of the Bartender's Guide is intended for people who are interested in a good drink which is also low in calories.

CALORIES

One gram of alcohol metabolized in the body yields seven calories which adds up to approximately 200 calories per fluid ounce (approx. 30 milliliters) of absolute alcohol, or 100 calories per fluid ounce of 100-U.S.-proof distilled spirits. Rums, whiskies, and vodkas are equal in calories, per oz., to their proof and most range between 80-100 calories per oz. In beer, some additional calories, about four per ounce, remain from the surviving cereal content of the original grain. (These non-alcoholic calories, however, are now being eliminated by some manufacturers catering to the weight conscious.)

DIETERS' DRINKS:

Since liquor has as many calories per ounce as its proof, i.e. one ounce of 86-proof rum contains 86 calories—no alcoholic drink will help you lose weight. But there are lesser evils to choose from and these are among them:

Sprittzers: White wines mixed with club soda (50/50 ratio) makes a low calorie refreshment that can be touched up with a twist of lemon and ice.

Wines in general are better for the weight conscious than mixed drinks because many of the vitamins and minerals stick with the wine through fermentation. Distillation causes spirits to lose almost everything except potency and calories.

Highballs: Mix down the usual amount of liquor (say 2 tsps.) of Scotch, vodka, or gin per glass of soda.

Tomato Vermouth: Tomato juice is the least fattening juice mixer. Combine 4 oz. of tomato juice with 2 oz. of dry vermouth in a glass with ice; shake well. Strain into an old-fashioned glass and add ice.

Bitters and Mixers: Campari and soda, lemon juice and soda with a dash or two of Angostura bitters or Perrier water with a touch of lemon and a dash of creme de cassis all make good, non-alcoholic, low-calorie drinks.

ALFONSO COCKTAIL
(80 Calories)

1 oz. champagne
2 oz. grape juice
Several drops of
Angostura bitters

Combine; serve over ice.

APPLEJACK DAISY
(99 Calories)

½ oz. gin
½ oz. apple brandy
1 tbs. lemonade

Combine and serve over crushed ice.

APPLE PIE
(60 Calories)

1 oz. vermouth (dry)
2 tbs. apple juice
Cinnamon, nutmeg
Brown sugar

Combine the juice and vermouth over ice. Add dashes of the spices and sugar.

BARBIE'S SPECIAL
(75 Calories)

1 ½ tbs. apricot nectar
1 oz. defrosted vanilla ice milk
A few drops of gin

Combine and shake with ice. Serve straight up

BIFFY
(75 Calories)

½ oz. gin
2 tbs. pineapple juice
1 tbs. lemon juice

Combine and shake with ice. Serve over crushed ice.

BLOODY PICK-ME-UP
(50 Calories)

½ oz. gin
1 tbs. catsup
1 tbs. lemon juice
A few drops of Worchestershire sauce

Combine in a blender at high speed for 15 seconds. Serve over crushed ice.

CAMPARI SPECIAL
(70 Calories)

1 ½ oz. Campari
Ginger ale
A few drops of orange bitters

Combine over ice. Touch up with a slice of orange.

CARDINAL
(45 Calories)

¾ oz. dry vermouth
1 tbs. orange juice
1 tbs. tomato juice
Ripe olive

Combine. Serve chilled.

CARTHUSIAN COOLER
(60 Calories)

1 oz. port
Club soda
½ honeydew melon

Hollow out ½ honeydew melon. Blend fruit with port; pour into shell and fill with club soda.

CHAMPAGNE COBBLER
(82 Calories)

2 oz. champagne
1 oz. lemon sherbet

Combine over crushed ice. Decorate with a cherry.

CHERRY RUM
(106 Calories)

½ oz. rum
2 oz. canned sour cherries in syrup
1 tbs. light cream
3 oz. crushed ice

Blend at low speed; strain and serve straight up.

CITY STREET
(100 Calories)

2 oz. dry vermouth
2 tbs. cranberry juice
Several dashes orange bitters

Combine and touch up with an orange slice.

CLARE'S CUP
(62 Calories)

2 oz. dry white wine
1 cucumber
Mint leaves
Lemon slices
Grated lime rinds
Club soda

Hollow out the cucumber, flatten one end. Pour in the wine, add soda to fill and garnish with mint and fruit.

COFFEE NOG
(95 Calories)

½ cup dark coffee (freshly brewed and partially cooled)
1 cup light cream
1 egg, separated
1 tbs. brown sugar
A pinch of salt

Combine the coffee, egg yolk, sugar, and salt in the top of a double boiler; cook until thick. Remove from heat and allow to cool. In a separate bowl, beat the egg whites with the cream until foamy but not stiff; fold into the coffee mixture and serve immediately.

CORONATION
(80 Calories)

2 tbs. apricot nectar
½ oz. creme de menthe

Combine; serve over crushed ice.

CORONET COCKTAIL
(90 Calories)

1 oz. port
½ oz. gin
Several dashes orange bitters

Combine. Serve straight up.

COUNT CURREY
(95 Calories)

2 oz. champagne
½ oz. gin
1 tsp. maple syrup

Combine and serve with mint sprig.

COUNTRY CLUB COOLER
(50 Calories)

1 ½ oz. dry vermouth
¼ oz. grenadine
2 oz. club soda

Combine and garnish with a lime slice.

COWBOY
(78 Calories)

½ oz. whiskey
1 oz. flavored yogurt

Combine with ice, shake very well. Serve over ice.

CREOLE PUNCH
(60 Calories)

1 ½ oz. canned pineapple juice
½ oz. 86-proof rum
½ oz. lemon juice

Combine and serve chilled.

CREME DE CACAO FLOAT
(95 Calories)

½ oz. creme de cacao
1 tsp. chocolate
Ice milk

Float the ice milk on top of the liqueur.

CUBA LIBRE
(70 Calories)

2 tsp. lime juice
½ oz. 86-proof rum
½ oz. grenadine

Combine and serve over ice.

CURRIER
(78 Calories)

½ oz. whiskey
1 tsp. kummel
1 tsp. lime juice (unsweetened)

Combine and shake well. Serve straight up.

CYNTHIA
(60 Calories)

1 oz. dry vermouth
½ oz. sweet vermouth
1 tsp. gin
Mint sprigs

Combine over ice. Decorate with mint.

DILL MARY
(65 Calories)

3 oz. tomato juice
1 tbs. vodka
½ tsp. crushed dill
A pinch of salt and pepper
A few dashes of tobasco sauce

Place the dill on the bottom of a mixing glass; add the vodka and tomato juice and allow to stand for several minutes. Add the salt, tobasco sauce plus ice; shake well. Strain over ice. Garnish with pepper.

DRY PUNCH
(30 Calories)

⅔ oz. dried mint
2 cups boiling water
16 oz. cold water
3 oz. grenadine
Mint sprigs
Lime peels

Steep mint in boiling water for 40 minutes. Combine with cold water and add grenadine. Float the lime peels and garnish with mint.

ENGLISH POSSET
(61 Calories)

1 oz. dry sherry
½ oz. light cream
Nutmeg

Combine and serve chilled. Garnish with nutmeg.

FIG LEAF FLIP
(90 Calories)

1 oz. creme de menthe
1 tsp. gelatin
1 oz. water
3 oz. crushed ice

Boil water and combine with the gelatin in a blender at high speed for 30 seconds. Add the creme de menthe and blend again. Add ice and blend one final time. Serve as a dessert.

FIRE AND ICE
(100 Calories)

½ oz. Cherry Herring
1 tbs. Kirsch

Combine with an ice cube. Stir until the ice begins to melt. Decorate with an orange slice.

FULL IN BED COCKTAIL
(65 Calories)

½ oz. port
⅓ cup apple juice

Combine and serve on ice.

GIN COCKTAIL
(65 Calories)

¾ oz. gin
A few drops of orange bitters

Serve over ice. Add a twist of lime.

GEORGE'S BEAUTY
(95 Calories)

½ oz. brandy
2 tsp. lemon juice
1 tsp. grenadine
1 egg white

Combine with ice; shake well. Strain and add ice.

HONOLULU SLING
(95 Calories)

1 tbs. vodka
1 oz. sherry
1 oz. Hawaiian Punch

Combine with ice; shake. Strain over crushed ice.

HONOLULU SPECIAL
(75 Calories)

1 oz. low proof rum
1 tbs. lemon juice
1 tsp. grenadine
1 tsp. pineapple juice

Combine with ice. Garnish with pineapple.

ISLAND TEA
(40 Calories)

 3 oz. freshly brewed
green tea
1 oz. grenadine
Fresh mint
1 tsp. lemon juice

Combine and decorate with mint.

LORENZO
(85 Calories)

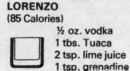 ½ oz. vodka
1 tbs. Tuaca
2 tsp. lime juice
1 tsp. grenadine

Combine; serve over ice.

LOW-CAL EGG NOG
(80 Calories)

3 oz. evaporated
Skim milk
8 oz. water
1 egg
Several drops of
low-proof rum
1 tsp. grenadine

Combine with ice. Shake and serve straight up. Garnish with nutmeg. (Serves two).

LUMBERJACK
(75 Calories)

 ½ oz. whiskey
1 oz. apple juice
(unsweetened)
1 tsp. brown sugar
Cinnamon and
nutmeg

Add the sugar to the juice and whiskey. Garnish with spices.

MASS TEA PUNCH
(70 Calories)

 3 oz. orange juice
1 tbs. lemon juice
1 oz. iced tea
1 tbs. crushed
pineapple
Tonic water

Combine and shake. Strain over ice. Add a twist of lime.

NETHERLAND
(90 Calories)

 ½ oz. brandy
A few drops of
Curacao
1 tsp. cranberry juice
Several drops of
Angostura bitters
1 cucumber shell

Combine and add ice. Serve in the cucumber. Add a twist of orange and lemon.

NORTHERN HONEY BEE
(103 Calories)

 1 oz. brandy
½ oz. lemon juice
1 tsp. honey

Warm the honey in a ladle over a low flame. Combine with the juice and brandy. Serve warmed.

OUZO RICKEY
(80 Calories)

 ¾ oz. Ouzo
½ oz. cognac
1 tsp. lime juice
Club soda

Combine and stir. Add soda to fill glass.

PANSY
(75 Calories)

½ oz. Pernod
Several drops of grenadine
A few dashes of Angostura bitters

Combine with ice; twist in a lemon.

PINK SQUIRREL
(75 Calories)

½ oz. gin
1 tsp. creme de noyaux
1 oz. lemon juice

Combine with ice. Shake and serve over ice.

PLANTER'S COCKTAIL
(60 Calories)

½ oz. rum
1 tbs. orange juice
1 tsp. lemon juice

Serve over crushed ice. Decorate with mint.

SHOOT
(85 Calories)

½ oz. Scotch
½ oz. dry sherry
1 tsp. lemon juice
1 tsp. maple syrup

Combine with ice. Shake and add ice.

SHRINER
(90 Calories)

½ oz. brandy
½ oz. sloe gin
A few drops of Peychaud's bitters
1 tsp. grenadine

Combine and serve straight up.

TOBAGO
(90 Calories)

½ oz. low-proof rum
½ oz. gin
1 tsp. lime juice
1 tsp. guava syrup
1 oz. crushed ice

Combine and blend. Serve over crushed ice.

TROPICAL SLING
(70 Calories)

½ oz. gin
1 ½ tsp. lime juice
1 tsp. grenadine
½ tsp. maraschino
club soda
Sprigs of mint

Combine everything except the soda and mint. Shake. Add ice and fill with soda.

WAVERLY
(90 Calories)

½ oz. gin
1 tsp. creme de cassis
1 tbs. orange juice
Crushed ice

Combine and touch up with an orange slice.

WEST INDIAN PUNCH
(70 Calories)

1 oz. dry sherry
1 tsp. limeade
1 tsp. guave nectar
2 oz. dark, cold tea

Combine and twist in a lime. Shake.

YOUR OWN RECIPE

YOUR OWN RECIPE

INDEX

BRANDY DRINKS

BREWS

CAMPARI DRINKS

422

423

CURACAO DRINKS

433

ICE CREAM, MILK, AND YOGURT BASED DRINKS

MARTINIS

PERNOD DRINKS

443

PORT WINE DRINKS

RYE DRINKS

SAKI DRINKS

SAMBUCA DRINKS

SANGAREES AND SANGRIAS

SAUTERNE DRINKS

SCOTCH DRINKS

SHERRY DRINKS

VERMOUTH DRINKS

VODKA DRINKS

WHISKEY DRINKS

461

WHITE WINE DRINKS

462

We Deliver!
And So Do These Bestsellers.

Special Offer
Buy a Bantam Book
for only 50¢.

Now you can have Bantam's catalog filled with hundreds of titles plus take advantage of our unique and exciting bonus book offer. A special offer which gives you the opportunity to purchase a Bantam book for only 50¢. Here's how!

By ordering any five books at the regular price per order, you can also choose any other single book listed (up to a $4.95 value) for just 50¢. Some restrictions do apply, but for further details why not send for Bantam's catalog of titles today!

Just send us your name and address and we will send you a catalog!